Veronica Brady was born in Melbourne in 1929. She is Associate Professor of English at the University of Western Australia and is a regular contributor to national and international literary journals. A member of the Loreto Order, her interests are wide-ranging—Australian literature, Aboriginal Australia, social justice, human rights and questions of belief. She has been a member of the board of the Australian Broadcasting Corporation, and is currently on the board of the Library and Information Service of Western Australia.

CAUGHT
IN THE
DRAUGHT

VERONICA BRADY

Angus&Robertson
An imprint of HarperCollins*Publishers*

An Angus & Robertson Publication
Angus & Robertson, an imprint of
HarperCollins *Publishers*
25 Ryde Road, Pymble, Sydney NSW 2073, Australia
31 View Road, Glenfield, Auckland 10, New Zealand

National Library of Australia
Cataloguing-in-Publication data:

Brady, Veronica.
Caught in the draught: essays on contemporary Australian society and culture.
ISBN 0 207 17943 3.
1. Aborigines, Australian. 2. Australia—Civilization—1965–. 3. Australia—
Social life and customs—1965–. 4. Australia—Social conditions—1965–.
5. Australia—Intellectual life—20th century. 6. Australia—Religion—
20th century. I. Title.
306.0994

Cover photograph by Peter Robinson.

Typeset by Midland Typesetters, Marysborough, Victoria.
Printed in Australia by McPherson's Printing Group, Victoria.

9 8 7 6 5 4 3 2 1
99 98 97 96 95 94

Foreword

Who is Veronica Brady, and how to introduce her? An important teacher? A significant critic (Patrick White at one point would be interviewed by no other)? A kind of theologian? A public conscience? Those who have known, read, been taught by or worked with her know these things anyway, and those who have not will probably find them all here. Whatever else she is—and she is clearly much else (a voracious reader, a tireless activist, an uncompromising thinker)—Veronica Brady is a writer. Yet her profile as a writer, as for many teachers whose best writings are for the most part for their students, has so far almost cruelly belied her production and the significance of her texts.

This is no small matter. In fact, where this book is concerned, it is everything. She has done something *in* and *to* and *through* writing, and that thing is as synechdochic as it is central to all else that she does. My impression, over the twelve years of our friendship, is of someone writing within and through all the other events and activities of her life so consistently and in such a way as to blur radically and importantly the edges of the writing and the living. They lean or bleed into one another, so that life—sinew—becomes textualised and text becomes sinewed. Early in the morning or late at night, before those who will hear or read her have risen or after they have gone to bed or at this and that part of the day when other calls upon her have left moments free, Veronica Brady is writing lectures, speeches, reviews, articles, essays, submissions, references, reports, letters, so that their rationales, their subjects intertwine, and one—*any* one—becomes imbued with the others. Literature looking at government, theology at bureaucracy, outrage at canticle, instruction at politics or prayer: all, however much they might try to turn their backs, live and breathe with and because of this context, and are held responsible to one another in this twisting and always-uncomfortable (if often comforting) discourse.

It would be wrong, then, to call her one thing or another—critic, nun, teacher, activist, even friend—that did not acknowledge the presence and inhabitation of the rest; wrong to expect her to write one thing, or one set of things, that was not also others. These essays bear evidence. On literature, on aesthetics, on belief, on human rights, on issues of Aboriginality, perhaps quintessentially on the nature, place and responsibilities of Australian identity, they dispute the fragmentation and placelessness and pastlessness and godlessness that are supposed among the reigning orthodoxies of our time, and challenge us with possibilities of bringing together, of connecting, when so much would excuse or distract us from that task.

David Brooks

January, 1994

CONTENTS

INTRODUCTION

The anthropologist Tom Lowenstein tells of revisiting an Eskimo village he had lived in for some time a few years earlier. The crucial change he noted lay, he said, in a complaint made to him by one of the young men: 'our old people aren't *real* old people any more'. He was no longer able to go to the old people for advice. He was now part of another culture, the white man's culture, which would not allow him to ask the kind of questions he used to ask of them.

This is a collection of essays by an 'old person'. The kind of questions I am concerned with are traditional and not very often asked today, questions about value, about meaning and purpose, even, some of them, about 'God'—whatever that word may mean. Our culture in general, and literary subculture in particular, is shy about these questions. Contemporary criticism is usually more 'scientific' and theoretical, more self-reflexive, more modest and more ironic; 'meaning' is a suspect term and 'humanism', if not a dirty word, is at least a sign of intellectual slackness and possibly also class complicity. Generally, literary scholarship is determinedly professional, secular, and increasingly international in its concerns and practices.

At the other end of the scale, away from literary culture, those still interested in questions of value and meaning grow increasingly fundamentalist, giving themselves up to totalist and totalising systems which excuse them from thought, delivering them over to the consolations of power and certainty. They, too, no longer look to the 'old people', to the long tradition of nuanced thought and feeling, of sympathy and tolerance based on belief which knows how to combine commitment with irony and how to acknowledge and respect the beliefs of others.

These essays, I suspect, will not please either group. Nevertheless, I have always been an admirer of Don Quixote. In particular I cherish the story of his 'terrible and undreamed of adventure with the

1

windmills' in which he charged windmills not only in the firm conviction that they were giants but also in the even firmer conviction that it was his business to contest giants. It was, he believed, 'God's good service to wipe so evil a breed from off the face of the earth'. However unfashionable it may be, it seems to me that those who think windmills are only windmills and are not prepared to do battle with giants are much less fortunate, and certainly less important in the scheme of things, than those like Don Quixote who do not and are so prepared. Commonsense matters, of course. But Don Quixote's dream of a world in which words like 'chivalry' and 'human' mean something, and in which it is the task of those who are educated, privileged or powerful to respect, care for and empower the powerless and vulnerable, in my view, matters even more.

In this spirit, then, I am prepared in these essays to unfurl an old and tattered banner, to reinvoke the notion of the 'liberal imagination', using the word 'liberal' not in its now almost meaningless political sense but according to its root meaning which derives from the Latin word *liber*, the free person. Used in this sense, the word denotes ideas, feeling, behaviour or conditions worthy of free people; people, that is, who are able and willing to take the risk of choice. It also has to do with generosity, an openness of a heart and mind which is flexible and ready for change, innovation and play. In the long run, I believe, we human beings are the key point of the world, however much we may have damaged and now threaten to destroy it.

The wind does not hear itself but we hear it; animals communicate among themselves but we humans each talk to ourselves and communicate with the dead and with the not yet born. The human clamor is the wind that knows that it is wind, language that knows that it is language and the means whereby the human animal knows that it is alive, and by so knowing, yearns to die.[1]

That has always been the central belief of Western culture; it is more important than ever, I believe, not to lose it now, faced as we are with the challenge of survival on this planet and, more specifically, in Australia, of remaining a relatively humane and decent society. It is this kind of spirit, I would like to think, which is, or should be, engendered by reading and by thinking and talking about reading.

It is true that in a society preoccupied with success, efficiency and technological rationality, these may seem forlorn thoughts, foolishly romantic and literary in the worst sense, that is, not merely impractical but a distraction from the proper tasks of thought which have to do with productivity and increasing efficiency. In the contemporary university they will seem even more useless, and certainly unlikely to qualify as 'research' and attract funding. But it may be that we need to rediscover our ideals. For lack of a vision, a people perish—and you do not need to live where I do in Western Australia in the disillusioned aftermath of WA Inc. and Mabo to be aware of that. The signs are all around us of anomie, of hopelessness, of a certain homelessness in the sphere of value.

In Australia today there exists no large social consensus, little rational frame for our living together, apart from the pursuit of economic goals. For most of us the self is an emptiness waiting to be filled, unsituated historically and unanchored in any traditional community—Aboriginal people are the exception here, of course, but an exception we prefer to ignore. Power today no longer grows out of the barrel of a gun but out of the cathode-ray tube. Those who control the media set the agenda for politics, the economy, and even the behaviour and lifestyle of most people because they work on our dreams, ambitions and aspirations. Self-interest has become a rule of life, pleasure a good, and money-getting, money-having and money-spending a life task. If society is not to fall apart into warring factions, we need to rethink our values and recover the ideal of citizenship, a sense of working together for the 'common good'.

At the risk of sermonising, I suggest that ideas and ideals of the kind I am canvassing here have never been so important. Seldom before has what we call 'civilisation' depended for its survival on the quality of thinking and feeling, on steadiness and trust, on the will for community and/or respect for a world in which living is not a mere machine for us to drive to its and our destruction. For this we need reason and creativity, sympathy and compassion. We need people who are deep, wise and humble, ready to share themselves and their insights, who not only know about but also believe in the society and culture we live in, its history, for ill as well as for good, and its possibilities.

These at least are the qualities which concern me here. Some of these essays are about injustice and cruelty, especially about the oppression and suffering of Aboriginal Australians, since I believe that it is important to name evil if we are to contest it. Complacency can not only be a form of dishonesty, it can also constitute a form of injustice. In contrast, however, the liberal imagination, to use that unfashionable phrase again, knows that the world is complex and often unexpectedly cruel and vicious, and insists that this should be acknowledged. Indeed, it knows that that acknowledgment is its opportunity and its obligation, that we are obliged to contest what is inhumane in the name of that 'humanity' which it constantly attempts to define, defend and enlarge.

This is a complicated as well as quixotic enterprise. But perhaps not so complicated as it first appears. As Wittgenstein reminds us:

The aspects of thing that are most important for us are hidden because of their simplicity and familiarity. (One is unable to notice something—because it is always before our eyes.) The real foundation of his [her] enquiry do not strike one at all. Unless that fact has at one time struck us.[2]

This proposition, I think, suggests the special importance of literature, especially of Australian literature. Defamiliarising what we take for granted, it allows us to see ourselves and our society from outside.

Looking back, I realise that this is a position I was almost bound to take. I was interested in Australian literature from childhood— my father read Henry Lawson and Banjo Paterson to me—I bought the collected poems of Bernard O'Dowd with the money from my first school prize—and, as an undergraduate just after the end of

World War II, I breathed in the air of enthusiastic but intelligent patriotism current at that time. Coming in contact with the Melbourne history department, with people like R.M. Crawford and Norman Harper—Manning Clark had just left to teach at Geelong Grammar—reinforced this interest, and the first stirrings in the English department of Leavis's ideas made me aware of the connection between writing and reading and quality of social, as well as merely individual, life. But Catholicism had something to do with it also. Growing up cheerfully Catholic—mine was not, it seems, the 'Catholic childhood' which has become almost a literary sub-genre of Australian literature—I also grew up with a sense of reality as polyphonic, not merely one-dimensional. For me, Catholicism was not a matter of ideological or moralistic rigidity but a licence to live beyond mere matter-of-fact, to believe that the supreme fact may be a kind of fiction, of poetry, 'a tune beyond us as we are', as Wallace Stevens put it, which also plays within us, composing us and at the same time drawing us to compose ourselves and the world in which we live. A concern for social justice came to be an aspect of that poetry.

Since then, of course, I have read and thought a great deal, and lived an interesting life. In the process I have also learned about the impurity of mere reason, the ways in which it is entangled in history and can become an aspect of power and, at the personal level, of self-interest. I now understand better the dangers of subjectivity in general, and religious feeling in particular; the delusions, dishonesties and distortions they make possible. Yet for me it remains undeniable that existence is dialectical, that there is an interdependence between what we know and some larger reality:

A dream (to call it a dream) in which
I can believe in the face of the object,

A dream no longer a dream, a thing
of things as they are

which also

Gives the touch of the senses, not of the hand,

But the very sense as they touch
The wind gloss.[3]

But this is not, I hope, a complacent belief. Growing older, I have grown more worldly-wise and come to think of myself more as a native of this world, thinking more as a native thinks rather than as the intellectual and emotional visitor I once was, increasingly aware not only of the world's painfulness but also of its absurdity. One of Salman Rushdie's characters expresses this awareness far better than I can:

'The world is incompatible, just never forget it: gaga. Ghosts, Nazis, saints, all alive at the same time; in one spot, blissful happiness, while down the road, the inferno. You can't ask for a wilder place'.[4]

That means the end of God as the divine watchmaker and patron of middle-class complacencies, of course. But for me, at least, it also means the beginning of a real sense of mystery, the sense expressed by another writer, Chinua Achebe:

That we are surrounded by deep mysteries is known by all but the incurably ignorant. But even they must concede the fact, indeed the inevitability, of judiciously spaced, but nevertheless certain, interruptions in the flow of their high art, to interject the words of their sponsors, the divinity that controls, remotely but diligently, the transactions of the market place that is their world.[5]

True, these 'words from the sponsor' become increasingly troubling as I grow older, rather than consoling, and Patrick White articulates for me the cruelties as well as the splendours under the surface of suburban life. A brief experience during the 1970s on the Appeals Tribunal of the Department of Social Security enlarged this perception and living in Western Australia, on the frontier, where racism and the spirit of conquest still flourish, helped also.

The German theologian Dietrich Bonhoeffer, executed for his opposition to Hitler, was also important to me. I first came across his work in the library during my time at the University of Chicago—theology was intellectually respectable there. Another great theologian, still alive then, Paul Tillich, gave a series of lectures on the false gods of our time, and another religious thinker, Mircea Eliade, was lecturing on Comparative Religion. It was the late 1960s. The civil rights movement was swirling around the university, situated on the southside, in the black quarter, and the Vietnam War was expanding and with it the protest movement, and here were theologians insisting that God was to be found at the centre of these concerns, not on the periphery. God showed himself in Jesus, Bonhoeffer argued, the 'man for others', done to death because of the challenge he offered to the rich and powerful of his day. God was not someone mysterious and aloof but to be found here and now.

Since then his theological understanding has deepened and Jürgen Moltmann's *The Crucified God* has been especially important in helping me to understand theologically the significance of our treatment of our Aboriginal sisters and brothers. This is an understanding which has also enlarged my commitment to literary and social criticism, making me aware that the 'meaning' of a text, whether it be literary or social, depends in large measure on its historical and ideological context. Learning more about language and the process of communication, I have also come to realise that the function is never merely aesthetic; language is the medium we use to display the world to ourselves and to one another, and solve the problems that arise within it. Reading and writing are political acts, less immediately influential than newspapers, advertising or the electronic media, but perhaps more enduringly influential since their effects are more long-lasting.

In these essays, then, I have tried to come at writing and living from different angles—literary, social and theological. Throughout, however, the central concern is with questions of value. I hope that does not make them fanatical: a faith which is not tempered with a certain amount of doubt seems to me dubious, given that its object is beyond comprehension—as St Paul insists, the idea of a crucified God is foolishness to human reason. There is no map of paradise or of the way there. We have to go there as free people, approaching by vigilance, imagination and love. But irony, a sense of proposition, is essential also. We cannot take for granted what we know or our method of knowing it if newness is to enter the world—that, for me, constitutes the importance of literary theory. But communication is essential, too, if one is to preserve the notion of community, of citizenship. That is why I suspect jargon and still cherish some notion of a 'common reader', interested in ideas and open to feeling, if not necessarily in touch with the full range of professional discourse.

This brings us to my last point, the preoccupation with the question of Australia. None of us lives at the originating point. We do not become who or what we are entirely by our own decision or learn all we know by personal experience; we are all part of a process of acculturation and socialisation. Thus my first influence was my father, a man who had travelled and continued to like travelling but who was also, perhaps for that reason, self-consciously and assertively Australian—his Irish ancestry was probably part of this, too. So I grew up interested in interpretation, trying to make sense of my world socially and politically as well as personally and ethically. Most people, particularly most academics and 'religious' people like me, take their environment more or less for granted. But thanks to him, Australia has always been for me a 'country of the mind' as well as a physical or political fact. So that I suppose I have been more like the settler Paul Carter describes in *The Road to Botany Bay*,[6] attempting to enclose a place in which history may begin to occur, to make a clearing in which she/he can express herself/himself as she/he is.

For me, Patrick White has been crucial to this attempt. But so, too, have been my encounters with Aboriginal people and culture and with their suffering at our hands, still going on, especially in Western Australia. Much of the state is still lightly settled, so the Aboriginal presence is still strong. It is still, in this sense, a frontier society, the frontier being a place of encounter with the other, of what is culturally unfamiliar, not just with nature. Here, by and large, we have made the decision to exclude this other, claiming the right to 'develop' and 'open-up' the land, denying Aboriginal rights to it by denying their culture's significance, condemning it and them as 'primitive'. But the more I get to know of Aboriginal people and of the history of our dealings with them and the land, the more I see this as a disastrous mistake—disastrous environmentally and culturally, as well as morally.

No doubt this is partly because, born into an Irish–Australian family, I belong to the oppositional strain of our culture. Even as a child, my imagination moved against the imperial tide of events. As a young man, my father had refused to fight in World War I and all his life he had a keen eye for dishonesty and injustice. For that reason, as I grew up I did not take the world for granted but thought more about changing it, sympathising with the losers rather than the winners. So the troubling presence of Aboriginal Australia, the prehistory with which our official history has still to come to terms,[7] has grown. Today, it seems to me increasingly the point at which we, as a people, invaders of the ancient land and intruders upon its culture, are challenged to come to terms with our actual situation as distinct from the one we like to imagine for ourselves.

For that, of course, we have to be prepared to see through our illusions and let them go. We need to be able to stand in the truth, to have a way of describing ourselves and the world which actually fits. So we return to the importance of literature and to another proposition by Wittgenstein. All too often, he remarked, thinking that we are describing the way things are, we are merely tracing through the frame through which we look at it. A picture holds us captive and we cannot get outside it, since it lies in our language which repeats it to us inexorably.[8] Literature, however, draws our attention to this language, helps us to interrogate the picture which imprisons us, provoking us by the strangeness, the world-disclosive power of its language. Neither science nor politics can overcome the problems we face. What we need rather, I would argue, is a renewal of imagination. A transformation of the way we see the world.

NOTES

1. Octavio Paz, *The Monkey Grammarian* (Peter Owen, London, 1981), p. 88.
2. Ludwig Wittgenstein, *Philosophical Investigations,* trans. G.E.M. Anscombe (Blackwell, Oxford, 1974), 129, p. 50e.
3. Wallace Stevens, 'The Man With the Blue Guitar XVIII', in his *Selected Poems* (Faber, London, 1963), p. 63.
4. Salman Rushdie, *The Satanic Verses* (Viking, London, 1988), p. 295.
5. Chinua Achebe, *Anthills of the Savannah* (Heinemann, London, 1987), p. 102.
6. Paul Carter, *The Road to Botany Bay* (Faber, London, 1988), chapter 5.
7. Ibid., p. 295.
8. Wittgenstein, 113–15, p. 48e.

1. ABORIGINAL AUSTRALIA

MABO
A QUESTION OF SPACE

We Australians like to think of ourselves as decent, easy-going and tolerant. But in the light of the storm of protest roused by the High Court's Mabo decision, we cannot afford to be complacent. Much of the protest is orchestrated by vested interests, it is true. But the residue of anti-Aboriginal, even racist, feeling is disturbing. What is happening? The problem is deep-seated, and it takes us back to questions left unresolved since the beginnings of settlement, crucial questions of identity and our place in time and space.

By and large we still define ourselves in imperial terms, as heirs to a destiny of world conquest. Today, of course, people world-wide are increasingly rejecting the idea and the fact of such a destiny. Yet many of us still cling to it, seeing ourselves as superior to our Asian neighbours simply because we are 'white'. We look to the old imperial centres of power in Europe and, more recently, the United States for assurance and support. So we are still colonised in an imaginative sense just as we are in economic terms. We are colonised and we are colonisers, seeing ourselves as superior to Aboriginal Australians and with superior rights to theirs. Until the Bicentenary, there was little thought of the country's past or of the prior rights of its Aboriginal inhabitants. There was even less questioning of our right to be here.

This is strange because, as a predominantly European culture in South-East Asia, ours is a particularly anomalous situation. In actuality, however, we may be said to live in the cultural equivalent of Lacan's mirror stage, in a world more imaginary than real, caught up, in Paul Ricoeur's phrase, in 'the annulment of the real in an imaginary unreal'.[1] True, this annulment has been increasingly challenged lately by growing political pressure from Asia and by the economic realities of our situation. But the Mabo decision is perhaps the most important challenge of all—it strikes at the roots of our self-definition as a people.

By definition, the idea of a nationality is bound up with notions of circumscription and exclusion, with fixed outlines which define us against others. In Australia, we have also had the help of geography. As inhabitants of an island continent, our physical boundaries are clearly outlined. Our developing sense of ourselves has often relied on exclusion—on the White Australia Policy, for example, and, more recently, the regulation of immigration. Despite the lip-service paid to multiculturalism, we like to think of ourselves in terms of monolithic unity. According to Mary Douglas's classification, our society is based more on the grid than the group, preoccupied with unity and with defending frontiers.[2] However, the Mabo decision blurs the distinctions we have drawn between ourselves and the Aborigines, writing them back into a history from which we had written them out, and suggesting that our unity might not be as monolithic as we think, that the other still survives within it and, some think, may subvert our purposes of prosperity and peaceful enjoyment of that prosperity.

The High Court's rejection of the notion of *terra nullius*, which served as the legal justification for our occupation of the country, also calls into question our ideas of space as an emptiness waiting to be filled. However, as writers like Mircea Eliade and Raimundo Pannikar point out, space has an inner as well as outer dimension. Properly speaking, they argue, there is no outer without inner space,[3] without some transformation of physical fact into psychic reality. It is precisely its strength that traditional Aboriginal culture made this transformation and established an equilibrium between the two spaces, so that, for thousands of years, people and land lived in a symbiotic and mutually supportive relationship. In our case, however, we have tended to live only in physical space, exploiting the environment for economic benefit—to increasingly destructive effect.

Notions of time are different. Time for Aboriginal culture is cyclical, a great wheel turning on a timeless centre, the Dreaming, which provides a point of orientation and value. For us, time is linear and progressive, tending to eliminate the past in the interests of the future. Our notion of time also writes Aboriginal people out of history: they represent the merely 'primitive', a prehistory which has been superseded, and was doomed to give way before us, the spearhead of progress. The High Court's Mabo decision, however, has written this prehistory back into social, political and economic consideration. What is at issue is not merely political or economic but symbolic. Mabo represents a challenge to the way we have imagined ourselves, especially in the crucial relationship to space and time.

Notions of Empire and imperial rights depended on the idea of empty space. Even as a boy, Conrad's Marlowe, for example, was preoccupied with the 'blank spaces of the earth', the imaginative equivalent of *terra nullius*, echoing the conclusion of Milton's *Paradise Lost*.

The world [seemed] all before them, where to choose
Their place of rest, and Providence their guide.

These lines, and the idea implicit in them of being the Chosen People on the way to the Promised Land, echo through British history of the nineteenth and twentieth centuries. They also coloured attitudes to the indigenous peoples of these 'blank spaces', the imaginative equivalent of *terra nullius* to be filled in by the 'civilising' power of Europe. With this notion went a parallel sense of destiny, propelling Europeans to take possession of the world. Like Adam and Eve at the end of *Paradise Lost*, and the Chosen People passing through the Wilderness on their way to the Promise,[4] Europeans considered indigenous peoples to be 'lesser breeds without the law', destined by divine logic to give way before European settlement. As the architecture of early Sydney suggests and Robert Dixon has shown,[5] this sense of imperial destiny coloured official views of the first settlement of New South Wales. As the settlement's name suggests, it was, in the words of William Wentworth's prize poem, to be A New Britannia in another world.[6] Britannia being seen as the heir of imperial Rome, Erasmus Darwin greeted the first settlement as a new chapter of this imperial history, a beginning which echoes Virgil's vision of imperial Rome:

There shall broad streets their stately walls extend,
The circus widen, and the crescent bend;
There, ray'd from cities o'er the culture'd land
Shall bright canals, and solid roads expand.

As for the land itself, it is to become fruitful and productive:

Embellish'd villas crown the landscape scene,
Farms wave with gold, and orchards blush between.[7]

Nature here is the sign of property and property the sign of nature, methodised to ends which were essentially economic.[8]

The reality, however, was quite different. The land around Sydney was poor and the flora and fauna unfamiliar and threatening. Very soon a different note began to sound, a note of historical as well as spatial vacancy. Marcus Clarke's introduction to the *Poems of Adam Lindsay Gordon* is perhaps its classic expression. 'This, our native or adopted land', he writes, 'has no past, no story. No poet speaks to us'.[9] It is a dangerous emptiness, a place of dread, like the Gothic castles which haunted the Romantic imagination, haunted by a strange but dangerous absence which is also a presence.

The land was threatening because it did not fit the categories the colonisers wished to impose upon it. 'The trim utilitarian civilisation bred [then sank] into insignificance'[10] before its expanse and its strangeness. The Book of Nature, that central trope of the Enlightenment, seemed closed. All that the newcomers saw were 'the strange scribblings of Nature learning how to write',[11] returning them to the archaic beginnings left behind by imperial progress. But the Aborigines belonged there, and could read the Book of Nature closed to the settlers. So, imaginatively, they were subsumed into this vacancy and into the dread it provoked. This dread was intensified by the nature of their resistance— not the open, recognisable military resistance of the Maoris of

New Zealand or the North American peoples, but a guerilla war, fought in terms of long absences punctuated by sudden terrifying incursions of fierce and dangerous presence.

So many settlers failed to come to terms with their actual situation, projecting on to it both their hopes and their fears, and their sense of 'weird melancholy'.

Space and time remained a formless expanse, homogeneous in its fundamental strangeness and unreality,[12] a place of psychic displacement. Settlement in a new country, Mircea Eliade argues, is the equivalent of an act of creation, demanding the 'transformation of chaos into cosmos'.[13] But for many, chaos remained, and the Aborigines were associated with this chaos. As Marcus Clarke wrote:

The Australian mountain forests are funereal, secret, stern. Their solitude is desolation.

They seem to stifle, in their black gorges, a story of sullen despair. In other lands the dying year is mourned, the falling leaves drop lightly on their bier. In the Australian forests no leaves fall . . . From the melancholy gums strips of white bark hang and rustle.

The very animal life of these frowning hills is either grotesque or ghostly. Great grey kangaroos hop noiselessly over the course grass. Flights of white cockatoos stream out, shrieking like evil souls. The sun suddenly sinks, and the mopokes burst out into horrible peals of semi-human laughter. The natives aver, when night comes, from out of the bottomless depths of some lagoon, the Bunyip rises, and, in form like monstrous sea-calf, drags his loathsome length from out the ooze. From the corner of the silent forest rises a dismal chant, and around a fire dance native painted like skeletons. All is fear-inspiring and gloomy.[14]

The Aborigines figure here at the level of dream—not just at the economic level. This is a crucial point. As Ricoeur remarks, 'to manifest the "sacred" on the "cosmos" and to manifest it in the "psyche" are the same thing'.[15] Associated with the threatening strangeness of the land, the Aborigines become figures of evil—diabolical.

This sense is not exclusive to Clarke, of course. In 'The Creek of the Four Graves', the opening section of Charles Harpur's unfinished epic of settlement, for instance, they figure as devils, leaping out of the flames of the explorers' camp fire like 'hell's worst fiends', come 'in vengeance':

> . . . *being in their dread inherited fate*
> *Awful, vengeful as hell's worst fiends.* [16]

In Harpur's poem, however, the economic reason for the Aborigines' opposition to the expansion of white settlement is clear: the explorers the Aborigines attack and kill are moving into the interior

> . . . *to seek*
> *New streams and wider pastures for [their] fast*
> *Increasing flocks and herds.* [17]

This is also a prime reason advanced by the opponents of Mabo: to give Aboriginal people rights over land, it is said, would be to hold up economic development. On the evidence of the Northern Territory, where Aboriginal people have some control over land, this is not so. But the fear of Mabo's opponents, it seems, goes deeper than the merely economic. It is connected with the sense that Aborigines represent some kind of malign and threatening presence, corresponding to something unacknowledged in the self, as they do in Harpur's poem. A passage from Rosa Praed's *Lady Bridget in The Never Never Land* (1915) expresses this sense even more vividly:

> *Lower and lower sank the sun, and when at last his rim touched the horizon, the blacks, as it were, concentrated themselves for one last effort. They were not easy to see, those naked black figures, that seemed to understand how to assimilate themselves with the scrub and to take advantage of every bit of cover, but the two lonely men seemed to feel their presence all around them. There was a strange rustling in the scrub, a breath of wind sighted mysteriously, a twig snapped on the bank above, some pellets of earth fell down, gently, slowly, silently, as if afraid to break the stillness.* [18]

If, as Edward Said argues, the ideology of empire involves 'a *distribution* of geographical awareness . . . a certain will or *invention* to understand, . . . to control, manipulate, even to incorporate what is manifestly different',[19] the Aborigines' presence and appearance resisted and continues to resist this distribution and this will.

In this way, Aborigines gradually became figures of taboo—dangerous to contemplate, unable to be approached without risk. The reaction of many of the opponents of Mabo reflects this sense of taboo. But an earlier example of this notion can be found in Cecil Mann's response to Katherine Susannah Prichard's *Coonardoo*, one of the first novels to deal with relations between a white man and a black woman. Mann, a leading literary critic, was outraged by the book. It was, he wrote, almost impossible to make 'the Australian Aboriginal a romantic figure'.[20] Echoing the neo-Darwinian view that the Aborigines were the lowest form of human life, the 'missing link' between the human and the animal, he continued:

With any other native, from fragrant Zulu girl to fly-kissed Arab maid, she could have done it. But the Aboriginal, in Australia, cannot excite any higher feeling than nauseated pity or comical contempt.[21]

The extremity of this outburst suggests that what is involved here is what Paul Ricoeur calls 'peril of soul',[22] the fear of defilement. Evil is experienced as 'a material "something" associated with blackness that transmits itself by contact and contagion',[23] and, here, the inflation of the sexual is also characteristic of this fear.[24]

Having spoken of these unconscious factors, however, we should now return to the matter of economics. The original meaning of the word has to do with management of the household. In settler societies, this question of management looms large, especially at the beginning of settlement. Migration is usually traumatic. In the words of *The Recollections of Geoffrey Hamlyn*, it involves a 'disturbance of the household gods and the rupture of life-old associations'.[25] In a new place, especially one as far away and strange as Australia, the envelope of custom, habit and tradition is left behind and the newcomers are delivered over unprotected to the cosmic and oneiric.

Geoffrey Hamlyn captures this vividly:

Few know the feeling which comes upon all men when [this break is made] . . . the feeling of isolation, almost of terror, at having gone so far out of the bounds of ordinary life; the feeling of self-distrust and cowardice at being alone and friendless in the world, like a child in the dark. [26]

Add to that the fact that the majority of migrants have always been poor and oppressed, and the reasons for our preoccupation with material possessions and well-being become clear. As Hannah Arendt observes, 'abundance and endless consumption are the ideals of the poor . . . the mirage in the desert of misery'.[27] The apparent poverty of the Aborigines was frightening to these people. To the better educated and more prosperous, it was also troubling: if, as the Enlightenment assumed, humanity was always and everywhere the same, then they were the epitome of all that was degraded, their few possessions, wandering life and near nakedness, resembling the figure of the Wild Man which haunted the Middle Ages and Renaissance. This figure, Hayden White suggests, was a distillation of the anxieties underlying the three basic institutions of civilisation: 'the securities of sex (as organised by the institution of the family), *sustenance* (as provided by political, social and economic institutions) and salvation (as provided by the Church)'.[28]

Because they challenged these securities, then, the Aborigines had to be excluded from the 'humanity' they threatened. Neo-Darwinian notions were also useful here. In 1830, James, for instance, wrote that the Aborigines were 'nearest of all to the monkey or orang-outang' and therefore incapable of enjoying the same state of intellectual existence 'as white people'.[29] Four years later, Peter Cunningham placed them 'at the very zero of civilisation—constituting the connecting link between man and the monkey tribe'.[30] This was also convenient. As the missionary, Lancelot Threkeld, observed in 1853:

If it could be proved that the Aborigines were only a species of wild beasts, there could be no guilt attributed to those who shot them off or poisoned them, [31] as many of them did.

In this way, Henry Reynolds says, successive generations became 'hardened against the natives'.[32] These feelings were also reinforced by what has been called the 'Manichean Allegory' which justifies imperialism with the notion that 'white' is to 'black' as good is to evil, as superior is to inferior, civilised to savage, rational to irrational, and so on.[33] This sense of superiority was strengthened by the economic argument which tended to associate prosperity with virtue, and poverty with vice. In this version of Christianity

. . . the blessed prosper and their blessedness is reflected in their wealth and health, the number of their sons, their longevity, and their ability to make things grow. The accused [in contrast] wither and wander aimlessly on the earth—fearful, ugly and violent; and their fearfulness, ugliness and violence are evidence of their accursedness.[34]

Even today, Aboriginal poverty is seen by many as a sign not only of their innate inferiority but also of their viciousness.

For people not entirely sure of their own identity, the Manichean allegory was and is particularly reassuring. The settlers may not have known the precise content of their own humanity, but at least they could assure themselves that they were 'not like that', seeing themselves as 'civilised' and the Aborigines as 'savage', 'Christian' where they were 'pagan' and so on.[35]

As Hayden White remarks, this kind of definition is especially appealing to 'groups whose dissatisfactions are easier to recognise than their programs are to justify',[36] so its continuing appeal today in a time of economic and social crisis is not surprising. Nor is its influence on the Mabo debate. If we regard Aborigines as different from and inferior to ourselves, then the proposal to accord them the same rights as ourselves is outrageous. It is even more outrageous when their claims are seen to threaten the hard-won gains of the past and prospects for the future in which we take so much pride. Similarly, writing them back into history challenges the neo-Darwinian logic of progress upon which we rely for justification.

Given such entrenched attitudes and the influence of unconscious factors, reconciliation seems a forlorn hope. Nevertheless, the rule of ideology is never universal nor is it unchallengeable. To the extent that it relies on symbols which govern the process of imagining ourselves and our world, symbols may hold the key to change. Negative attitudes to Aborigines are the product of a certain set of symbols—of exclusion on the one hand, and of a dream of imperial power and prosperity on the other. What we need to do, therefore, is renew the symbols by which we live. This at least is what David Malouf suggests in his most recent novel, *Remembering Babylon*.

Throughout his career, Malouf has been preoccupied with questions of liminality, of space and transformation and the relations between self and other, language and silence. In *Remembering Babylon*, these questions are not only central but are posed in terms of relations between non-Aboriginal and Aboriginal Australians. These terms are seen as ethical, even metaphysical, as a choice between good and evil, between Jerusalem and Babylon of the title. It also offers an opportunity to learn a new language, a language of the earth.

In this way, the novel begins with the Manichean division which underlies the division between Aboriginal and non-Aboriginal Australians. But it also highlights the question of the frontier, of the definite lines we have drawn around ourselves and upon the map and of the need to move across them into new and unknown territory.

Set on the Queensland frontier in the 1840s, it initially highlights the settlers' reliance on imperial authority, represented by the Governor, whose power derives from a distant monarch, a power, they believed, which 'held them all, a whole continent, in its grip'.[37] But the novel also highlights the settlers' anxiety, and the threat the Aborigines occasion in their refusal to acknowledge this authority:

And all around, before and behind, worse than weather and the deepest might, natives, tribes of wandering myalls who, in their traipsing in this way and that were forever encroaching on boundaries that could be insisted on by daylight—a good shot gun saw to that—but in the dark hours, when you no longer stood there as a living marker with all the glow of the white man's authority about you, reverted to being a creek bed or ridge of granite like any other (p. 9).

This threat reaches panic proportions with the arrival in their midst of a young white man, Gemmy Fairley, who has lived for sixteen years with the Aborigines. He has thus crossed the line which divides white and black, on which they rely for authority. Suggesting that after all this line is not absolute, 'not to be fixed in real space . . . [but] could begin anywhere', (p. 38) his presence among them seems somehow treasonable. But even more terrifying, having shared the life, even learned the language of people they regard as savage and degraded, he now comes back to claim his right to live among them as a British subject or 'object', as he (perhaps rightly) puts it in the confusion of first encounter.

Malouf's account of the terror his presence arouses gives a vivid sense of the effects this reminder of the other world they have rejected in the name of civilisation has upon them, of

. . . the horror [Gemmy's appearance] carries . . . not just the smell, in your own sweat, of a half-forgotten swamp world going back deep in both of you, but that for him as you meet here face to face in the sun, you and all you stand for have not yet appeared over the horizon of the world (p. 43).

There is a contemporary parallel in the panic Mabo has occasioned. The notion that Aboriginal people have rights as we do, like Gemmy's crossing of the line drawn by the settlers, threatens our sense of superiority and even of identity. Looking at him

. . . all the wealth of [civilisation] goes dim [for the settlers] . . . then is cancelled altogether, and you meet at last in a terrifying equality that strips the last rag from your soul and leaves you so far out on the edge of yourself that your fear now is that you may never get back (p. 43).

In the novel the settlers respond by driving Gemmy out of the settlement and back to the Aborigines where he is later killed by a group of whites, 'ridden down and brought to earth by blows from a stirrup iron at the end of a stirrup leather—an effective weapon, when used at a gallop for smashing skulls' (p. 196). This is true to the brutalities of history. But Malouf is also concerned with the possibility of change. Among the settlers, two characters, two of the three children who first met Gemmy—Janet McIvor and Lachlan, her cousin—are changed forever by this meeting, open out to the possibilities Gemmy represents.

For Janet, this involves an experience which is profoundly dangerous, a moment in which a swarm of bees descend upon her, surrounding her with a thick and dangerous darkness. Where colonial society shrinks from this kind of danger, she allows herself to be drawn into it, moving across the frontier into a danger which is initially physical—the bees could kill her—but ultimately psychic, an experience of 'the process and mystery of things' (p. 143) of the sacred, the *mysterium tremendum et fascinans*.

Colonial society has located itself resolutely in profane space. But here she lets herself be drawn into a sacred space, the space of traditional Aboriginal society. She is prepared for this by an earlier scene in which, picking at a scab on her knee she discovers under it another skin, 'lustrous as pearl':

A delicate pink, it might have belonged to some other creature altogether, and the thought came to her that if all the rough skin of her present self crusted and came off, what would be revealed, shining in sunlight, was this finer being that had somehow been covered up in her (p. 59).

Her world ceases to be monolithic, the unitary world of a society intent upon the merely material. When she gets up and walks out into the paddock, her world is transfigured:

All the velvety grass heads blazed up, halved with gold, she felt under the influence of her secret skin, suddenly float, as if she had been relieved

of the weight of her own life, and the brighter being in her was very gently
stirring and shifting its wings (p. 59).

Colonial space is a matter of exclusion and exteriority, of drawing
lines, building barriers and accumulating material things, of defining
ourselves by appearances and marking what is different with the signs
of our power. But here Janet is moving out into a richer sense of
reality, aware of another kind of power.

This seems a long way from the harsh social, political and
economic realities of the Mabo debate and the long history of
prejudice, fear and violence between Aboriginal and non-Aboriginal
Australians. But it may be that we non-Aborigines will remain captive
to our injustice and, worse, to the pretence that we are innocent,
until we learn to expand our world view to a larger sense of good
and evil than the one we currently have, which confuses the
cosmobiological with the ethical—confuses *fairing* ill with doing ill.[38]

If Homi Bhabha is right—that colonial authority rests on
empiricism idealism, mimeticism and monoculturalism[39]—then the
move here towards the sacred and a more polyphonic sense of self
and world represented here is important. It could represent that
ceremonial taking possession of new territory of which Eiliade
speaks, a ritual in which space is transformed from threatening chaos
to cosmos and we are made at home in the world in the largest
sense[40]—as Aboriginal people are in their culture, in which existence
is totally symbolic, and the psychic and the physical are two aspects
of the one reality.

This may seem exalted. But as Homi Bhabha points out, the battle
between colonisers and the colonised is as much a battle for the
status of truth as for the possession of land and resources.[41] We
rejected Aboriginal culture and everything it stood for, attempting
to impose our own monolithic and one divisional notions of reality
on them. Legally, the High Court's decision allows for their
difference, for their different relationship with the land. But
acceptance of difference needs to go further, to extend to a
recognition of their culture and its different notions of reality and
value. This kind of transition will not take place over night, however,

and it will demand significant adjustments and recognitions. This is where the figure of Lachlan becomes important in Malouf's novel.

From the beginning, Lachlan is the typically boyish, idealistic settler of legend, 'full of bright schemes for the future', heroic visions in which his limitations would at last be transcended. Confident that life is essentially rational and manageable, he feels that if only he could spell out these visions clearly 'they would be up there, up ahead, waiting for him to catch up bearing the details at last of place and time (p. 60)'. But Gemmy's arrival confuses things, challenging the clear lines drawn up to distinguish black from white, civilised from savage, good from evil, and so on.

Externally, Lachlan goes on living as the others do, becoming rich and successful and eventually a member of Parliament. But long after his disappearance, the memory of Gemmy continues to trouble him. The climax comes when he discovers the bones of Gemmy and his Aboriginal companions killed by a group of marauding whites.

He looked at one dry bundle, then another—they were not distinguishable—and felt nothing more for one than for any of them . . . He sorrowed quietly for all, in the hope that it might also cover his *bones, if they were here (p. 197).*

It is fifty years since he last saw Gemmy. But 'what he had touched off in them was what they were still living' (p. 197), the realisation that the frontier opens out to difference and need not, must not, exclude it. So the ragged figure, as they first saw him balanced on the fence, the frontier between his Uncle's farm and the unknown country beyond, 'impenetrable dark' (p. 8), remains with him:

the figure outlined there against the streaming sky. Still balanced. For a last moment held still by their gaze, their solemn and fearful attention, at the one clear point, till the last, where they were inextricably joined and would always be (p. 197).

What had begun with this meeting, he understands, 'would end only when they were ended and maybe not even then' (p. 197). They

26

would keep coming back to this point of encounter.

If the fearful enclosure of colonial society can be summed up in J. M. Coetzee's image of the 'Man with the Gun', driven by the fear that all life is trapped within him, and that his life may be the only life there is, that there is nothing outside the self[42] (an image replicated in Sidney Nolan's Ned Kelly), here Lachlan has laid down his arms. He is open to the other, ready to stand on the same ground of humanity with the Aborigines. When he tells his uncle of his discovery of the remains of the massacre and that Gemmy is dead, it is as if he is 'tying up one of the loose ends of his own life, which might otherwise have gone on bleeding forever' (p. 197). Lachlan is facing the darkness within himself, acknowledging his own complicity in the killings and dispossession of a people.

Some people say that this kind of acknowledgment means indulging in guilt. But guilt is best defined as feeling responsible for not being responsible.[43] To face up to the injustices of the past and to admit that we still benefit from them, from our occupation of the land, acquisition of its resources and dispersal of its Aboriginal inhabitants, is at least to acknowledge responsibility and thus come to terms with guilt. The Mabo decision points to one way of beginning to right these historic wrongs, a way to begin to move, as Janet does at the very end of the story, into the rich, more polyphonic sense of reality characteristic of Aboriginal culture.

Watching the moon rise over the water and looking back over her life since the meeting with Gemmy, Janet is drawn once more into a sense of 'the process and mystery of things' (p. 143).

Out beyond the flat land the line of light pulses and swells. The sea, in sight now, ruffles, accelerates. Quickly now it is rising towards us, it approaches.

As we approach prayer. As we approach one another (p. 200).

This is not a way likely to recommend itself to politicians or pragmatists, of course. What it suggests, however, is the need for non-Aboriginal Australians to move out of the narrow ideological enclosure in which we have been living to recognise the other,

Aboriginal Australia, its history and its claims upon us in the name of justice. This at least is what Janet in *Remembering Babylon* recognises, as in the full light of the moon 'in a line of running fire, all the outline of the vast continent appears, in touch now with its other life' (p. 200).

NOTES

1. Paul Ricoeur, *The Symbolism of Evil* (Beacon Press, Boston, 1967), p. 13.
2. Mary Douglas, *Natural Symbols* (Penguin, 1973), pp. 77–92.
3. Raimundo Pannikar, 'There Is No Inner without Outer Space', *Cross Currents*, 43, 1 (Spring 1993), pp. 60–81.
4. Hayden White, *Tropics of Discourse: Essays in Cultural Criticism* (Johns Hopkins University Press, London, 1986), p. 159.
5. Robert Dixon, *The Course of Empire: Neo-Classical Culture in New South Wales 1788–1860* (Oxford University Press, Melbourne, 1986).
6. Ian Turner, *The Australian Dream* (Sun Books, Melbourne, 1968), p. 12.
7. Ibid., p. 2.
8. Simon Ryan.
9. Ibid., p. 101.
10. Ibid., p. 102.
11. Ibid.
12. Robert Moore, 'Space and Transformation in Human Experience', in Robert Moore and Frank Reynolds (eds), *Anthropology and the Study of Religion* (Centre for the Scientific Study of Religion, Chicago, 1984), p. 129.
13. Mircea Eliade, *The Myth of the Eternal Return or Cosmos and History* (Princeton University Press, 1971), p. 10.
14. Turner, p. 101.
15. Ricoeur, p. 16.
16. Harry Heseltine (ed.), *The Penguin Book of Australian Verse* (Penguin, 1979), p. 59.
17. Ibid., p. 55.
18. Rosa Praed, *Lady Bridget in Never Never Land* (Paladin, Sydney, 1987), p. 89.
19. Edward Said, *Orientalism* (Penguin, 1978), p. 12.
20. Ric Throssell, *Wild Weeds and Wind Flowers: The Life and Letters of Katherine Susannah Prichard* (Angus & Robertson, Sydney, 1975), p. 54.
21. Ibid.
22. Ricoeur, p. 12.
23. Ibid., p. 69.

24. Ibid., p. 28.
25. J. S. D. Mellick, *Portable Australian Authors: Henry Kinglsey*, (University of Queensland Press, 1982), p. 134.
26. Ibid.
27. Hannah Arendt, *Of Revolution* (Penguin, London, 1973), p. 139.
28. White, p. 166.
29. John Harris, *One Blood; Two Hundred Years of Aboriginal Encounter With Christianity: A Story of Hope* (Albatross Books, Sydney, 1990), p. 24.
30. Ibid.
31. Ibid., p. 25.
32. Henry Reynolds, *Frontiers* (Allen and Unwin, Sydney, 1989).
33. Abdul Jan Mahomed, 'The Economy of Manichean Allegory: The Function of Racial Difference in Colonialist Literature', in Henry Louis Gates (ed.), *'Race', Writing and Difference* (Chicago University Press, London, 1986), pp. 78–106.
34. White, p. 160.
35. Ibid., p. 151
36. Ricoeur, p. 12.
37. David Malouf, *Remembering Babylon* (Random House Australia, Sydney, 1993), p. 5. Henceforth page references given in the text of my essay.
38. Ricoeur, p. 27.
39. Homi Bhabha, 'Signs Taken For Wonders: Questions of Ambivalence and Authority Under A Tree Outside Delhi'. In Gates, p. 169.
40. Eliade, p. 10.
41. Bhabha, p. 171
42. J M Coetzee, *Dusklands* (Penguin, London, 1971), p. 61.
43. Ricoeur, pp. 100–1

POLYPHONIES OF THE SELF
THE CHALLENGE OF ABORIGINAL AUSTRALIA

This is a difficult paper to write; to some non-Aborigines it will seem inappropriate and to some Aborigines yet another act of appropriation. It is about the crucial problem facing Australian culture, reconciliation between Aboriginal and non-Aboriginal Australians. For Aboriginal people we were 'the bringers of death' (Mudrooroo Narogin). But there is also something lost in and to those who bring death, and my argument will be that non-Aboriginal Australians need to come to terms with this aspect of our culture and of ourselves, that our sense of who we are in relation to the Aborigines is the key myth—to use Levi-Strauss's term—of our culture. What is involved, that is to say, is an attempt to move from ethnology to anthropology, arguing that, in this case at least, Aboriginality can be seen as an aspect of ourselves, as a psychic, ethical, perhaps even metaphysical fact. That is not to deny the actual existence of Aboriginal people and their culture—that is the ultimate assimilation. But it is to say that in non-Aboriginal experience as the Aborigines have perhaps come to represent the shadow, 'the sum of all those unpleasant qualities we like to hide, together with the insufficiently developed functions and contents of the . . . unconscious'.[1]

By definition, this arises out of our colonial situation. As far as Aborigines are concerned, we are colonisers. Yet the 'Manichean allegory' of colonisation in which white is to black as good is to evil[2] also has its effects on us, locking us into a position of false superiority and out of our own hearts, sometimes our own bodies, leaving us with deep feelings of inadequacy which issue, on the one hand, in authoritarian habits of mind and heart and, on the other, the desire to be noticed and to please some distant metropolitan centre, formerly London but now more often New York. For all our talk of 'multiculturalism', Australian society thus remains defensive, essentially ethnocentric and monological, tight-lipped and preoccupied with objective reality, living in what Patrick White calls 'the Great Australian Emptiness' overwhelmed by the meaninglessness of profane existence and the ghost-like character, the somewhat sinister loneliness of much of our writing.

This is not the general view of Australian culture, I know. But it is the view of us increasingly appearing in Aboriginal writing. In his novel, *Master of the Ghost Dreaming*, Mudrooroo Narogin, for instance, shows us to ourselves through the eyes of the Aborigines in the first stages of the encounter between us, as ghosts, refugees from the other side of the world, 'a cold and forbidding place filled with so much suffering a human being could not survive in it'.[3] To them, we 'seemed to have a horror about humanity' and our whole bodies seemed to be 'made of solidified fog . . . [which] if they went unclothed for any length of time . . . would slowly begin to evaporate.'[4] In this view we have become what the Aborigines often are to us, a figure in a nightmare.

But nightmares can influence social reality, as the increasing violence between Aboriginal and non-Aboriginal Australians suggests. It is surely crucial, therefore, if we are to waken from it, to see ourselves through the eyes of others, particularly the others with whom we share this land. Indeed, I want to argue that it is essential if we are to discover who we really are. According to Bakhtin, for example, it is impossible to conceive our being or even to imagine ourselves to ourselves, much less to others, except through relations which link us to the other.[5] Our culture needs to be decentred verbally and ideologically if we are to break out of the enclosure of our self-sufficiency and become conscious of ourselves in relation to other cultures and languages and thus other ways of being human. For this, according to Bakhtin we need a 'transgredient' element of consciousness which is external to it yet necessary for its completion.[6] The Aboriginal people and their culture, I would argue, constitute this element, the lost Other side of ourselves and our present sense of ourselves is incomplete without it. Every person and culture, Bakhtin says, has an absolute need:

. . . for the other, for the other's activity of seeing, holding, putting together and unifying, which alone can bring into being the externally finished personality; if someone else does not do it, then the other presently will have no existence. [7]

The other people and cultures who and which are becoming increasingly important in 'multicultural' Australia, do not have the same valency as the Aborigines because they are more or less external to this drama of identity which began in 1788, though the Chinese might be a possible exception. But the Aborigines are an essential part of the continuous sign chain of our way of life since then. True, in the course of time they have become what Bakhtin calls a 'diseased transgredient'. [8] What they represent has become morbid, a sign of guilt, of unacknowledged defilement and of our own ethical and existential failure. The fact is, however, that the disease is ours rather than theirs, and the chronic unconcern, the sheer indifference, if not hostility, with which most Australians try to deal with this issue is one of its symptoms. If we are to restore ourselves and our culture to health we must break and then relink the chain of significance within which we and they exist.

Here literature becomes important, providing a way out of the self, a means of 'finding oneself outside', by fictional models—act and reality, as Eliade points out, are a function of invitation. [9] In the present instance, then, action will come from disrupting the system of representation which has excluded Aboriginal people and our treatment of them.

The first stage in this disruption is not identification and empathy—that leads to assimilation—but the reverse, contemplating the Aborigine as the other, indeed a troubling other, and this is why the anger of Aboriginal writers is so important. But so, too, is the growing presence of Aboriginal people and culture in the work of writers as different as White, Stow, Keneally, Drewe, Koch, Hasluck, Winton, Moorhead, and, by powerful implication, in Jolley and Farmer. This presence echoes the question put in 1844 by Richard Windeyer. Notable apologist for white settlement and defence counsel for the white men involved in the Myall Creek Massacres, he still had to ask himself: 'How is it that our minds are not satisfied? What means this whispering at the bottom of our hearts?'[10] Troubling figures like White's Alf Dubbo, Moorhead's Oona or Winton's black Christ by the roadside and on the seashore keep these questions alive, suggesting that they, not we, are at the centre and that it is we who are marginal. '[Aboriginal] cultural heritage,' the Aboriginal dancer Ross Watson insists, for example, ' . . . is instilled into the very depths of this continent, into our very beings', whereas, as *Voss* put it, we are uneasily aware of ourselves clinging to the fringes of the continent and of ourselves.

This trope of the land is usually, and probably rightly, seen as the key to Australian culture since, as Ricoeur remarks, 'Cosmos and Psyche are two poles of the same expressivity.' We express ourselves in expressing the world, explore our depths in deciphering that of the land.[11] Significantly for us non-Aborigines, however, the land usually figures as a place of death, the 'dead heart', the desert at the centre 'out where the dead men lie', the equivalent of the Colossus for the ancient Greeks—vast, shapeless, immobile, emblem of the fixity of death set against the warmth and mobility of life.[12] In this way, the land figures forth the death we have brought to the Aborigines and their culture.

The official histories have repressed this violence. But in fact, as Henry Reynolds argues persuasively, settlement was marked by 'a line of blood'.[13] Certainly, the first settlers often saw themselves as engaged in a military operation, and at least 20 000 Aborigines and perhaps a quarter as many whites died in a long and bitter guerrilla war. To the extent that we deny or repress this, however, the Aborigine becomes a psychological as much as a physical presence, the embodiment of that which we are afraid of in ourselves, a figure of taboo, of the 'peril of soul' which it represents.[14] In this sense they belong to the oneiric dimension. But it is in dreams, of course, that we catch a glimpse of the most fundamental and stable aspects of ourselves. Consider in this respect the dream of an early squatter, E. Lloyd, published in a memoir in 1846:

I had a dream . . . It did not seem like a dream; of some gentle beings as in time past, speaking words of comfort and soothing; when they rejoiced I rejoiced with them, and when they wept, I sorrowed. Suddenly, the scene changed and I was conscious of a number of hideous black faces crowding round me with hostile intent, demanding tobacco. Wherever I retreated they followed; and still the sound of their voices came ringing in my ears . . . in a threatening tone and to the last their horrible visages, with this detestable sound, pressed on my troubled fancy. But a cold, chilly feeling came over me, and I awoke.[15]

J.J. Healy has also remarked on a 'sweaty anxiety' which seems to enter colonial writing whenever Aborigines are mentioned. They represent, it seems, something at once alien and terribly familiar, a part of oneself which has been suppressed but which returns with devastating effect.

The settlers' insistence on the Aborigines' 'savagery', ugliness and treachery thus takes on new significance. An early settler in New South Wales in 1820, for instance, writes of the horror of 'waiting, waiting, waiting for the creeping, treacherous blacks', and another of feeling them 'hovering close around us', living in 'constant dread'; and one senses here a fear of retribution. Similarly, for the West Australian Bessie Bussell, in 1837, the word 'native' was 'fraught with fatigue, fear and anxiety'.[16] It is the primitive anxiety evident here which often pushed and sometimes still pushes us to violence against those we have wronged.

Contemporary Aboriginal writing makes this clear, directing the violence back at us. The effect is cathartic, pointing to the violence implicit in the 'Manichean allegory' of racism, a way of giving moral authority to the superiority based on brute force, and suggesting that our hatred of the blacks may be self-hatred.

Challenging merely aesthetic categories, these texts thus demand a reading which is political and ethical, becoming for us as well as Aborigines a matter of self-discovery and perhaps even of self-reversal as we see ourselves and our culture through their eyes as brutal, degrading and destructive. That, of course, is the way to a proper self-knowledge since Bakhtin observes, 'there exists no death from the inside; it exists for no one, not for the dying, nor for others . . . I can die only for others', just as, 'conversely, for me, only others die'.[17] But this encounter with the other, the consequences of our destructiveness, can also be liberating. The strangeness of form and language in works like Narogin's *Doin Wild Cat* or the poetry of Lionel Fogarty, for example, is an encounter with other voices, other discourses, which represents new polyphonic possibilities for the self. True, they can also threaten disintegration and even insanity. But to the extent that we embrace rather than resist them a new, more expansive and inclusive sense of self begins to emerge from it.

This brings us to our last and perhaps crucial point, to the confrontation with death, the descent into the underworld or, to use a more characteristically Australian trope, the journey into the centre. This, B. Wongar insists, is the only way resolution will come, enabling non-Aborigines to be accepted into the Aboriginal spiritual world. Patrick White is the key writer here, and *A Fringe of Leaves* the key text. Here Ellen Roxburgh suffers a ritualised death, descending into the underworld of the 'savagery' which Western culture projects on to the Aborigine. But she also shatters the ultimate taboo, cannibalism, which represents the climax of the colonial repertoire of violence, the emblem of ultimate savagery, as all that we see as grotesquely different and disgusting. As Ellen's encounter is presented here, we are brought up before the source of this violence, the fear that the Aborigines were not so much our brothers and sisters but rather 'distant ancestors who had overstayed their time on earth'.[18] Recognising them as her contemporaries, owning what is 'archaic', the shadow within her, Ellen thus renounces the neo-Darwinian justification for our presence in this country, that justification which rests on the image of 'the unchanging savage [as] . . . the benchmark which could be used to measure the reality of colonial progress'.[19] The fact that the scene is comic, even parodic, in tone indicates the relief involved.

Between them, therefore, writing by Aborigines and non-Aborigines bears on this encounter between us, generating a new

35

sense of plurality. On the Aboriginal side, new power emerges, a new sense of themselves speaking within our culture and challenging us. On our side, a closed and defensive unity of self opens out to affirm the Aborigine not as an object but as another subject, an aspect of ourselves and our history and the moral problem we projected on to them is increasingly recognised as our own. In the past we have shrunk from this discovery, fearing the loss of our self-possession as well as our other possessions. Now it may be that recognition of the discourse of the other points us to a different kind of future. Let Mudrooroo Narogin have the last word: while 'souls must be given warmth, warmth love and forgiveness to all, allowed to flow through to all planes. The ways must be opened. Bitterness and hatred block the way to . . . empowerment.'[20]

NOTES

1. Anthony Storr (ed.) *Jüng: Selected Writings* (Fontana, London, 1983), p. 87.
2. Abdul JanMohamed, 'The Economy of Manichean Allegory: The Function of Racial Difference in Colonialist Literature', in H.L. Gates (ed.), *'Race', Writing and Difference* (Chicago University Press, London, 1986), pp. 78–106.
3. Mudrooroo Narogin, *Master of the Ghost Dreaming* (Angus & Robertson, Sydney, 1991), p. 32.
4. Ibid., p. 52.
5. Tzoetan Todorov, *Mikhail Bakhtin: The Dialogical Principle* (Manchester University Press, Manchester, 1985), p. 9.
6. Ibid., p. 95.
7. Ibid., p. 101.
8. Ibid., p. 99.
9. Mircea Eliade, *The Myth of the Eternal Return: Or, Cosmos and History* (Princeton University Press, Princeton, 1974), p. 12.
10. Henry Reynolds, *Frontier: Aborigines, Settlers and Land* (Allen & Unwin, Sydney, 1987), p. 162.
11. Paul Ricoeur, *The Symbolism of Evil* (Beacon Press, Boston, 1969), p. 13.
12. Jean Pierre Vernant, 'La Categoire du Double', In *Mythe et Pensée Chez Les Grecs* (Maspew, Paris, 1982), pp. 65–78.
13. Reynolds, p. 196.
14. Ibid., p. 10.
15. Ricoeur, p. 12.

16.   Reynolds, p. 11.
17.   Todorov, p. 98.
18.   Reynolds, p. 128.
19.   Ibid., p. 123.
20.   Narogin, p. 88.

THINKING AS FEELING
BILL NEIDJIE'S STORY ABOUT FEELING

A t the first Conference of Aboriginal Writers at Murdoch University in 1983 there was a great sense of pride. As they saw it, writing by non-Aboriginal Australians had little to say—MudroorooNarogin (Colin Johnson) called it boring and derivative, criticising its utter complacency, and its unawareness that it was 'becoming more and more irrelevant to the society with which it seeks to deal'. Aboriginal writing, in contrast, 'is and can be more vital in that it is seeking to come to grips with and define a people, the roots of whose culture extend in an unbroken line far back into a past in which English is only a recent intrusion.'[1] They were also very conscious, however, of the difficulties they faced. The most important of these was mechanical; getting their works published in the first place. Next was finding publishers sympathetic to what they were trying to do, who would not therefore change or censor their work to please white readers and their sensibility and would then have these works properly distributed.

Story About Feeling suggests that the first of these problems is on the way to being solved. Founded in Broome in 1988 as a project of the Kimberley Aboriginal Law and Culture Centre, Magabala Books had already published a number of books by Aboriginal writers. These books speak in a peculiarly Aboriginal voice about peculiarly Aboriginal concerns. True, the distribution problem remains. It is not always easy to get hold of Magabala books, though they respond very promptly to enquiries—PO Box 668, Broome, 6725, Western Australia. Nevertheless, this venture not only marks a significant milestone for Aboriginal writing but is also a model of its kind; the white people involved offer their services respectfully as well as enthusiastically. Keith Taylor who transcribed and edited the tapes of his talks with Bill Neidjie to make *Story About Feeling*, for instance, makes no attempt to explain or interpret Bill's story, insisting in his preface that, in Bill's words, ' "Someone can't tell you. Story telling you yourself".' In the design, too, Peter Bibby is scrupulous in his use of paintings by Aboriginal artists who have all given permission for their use. The photographs by Brian Stevenson, Ian Morris and Greg Miles, too, all respect the spirit of the text.

This is an important book, then, for Aboriginal people, because it puts down in writing a tradition of knowledge and love of the country which is in danger of being lost, with the present breakdown of traditional Aboriginal culture. True, there are dangers in this. Traditional culture is oral, not written, and thus knows nothing about the anxiety with meaning which is bound up with writing and with reading, the desire to stabilise 'reality' and take hold of, explain, control and even possess the world. In this sense, writing stories down could mean endangering them, drawing them into the ambit of Western culture which has also attempted to assimilate Aboriginal people. There is, after all, a profound symbolic relationship between the discursive and material practices of imperialism. Against this, however, one must set the impact of a book of this kind on us non-Aboriginal people, the colonisers. It is on this impact that I want to focus since it is surely impertinent as well as impossible for a non-Aboriginal reader to canvass possible Aboriginal readings. This importance for us is clear, almost self-evident. Keith Taylor puts it this way in his Preface:

In a world where our vision becomes even more blinkered by the dominance of a single cultural way and where such dominance threatens the survival of other ways of thinking and being, there is an urgent need for more stories like this.

That said, however, complications begin to appear. The first of these is the matter of a beginning. Every beginning, according to Edward Said, raises a number of questions about reception, interpretation and response.[2] Just as 'facts' are only facts within a certain perspective of understanding, so reading any text draws on the training we have received and is influenced by the context in which we are reading it. It also raises questions about the material it uses—the world it reworks, about its point of departure from that world and what it therefore presupposes about relations between 'reality' and textuality and about the conventions, existential as well as aesthetic, which govern it.

These questions become particularly urgent with Bill Neidjie's *Story About Feeling* since it makes few concessions to our notions of reality or textuality and works by different conventions. Aboriginal novelists like Mudrooroo Narogin, playwrights like Jack Davis or poets like Oodgeroo Noonuccal (Kath Walker) borrow their forms from non-Aboriginal culture, though in the process they also modify them, using them for their own ends. But *Story About Feeling* appears to the non-Aboriginal reader to have no recognisable form, seeming to be just a series of personal reflections and thus of no particular significance apart from a personal or even vaguely anthropological interest. The first problem it poses, therefore, is hermeneutical, how to read, and where to find significance.

This might seem a minor matter, but it is not. More than most, Australian culture is profoundly ethnocentric and logocentric— witness the problems we have in coming to terms with what we like to call 'migrant writing', to say nothing of cultures very different from our own. If Europeans tend to take the consciousness of ourselves as, in Daniel Defert's words, 'a planetary process rather than as [the product of] a region of the world',[3] then Australians probably take that consciousness to extremes, regarding ours as the only possible culture and English (as we speak it) the only possible language. Being Australian is thus an extreme form of Orientalism,[4] 'a self-confirming business'—hence the anxieties caused by any challenge to our self-identification. I have argued elsewhere that these anxieties have a great deal to do with our racism in general and with the peculiar virulence of attitudes towards Aboriginal Australians and their culture. At the moment, however, the concern is with responses to Bill Neidjie's *Story About Feeling*, and about the difficulties its difference entails.

First of all, comes the need to accept and tolerate this difference, learning to read in a different kind of way. The European conquest of other cultures, as Todorov suggests, was in part justified by our understanding of biblical universalism, the belief that it was given to us to 'convert' the whole world. It succeeded not by the moral superiority but by the superior power of this ideology grounded as it was in domination rather than acknowledgment[5]. What was different from us was seen not merely as different or inferior but wrong. Aboriginality thus became part of what Abdul JanMohamed has called the 'Manichean allegory' which provides the supreme rationale for colonialism, transforming cultural difference into social and even metaphysical difference, and assuming the superiority of the European and the inferiority of everything Aboriginal.[6]

The political and social consequences are obvious and apparent around us. But the effects on sensibility are perhaps not so apparent since they affect the way we perceive the world and thus the origins of feeling as well as thought. Put simply, the point of departure for reading *Story About Feeling* is thus, to a greater or lesser extent, a point of misunderstanding. This misunderstanding is complicated by our conventions of reading—though, as I shall be arguing, recent developments in the theory help to solve some at least of these problems. Reading this little book which seems at first simply an expression of personal feeling, it is easy to be condescending, to fit it into unconscious assumptions about race and to praise it for unexpected subtlety and sophistication—Bill Neidjie is already a hero of this kind as the original 'Kakadu Man'. Alternatively, we may appeal to the other and more positive, but equally exaggerated, side of the trope of difference, the notion of the Noble Savage. Reading lines like:

I love it tree because e love me too.
E watching me same as you
tree e working with your body, my body,
e working with us,

for instance, it is possible to indulge ourselves in the fantasy of Aborigines as people of childlike, even childish innocence, freedom and naivety, inhabitants of an unfallen world living in tune with nature. Quite apart from the repression this fantasy involves of the tragic history of what we have done to this culture, it commodifies Aborigines and their culture, turning them into a series of stereotypes to be used for our own pleasure and self-justification, projections of our own need for what is not so much innocence as irresponsibility.

The first step towards a proper appreciation of *Story About Feeling* and other texts like it, therefore, is to be aware of these problems. Our culture is essentially narcissistic, working to absorb and assimilate all that is different and then fixing it in an unchangeable position, an element in the system of differences which we call 'human nature' and the world of human experience. So we need to recognise this, to acknowledge the way in which we tend to absolve difference, homogenise Aborigines into a collective 'they', the distillation of particular traits, beliefs and practices which we take to be 'typically Aboriginal' and thus enabling us to classify and understand, making Aboriginality a kind of mirror in which we see the face of our own desires.

So, next, we need to break the mirror, to recognise that what we like to call 'reality' is parabolic, a series of 'images projected on the white screen of chaos' (J.D. Crossan), and that our culture, like theirs, is a series of projections, not something given, which offers only one of many possible images of the world. This, of course, is where contemporary theory is helpful. As Barthes writes, reflecting on the problems facing those historians who see themselves as dealing with 'just the facts':

The paradox comes full circle: narrative structure was evolved in the crucible of fiction (via myth and the first epics), yet it has become at once the sign and proof of reality. It is clear that the attenuation (if not disappearance) of narrative in contemporary historians . . . represents . . . a fundamental ideological transformation . . . from now on the touchstone of history is not so much reality as intelligibility.[7]

Intelligibility in turn becomes a matter of story, and of finding a story which fits the way we conceive things to be. The poets have known this for some time, of course.

Only the imagination is real!
I have declared it
time without end.
    (William Carlos Williams)

and

So, say that final belief
Must be in a fiction
    (Wallace Stevens)

But so, too, have Aboriginal people. Bill Neidjie's poem suggests, moreover, that they are aware of it in an equally sophisticated way:

This story e can listen careful
and how you want to feel on your feeling.
This story e coming through your body
e go right down foot and head
fingernail and blood . . . through the heart
and e can feel it because e'll come right through

Compare this with Werner Heisenberg's words about changes in scientific method:

The . . . method of analysing, explaining and classifying has become conscious of its limitations, which arise out of the fact that by its intervention science alters and refashions the objects of its investigation. In other words method and object can no longer be separated. The scientific world view has ceased to be a scientific view in the true sense of the word.[8]

It is this which gives us our cue. Bill Neidjie's stories, which are about plants and animals, birds and fishes, rocks and the earth itself as well as human beings, are part of an investigation of this kind, and one which has profoundly personal and social consequences. Their language, that is to say, is the language of promise, since it is involved with concrete things, brought to full sensuous contact with a living world laden with possibility because in it ancient traditions of living are preserved and renewed:

Listen carefully, careful
and this spirit e come in your feeling
and you will feel it . . . anyone that
I feel it . . . my body same as you.
I telling you this because the land for us,
never change round, never change.
Places for us, earth for us,
star, moon, tree, animal,
no-matter what sort of animal, bird or snake . .
all that animal same like us. Our friend that.

Stories of this kind can only be understood from inside their own world. They are revelatory only to insiders because their effect is textual, because, calling to us to listen carefully, they call us to become what we hear. This is not only a spoken text therefore but also a ritual text, one which enacts a way of living.

The great temptation of the black writer is, perhaps, in Fanon's words, to 'turn white or disappear', but Neidjie knows nothing of this temptation. Even though he has lived for much of his life away from his traditional country, working in timber-mill camps or in luggers or labouring jobs in Darwin or for the air force during the war, he insists on the tradition of his people. Nor does he seem to know much about that other strategy of black writers, the strategy of camouflage or mimicry; black skins speaking through white mouths. The voice which speaks here is Aboriginal. Even though it speaks English, Neidjie puts his own cultural mark upon it, colonising it with his own intentions and intonations, appropriating the words and adapting them to his own needs, experience and aspiration. In writing, the author is usually absent from his/her creation. But this is essentially a spoken text, since it is suffused with and indistinguishable from Neidjie's originating presence, and models his world, one in which all things share the one life, expansive and vibrant. As he reflects on a cave painting, the world appears as process, not something static; time as not linear but as continuing presence, and the cosmic personal.

We don't know how many thousand years
that painting was there.
Our Aborigine never writing, no date, no anything.
No one bin make everything . . .
only painting and stone axe.
Ironwood—spear, bamboo . . . all burn, you can't see.

What is invisible like this, however, matters as much as what is visible. Our culture, in contrast, fears and dislikes what cannot be seen. Finding its apparent disappearance threatening, it suspects what has to do with the process of becoming, of moving from one state to another, preferring fixity to fluidity even in our description of the world—in defiance of fact, of course. But in Aboriginal culture visible and invisible are part of the one process of being which at the same time repeats the one pattern.

The world of *Story About Feeling* is, therefore, dialogical; an open and reciprocal relationship between self and self, self and other selves and with the world itself as another self. Seen in this way the passage quoted earlier takes on a new significance:

I love it tree because e love me too.
E watching me same as you
tree e working with your body, my body,
e working with us . . .
That tree, grass . . . that all like our father.
Dirt, earth, I sleep with this earth.
Grass . . . just like your brother.
In my blood in my arm this grass.
This dirt for us because we'll be dead,
we'll be going this earth.
This the story now.

The locus of these poems, as of life itself, is not so much place as this relationship, this assembling of all living things in the story which brings them together and makes them whole. But it is not merely self-referential because it does not refer but presences, and celebrates this bringing together. Nor, in contrast with our kind of aesthetics, is it self-justifying either, because this presence comes when it comes without any attempt on the storyteller's part to control it, and comes as a kind of gift, a proof of the goodness of things.

Our culture sees the external world as a source of information, something external to us to be exploited and developed for economic purposes or looked on for pleasure as a kind of panorama. But here it is an aspect of self to be listened to, accepted in reverence and lived out:

That tree now, feeling . . .
e blow . . .
sit quiet you speaking . . .
that tree now e speak . . .
that wind e blow . . .
e can listen.

Our aesthetic attitudes usually have to do with a fantasy of domination and control, separating self off from world, and effacing our presence in it. But here, though and indeed because it is part of the whole, the self is central; a speaking, listening, feeling, erotic self. The world, too, is a living experience, not something dead and inert but a state of mind, the product of 'dadirri', an inner deep listening and quiet still awareness, a waiting which is profoundly reverent and essentially trustful. Where our attitude to the world and the authority we assume over it is antagonistic, this is agonistic. Self and world are intimately interrelated, living and moving together as lovers do.

For all its apparent simplicity, therefore, this is a very important book. It is important, first of all, for the challenge it offers to our notions of textuality and thus of reality, calling us in a sense to rewrite ourselves and our world and reinscribe ourselves within it.

As Foucault reminds us, our discourse is in a sense our life. The way we describe and inscribe ourselves into the web of relationships which binds us to ourselves, other people and cultures and to the natural world is thus a crucial determinant of behaviour and culture. Our scientific and technological culture not only tells us, for example, that we are the primal self-referent of all language but makes us act as if we were. *Story About Feeling* however, weaves language into the whole of reality, seeing everything as textual, ourselves as part of a cosmic story, or dance rather than its author, investigator or master.

This cannot, I think, be dismissed as mere nature mysticism. The parallels with contemporary physics are striking and significant. But Neidjie's world view also throws light on Derrida's proposition that there is not only 'no outside text' but also 'nothing outside of the text'. Any reading which refers to anything outside this text, this world as signifying process, is not only illusory but destructive since it destroys the otherness in which we are situated and which in a sense we also are.

All this may seem merely theoretical but its consequences are profoundly ethical and even political. Making contact with what is not only unthought in our tradition but, to use Derrida's phrase, 'that-which-cannot-be-thought', Neidjie's stories destroy the basis of the Manichean allegory of racism, its assumptions of universality on the one hand and of its own superiority on the other, undercutting this fantasy of difference by writing it into its own text, showing us ourselves as the other sees us:

Well e can make money.
E get im from underneath, riches in the ground,
E make million, million might be.
But trouble is . . . dying quick!
People . . . bit mob they die because lot of money.

Neidjie's view of the history of European–Aboriginal relations is equally ironic and subversive. It begins, for instance:

47

But wasn't Aborigine fault.
White-European didn't make friend with Aborigine.
That first go e put chain!

Neidjie recognises that he and his people occupy the space into which we Europeans have attempted to write our culture and write out Aboriginal culture. But he resists this attempt, claiming the authority of his own kind of truth, making white people, not Aborigines, the incompetents, the foolish ones. The effect on the reader is thus to call into question notions of power and assumptions about reality, interrogating our culture by offering glimpses of other modes, other definitions, and suggesting that existence is polyphonic not monolithic. Our grammar, it seems, is not the only one, nor is it the infallible guide to reality, to what is actually the case.

This is easy to say, of course. But the adjustments involved are both profound and complex. They demand, in fact, a virtual revaluation of value. Profoundly troubling at any time, this is perhaps particularly so today when so much else seems to be in a state of flux and called into question, when most of us lack a world view which has the capacity for this otherness, for making the move towards a more polyphonic world. For this reason, reading texts like *Story About Feeling* will remain difficult.

Maybe therefore the place to begin is within the self, recognising that the discriminatory image we have made of Aborigines which closes us off from them, is just that, an image, the embodiment of what Jung calls the 'primitive shadow', our disowned and uncon-scious self. As Jung also points out, however, the shadow is also a moral as well as psychological problem. Precisely because it embodies the dark aspects of ourselves, its recognition challenges the very image we have made of ourselves and demands considerable moral effort.

Story About Feeling, however, makes this process much less challenging that it might otherwise be. Aboriginality here is not particularly threatening, being more intent upon itself than us. The contradiction it offers to our world view, therefore, functions less as a threat than as a kind of heuristic device, leading us out from our own limited order into a more inclusive and insightful way of conceiving the world and our place within it, enabling us to make an option for otherness, which is shown not as dangerous but bountiful and an opportunity for expansion, enlarging the possibilities of existence. Pointing behind the narrowness of the merely literal and empirical, these stories remind us of the way 'reality' is bound up with the imaginary and thus setting us free to reimagine who we are and where we are situated.

The question then, becomes whether in fact there is any other way to live or any other way of knowing reality than the way these poems do, textually, living and knowing in parables. Let us conclude therefore with another parable, one of Kafka's:

Why such reluctance? If you only followed the parables you yourselves would become parables and with that rid of all your daily cares. Another said: I bet that is also a parable. The first said: you have won. The second said: but unfortunately only in parable. The first said: No, in reality: in parable you have lost.[8]

Bill Neidjie would understand, I think.

NOTES

1. Jack Davis & Bob Hodge (eds), *Aboriginal Writing Today* (Australian Institute of Aboriginal Studies, Canberra, 1985).
2. Edward Said, *Beginnings: Intention and Method* (John Hopkins University Press, Baltimore, 1978).
3. Quoted in Marie Louise Pratt, 'Scratches on the Face of the Country: Or What Mr Barrow Saw in the Land of the Bushmen', in H.L. Gates (ed.), *'Race', Writing and Difference* (Chicago University Press, London, 1986), p. 144.
4. Edward Said, *Orientalism* (Penguin, Melbourne, 1985).
5. Quoted in J.B. Metz, 'Unity and Diversity: Problems and Prospects for Inculturation', in *Concitium*, 204 (August 1989), p. 82.
6. Abdul JanMohamed, 'The Economy of Manichean Allegory: The Function of Racial Difference in Colonialist Literature', in Gates, op. cit., pp. 80–3.
7. Quoted in John Dominic Crossan, in *Parables: The Challenge of the Historical Jesus* (Harper & Row, New York, 1973), p. xv.
8. Ibid.

TOWARDS RECONCILIATION?

After the bicentenary, the centenary of the Australian federation is approaching. Celebrating the foundation of the Commonwealth, many would argue, is far more significant than celebrating the beginnings of a penal colony. But the word 'commonwealth' and the aspirations it encapsulates point also to unfinished business; to the fact not only that Aboriginal Australians do not and never have shared in the 'commonwealth' of this society but also that its very existence rests on invasion, killings, dispossession and oppression. The Australian parliament, however, has instituted a Council for National Reconciliation, charged with the task of exploring ways and means of bringing about reconciliation between Aboriginal and non-Aboriginal Australians and of developing a strategic plan to that end.

This council is the last in a series of attempts which began in 1979 with a senate committee, set up to investigate the possibility of a treaty between the Commonwealth and Aboriginal people. In turn, this committee was the result of pressure from a group of distinguished Australians which included figures like H.C. Coombs and Judith Wright. Its results, however, were disappointing since it was advised that such a treaty was impossible without a referendum. Shortly afterwards the National Aboriginal Council, disliking the idea of a treaty, proposed instead the Aboriginal notion of an agreement, a *maccerata*, to be drawn up in terms of Aboriginal law. But that ideal also failed to take hold.

The matter rested there until the bicentennial year, 1988. In that year the then prime minister, Bob Hawke, visited Barunga in the Northern Territory. There the Aboriginal people presented him with a set of demands, for land, control over their own culture, over mining on their land and over national parks, and for genuine equality before the law. They also presented him with a painting done by traditional people, asking him to arrange for it to be displayed in parliament as a reminder to politicians of the need to settle the difference between Aboriginal and non-Aboriginal Australians. The next day, Mr Hawke spoke on Aboriginal radio and promised to work towards a 'compact' between the two peoples.

A compact, of course, is much weaker than a treaty, since it is without any binding legal force. But probably the calculation was that it would thus be more acceptable politically, since the Opposition had declared itself opposed to any treaty and threatened to repudiate it, if made, when they came to power. They argued that it would be divisive and 'racist' in that it gave 'special privileges' to one group of Australians, setting them apart from the rest.

Until the Council for National Reconciliation was set up, therefore, little was done in the matter. At a federal level, ATSIC, the Aboriginal and Torres Strait Islander Council has been set up and the Royal Commission on Aboriginal Deaths in Custody has released its findings. But little has changed for Aboriginal people. Not surprisingly, many of them regard the Council for National Reconciliation as yet another piece of window-dressing, a gesture for white consumption. The fact that Aboriginal organisations were given a mere two months, and that over the wet season, to comment on the nearly 400 recommendations of the Royal Commission, giving them little opportunity to make a substantial input gives weight to this suspicion. At a state level, especially in Western Australia and Queensland, states with the largest number of Aboriginal citizens, there seems even less reason for optimism. Indeed, with the recession, the influence of mining companies and developers seems to have increased rather than diminished and land rights, the central goal of most Aboriginal people, seem further away than ever. In Western Australia, to add to this sense of disillusion, recent amendments to the Crimes Act which affect young Aborigines in particular, have intensified this feeling.

In this context it seems they have every right to be sceptical, not only about the Council for National Reconciliation but also about non-Aboriginal Australians' will to be reconciled. As they see it, the council arose out of a context of political manoeuvre and in the view of some represents, for that reason, a lessening of political will to see justice for Aborigines. Faced with the intransigence of the Opposition towards land rights and the constitutional difficulties of a treaty, it is no doubt at best a compromise, at worst a face-saving device for a government which, despite statements by the prime minister, Paul Keating, continues to profess its good intentions towards Aboriginal people but seems to have done little to implement them, though it may also reflect a new awareness of growing international concern about the plight of Australia's black minority—and that is something positive as far as Aborigines are concerned. Yet it remains that the council may be merely a political gesture, an opportunity for enhancing the celebrations of the year 2001.

To many Aborigines, therefore, the council seems a distraction from what they see as the essential issues: the land, their rights to it and thus their rights to their own culture, to some control over their own lives and economic circumstance, as well as justice before the law and the ability to bring up their children in their own as well as in European Australian culture. West Australian Aborigines are perhaps especially suspicious; they recall the way their hopes were betrayed by the state government of Brian Burke which promised them land rights before the 1983 election, which after the election set up a committee under Mr Justice Seaman to explore ways and means but, after the report was completed, did nothing. As one Aboriginal group put it:

The 1984 Seaman Inquiry was a big thing for Aboriginal people. They fronted this fellow up who wrote a lot of things about what people wanted to see done about the land for the benefit of the Aboriginal people, but none of these have happened.
. . . You know those people have been sent out to pick our brains and they think they know what our problems are but they haven't fixed things up. You and I are still sitting on the banks of the river today, still trying to meet the need of our young people that are coming up today.[1]

In their view, the Council for National Reconciliation may be just another trick. 'After the talk of land rights and then of a treaty they just turned the page of [the] book and said there is another word on this other page called "reconciliation", and that means let's be friends, let us forget the past' (p. 30). For Aborigines, however, that is not easy. Whites have to listen to them for a change:

What are the things we say we need? We want our land; we want our language; we want control over tourists and we want a better lot of rules of how miners should behave. Some of these things should be put to the government first and say listen to this rule here. Fix some of these things up first, then we'll talk about shaking hands (p. 30).

For all that, there are some Aborigines who see the notion of reconciliation as an opportunity to make some gains, if only to convince

'the gadiya [white people] that it is important for them to get to grips with the way they treated black fellas. To come to grips with the way they're continuing to do that . . . To say alright, I want to be your friend. It'll take a long time but we have got to work on it' (p. 30).

In this respect it is perhaps significant and hopeful that Aboriginal people are to form the majority of the council's twenty-five members who will be appointed for three years. But it also includes representatives of mining companies, the farming community, trade unions, churches, the media and the entertainment industry; all people most Aborigines believe need educating in their ways. True, these members have been appointed by the government with the approval of the Opposition. But as far as the Aborigines appointed to it are concerned, once appointed they should consult with, report back to, and represent the interest of their communities, thus enlarging their sphere of influence.

Moreover, the fact that it is a different kind of body from ATSIC, though ATSIC's chair and deputy chairperson are members, means that it will perform a different, more wide-ranging function. It need not be concerned merely with funding or with specific projects, but with raising the consciousness of Aboriginal needs throughout the community. Its chairman, Pat Dodson, has a long record in this regard.

It has no set agenda and its task extends over a decade. Thus the council is not caught up in day-to-day administrative matters as ATSIC is. This gives it flexibility, enabling it to set its own agenda and pick up issues as they arise—issues like the return of Aboriginal remains from overseas, for instance, or media treatment of Aboriginal issues. But since it is concerned with initiating and developing a process, the growth towards mutual understanding, it will be able also to give attention to long-term matters; Aboriginal control of national parks situated in traditional areas, for example, or white prejudice against black Australians. But because their mutual understanding needs to develop primarily at the grassroots level, it is also possible that the council may be able to bring about agreements between Aborigines and non-Aborigines in local communities; agreements about education, for instance, or between police and Aboriginal communities. Certainly, agreements like this are essential if the whole project is not to disappear in a cloud of fine feelings and uplifting statements.

From an Aboriginal point of view, however, the first necessity is that we non-Aboriginal Australians listen to them. In Australia, unlike South Africa, for instance, our racism is often largely unconscious. Thus even well-meaning people tend to regard Aborigines still as 'different', less able and less intelligent than ourselves, needing to be looked after and spoken for by white people. But to Aboriginal people this is deeply offensive:

There are gadiya (white people) that write about black fellas every day of the week. They write reports trying to explain what we like, what we need, why we don't get what we want. They try to explain everything. The whole lot, and yet we are still waiting for something to happen (p. 23).

As Aborigines see it, everything, even attempts to promote Aboriginal interests, is done on white fellow terms, often to satisfy white fellow needs and sometimes their consciences. But in either case, the effect is to undermine Aboriginal culture, to deny its autonomy and to try to make Aborigines conform to non-Aboriginal culture.

For all these reasons, therefore, it is important to hear from Aboriginal people; their views of the idea of reconciliation in general, and of the Council for National Reconciliation in particular.

ABORIGINAL VIEWS

The following, then, are the views of a group of Aboriginal leaders from the Kimberleys, people still in possession of their own culture, though very much aware of the destructive inroads made by the dominant culture of non-Aboriginal Australia. They are not necessarily representative of the views of all Aborigines throughout Australia. But they do represent the views of their people and are therefore, I believe, significant.

Nowhere, perhaps, are these views more significant than in their strong conviction that the time has come for Aboriginal people to make a stand, to regain control of their lives and culture. They are aware that things are changing in the white community and that a growing number of non-Aboriginal Australians are beginning to be aware of the other side of Australian history; of the offences and injustices committed against the Aboriginal inhabitants and of their continuing oppression and exclusion. For that reason, they assert, 'today is a different day.' There is among them a new confidence, a new sense that 'today is the day when we start to talk' (p. 34). In the past, oppression and lack of hope have made Aborigines submissive. 'Our mind [has been] . . . locked . . . [making] us say, 'Oh the gadiya he is the boss.' (p. 34). But now they are beginning to recover a sense of their own power. They are more prepared to announce:

But no he's not the boss. He's boss for himself. He shouldn't be boss over us. That is what has got to be stopped.

If they want to do things they have got to come and 'negotiate'. They have to start to say, this is what we want to do and we have to say, well we don't like what you want to do because it doesn't allow us to do the things that we want to do. Now let us talk about that. Let us find a proper way where we can agree (p. 34).

In the first instance, their objections are directed against mining companies and government departments and officials. But there is also a growing sense of the larger need to claim equality for their own Law and Culture and to resist the encroachment of white law and culture more generally. In their words:

The gadiya have their own culture, own business, own law, own hand reaching for what he wants and some of us get sucked into what he wants because of many reasons, and it can take us away from the culture. We can get caught up in letting his mind get on top of our minds. Letting his spirit crush our spirit; letting his rule try and run our life. So that we end up in a shadow, nowhere (p. 27).

Hence they must carefully examine every scheme proposed by white people in business or in government:

Ever since gadiya have come to this country they have had a plan for Aboriginal people and are forever telling Aboriginal people what to do and how to do it. None of these plans have worked, but they have affected and determined the lives of Aboriginal people (p. 35).

Whether or not it is true that people in business or government have any coherent plan for Aborigines—it is probably more true to say that the assumption was that they would 'die out', such was the influence of neo-Darwinian thought, and that therefore there was no plan—there can be no doubt that governmental policies, economic practice and social attitudes have been destructive, as far as Aborigines are concerned. It is time for us to admit it.

For their part, picking up on current rhetoric about multiculturalism, many Aborigines see it as the time to assert 'the primacy of indigenous cultural rights in a multicultural Australia' (p. 6). 'No one ever agree for the gadiya to come and take the country' (p.

35), they declare, and the gadiya have to be reminded that this is so:

Instead of people who stand back, we have got to stand in front and say come here to the table don't wait over there in Canberra or Perth or in some office in Derby or Kununurra or Broome or wherever. Come here and sit down and talk. Then we can talk to them properly (p. 35).

Thus it appears that the word 'reconciliation' is more ambiguous than it might seem at first; a word which suggests bringing people back again into friendly relations after an estrangement, it may also highlight that estrangement. Seen through Aboriginal eyes, for instance, 'friendship' is hardly the word to describe relations in the past; for most of them, it is a story of brutality, ignorance and injustice. 'Some of the people out there are powerful and they don't like Aboriginal People' (p. 34). These people, it should be noted, include politicians and bureaucrats as well as mining companies, some pastoralists, police and white racists. Thus, Aboriginal people have little access to systems of power. White people's interests continue to be preferred to those of Aborigines. On the failure of Bardi people to obtain a licence for a pearl farm they remark on the apparent injustice:

Gadiya get up their laws and say alright Aboriginal People you can't get a licence to set up your pearl farm or you can't get a licence to do this because we've already given them out to everyone else (p. 35).

In the area of justice, the report of the Royal Commission into Aboriginal Deaths in Custody suggests that this kind of ill-treatment is not yet over. Aboriginal people throughout Australia are twenty-seven times more likely to find themselves in police custody than other Australians.

To Aborigines, there is a historical component to their feelings of injustice. Initially, Aboriginal people offered friendship to white explorers and settlers, acting as guides, leading them to water and pasture for the flocks and later working for them on their stations.

But for them there has been little return. The land was taken from them. The women were taken away and Aboriginal stockmen were often slaves on their own land, they were paid a pittance and often harshly treated. When it suited the owners or when, in the 1970s, they were obliged to be paid the same wage as white stockmen, they were turned off the land and driven to live on the fringes of towns like Roebourne and Wyndham, dispossessed of the land to which they belong and where they find their identity.

In this sense, it seems to many Aborigines that things have not changed much since the initial invasion. White people still try to dominate Aborigines, even if now with the best of intentions:

Gadiya keeps coming. New waves of them fly in from places like Perth and end up in the Kimberley. Their ideas are often developed in places like Melbourne and Canberra. They can drop in with a 'parachute' and land here and then they want to create what they left behind. That's happening now and it's what they've been doing all the time.

In the meantime our people get shifted out to the fringe. Little bit of sugar here, and a few crumbs there but no proper recognition of the people or their rights (p. 24).

There is little sharing of values—white culture is always taken as the norm—and little sense of equality or intimacy between people whose values and beliefs are so different.

To Aborigines, then, 'reconciliation' can seem like yet another way of bringing them into a state of acquiescence with, and submission to a situation which they see as essentially oppressive and unjust. If the Council for National Reconciliation means anything, therefore, it must mean adjustment on our side; a readiness to settle the injustices to bring about the kind of agreement which is necessary between people who have been at odds with one another. On the Aboriginal side it demands a new honesty and directness. But how might this happen?

In the first place, Aborigines must be released from the situation of subservience and given control of their lives and situation. As they point out, Aboriginal affairs are still controlled by government officials or by white people who own the land which Aborigines regard as their own and which their people have inhabited for thousands of years. They are still powerless in their own land; unlike most other Australians, they are almost entirely unable to participate in or influence decision-making processes of government and of the bureaucracy. Bureaucrats seldom attend bush meetings or negotiate with Aboriginal people about their needs, and politicians tend to fly in and fly out to talk and ingratiate themselves, but usually with little result. Nor do these politicians and bureaucrats see themselves as accountable to Aborigines. Their concern is with the bureaucratic system, with white law and white society. Thus as Aborigines see it, white interests, mining, farming, investment and so on, nearly always prevail over Aboriginal interests. Instead of serving and empowering them and defending their rights, Aborigines assert that the government tends to 'stop us from doing what we want to do' (p. 35).

White people may take this situation for granted, assuming the superiority of their needs over those of Aboriginal people, and confident that economic development is more important than Aboriginal Culture. But seen through Aboriginal eyes it looks very different:

We see mining companies drive in and out. They go to places which we can't go to. They can go on to a station and pay out their lot, put their drill down, dig around, pick up rocks and go away. If someone wants to go and visit their country, look for tucker, visit their sacred place and camp there, some bloke might say you can't go there. You might get shot. Or a policeman might come and move you from there. So we have to go back to the start. Who is the owner of the ground? What he brings to the country? Whose rights belong to the country and how do we bring these rights square in front of the gadiya government (p. 23).

Aborigines are tired of having their needs subordinated to those of others—hence their strenuous opposition to the plan of the West Australia government to provide for Perth's need for water by bringing water from the Kimberleys by pipeline, for instance.

The unfairness of this situation of exploration is clear to them:

We worked hard for the gadiya to build up the country. Now this is the time for us to work hard for ourselves and build ourselves up. Make ourselves strong (p. 30).

If it is to be genuine the process of reconciliation, therefore, will have to acknowledge these claims. For this it will have to recognise that what is at issue is ideological; a matter of attitudes and values, not a mere clash of politics or economics. What matters most to Aborigines is the preservation of the Culture, for them the source of life and value, whereas for us the economic imperative is dominant. For this reason it is worth spelling out here Aboriginal views on the matter of value.

Aboriginal and non-Aboriginal Australians live by two very different definitions of 'culture' and two different sets of values. For us, culture has to do largely with the way we live, our social practices and material circumstances. For Aboriginal people, however, it is a spiritual quality, a certain 'trueness in our hearts', so they believe it should be spelled with a capital 'C'.

Aboriginal culture connects people to what is generally called Dreamtime or Law or from the beginning. People today know what they know from before. Not just the history but also the Law, the Rules, the Values, the Knowledge, the memories on how to behave and live properly, how to look after people properly and how to look after the country and it's not just mine or an individual thing it belongs to people. Culture is belonging to a common mind, a common memory about these things. It's also continuing (p. 25).

But it continues by being lived, by telling its stories, 'making sure that those things are done properly and it's passed on' from the older to the younger and held in proper respect. 'Gadiya law' is always changing. But Aboriginal law, they argue, is unchanging and constitutes an unchanging source of life. 'It is for identity, unity, control, dignity and integrity' (p. 26), and is ultimately 'what makes us strong' (p. 23). But it is also 'written in the land' (p. 26). Travelling across the land Aboriginal people discover the Law and learn how to follow it, learning what their relationship and their obligations to the land are and what it has to give them. In this sense 'Culture is a map. The land is the map. It is recorded on the land' (p. 26).

Aboriginal attitudes to the land are thus very different from ours. For them, land is not a resource to be exploited but an object of belief, reverence and of responsibility. At the appropriate time they must visit certain places and carry out the ceremonies and tell the stories which make it flourish. This is why they have problems with pastoralists and mining companies who claim to 'own' such places and refuse them access to it. For them, it is a religious duty to go there 'to those places we belong to because the land owns us, we don't own that ground, that land owns us we have to go there' (p. 28) if life is to continue fruitfully. But these white people have shut them out because 'we don't have a piece of paper . . . to say that's your title' (p. 28). For traditional people unable to go there, this is a source of deep anxiety. It also occasions painful memories:

We know in the past, if you went there he [the white man]'d shoot you or he'd land with a helicopter and say what you doing here and he'll put a fine on you and that cuts at the very heart of what our life's about . . . That's what the gadiya has to learn and that's something we have to see changed (p. 28).

For Aborigines, 'everything comes back to land' (p. 28). Without land rights they are unable to exercise their Culture since it is from the land that the Law, languages and their whole way of life comes to them and continues. Land dispossession, therefore, leads to Cultural erosion, threatening their death as a people.

Seen from this point of view then, land rights, access to and control over their own land, becomes the central issue. But it is a matter of spiritual, not just material survival. This is difficult for many of us to understand, of course. In our culture the economic factor dominates and tends to subordinate; for example, every politician argues that Aboriginal opposition to mining is against the 'national interest'. For them, economic development is paramount and economic expansion imperative. But Aboriginal people, concerned to conserve the land, identify it with their continuing life as a people.

At the very least, it would seem that justice demands some recognition of this point of view in general. In particular it is important to realise the urgency of their demands to be allowed to negotiate directly with mining companies, and through their traditional leaders rather than younger people who may have lost a proper sense of their own Culture. In the traditional view the land still owns them and these claims cannot be abrogated by any white fellow's law, and if they deny their responsibility to the land, they are destroying themselves. That does not mean that they are not prepared to compromise, to accept white needs. What they ask, however, is that the mining companies tell them just where they want to make their explorations, ask their permission to do so, allow them to adjudicate what is and is not allowable, and abide by their decision. This, surely, is a matter of respect for their deeper needs as a people, a respect, moreover, guaranteed by the United Nations Charter of Human Rights.

This is not a view likely to appeal to many non-Aboriginal Australians, of course. But if we are serious about the need for reconciliation it must be taken into account. Therefore, we must also attempt to understand the premises from which they are operating. Indeed, we may even have something to learn from them, since the evidence suggests that our culture may be well on its way to destroying the fragile environment which Aboriginal Culture preserved and lived peacefully with thousands of years. As the Kimberley people remarked, 'the fact that people are more important than cattle is something the gadiya find very hard to accept' (p. 39). Nevertheless, it may be an important principle if our society is to survive. 'The principles and values that make money is what cuts across our beliefs and . . . what people want done' (p. 39), they observe. But these principles and values may also be in danger of seriously damaging, if not destroying, the environment.

To say that reconciliation means that non-Aboriginal Australians should learn more about and come to respect Aboriginal Culture is therefore not just a gesture of benevolence. It is something which matters for all of us. In the meantime, however, Aboriginal people are concerned to defend their Culture against the encroachments of ours. Thus they are deeply concerned about the effects of alcohol and drugs, which they see largely as a result of their young people's alienation from their own culture. White schooling, they believe, has something to do with this. Hence they demand the right to educate Aboriginal children in their own Culture for three days, leaving two days for white schooling. According to their own ways of learning, education is personal rather than institutional:

What you have in your head and your heart you learn from someone, from old people by looking, listening and sitting down talking. You don't need gadiya for that. You don't need schools for that. That is what you know, that's the power that has to come to people to walk strong in the future (p. 20).

In the sum, then, many Aborigines feel, like the Kimberley people, that it is 'a time to think about where Aboriginal People . . . have got to after all these years of gadiya dominating and controlling our lives. Where do we stand and where do we go' (p. 22). As they see it, there is first of all the need to preserve and live by their own Culture and then to 'get control over things that currently tend to control us' (p. 22).

That, for them, is what reconciliation is about; recognition of their rights as a people to their own Culture.

There may be differences in detail between different Aboriginal groups throughout Australia. But there is also profound unity and agreement about the essentials. 'We are united about the need for land rights, about the need for people to recognise our right of language, and on the way we want to live' (p. 39).

Whether or not non-Aboriginal Australians will be able to understand these needs and the claims they make as a consequence will be a mark of our maturity and our ability to make a truly pluralist society, one in which every citizen has equal rights to everything that makes for life and dignity. In the meantime, as far as Aborigines are concerned, there is a new determination and a new self-awareness. As the Kimberley Land Council meeting declared;

We have got little to lose and when you are hungry and you have to fight, you make a fairly formidable opponent. People find it difficult to deal with you. When you are organised and hungry they find it twice as hard to deal with you (p. 40).

On the non-Aboriginal side at long last, there is a growing need to begin to listen to these demands and to understand where they are coming from and the needs on which they are based; the need for Aboriginal Australians to live as free people in their own land. It may be that we shall learn a great deal from them in the process.

NOTES

1. Kimberley Land Council and Waringarri Resource Centre, 'Recommendations of the Conference of Resource Development, Kimberley Aboriginal Control', 11–13 September 1991, p. 19.

2. WHAT IS JUSTICE?

THE MEN WHO LOVED CHILDREN

My approach to incest which is based on the evidence of literature, of what is evidently self-proclaimedly imaginary, may seen unscientific. It will seem tainted with psychologism and even with religiosity. Yet it is possible that evidence of this kind will take us to the heart of the problem, to what is otherwise inexpressible; the actual set of experiences, in which victim and those responsible for the abuse seem to be enclosed and even trapped.

It is clear that no controlled research study of incest is possible. It is impossible to say exactly what happens psychologically or even socially to the child since we are here in the area of taboo, the 'peril of soul' associated with things forbidden, which cannot be approached without risk to self and society. Taboo being 'nothing else than this condition of objects, actions, or persons that are "isolated" or "forbidden" because of the danger involved in contact with them',[1] it follows that the attempt to discuss a taboo subject, like incest, leads us beyond the merely rational area of social analysis, even perhaps beyond the confines of what is called 'secular' life and thought,[2] at least if we are to attempt to understand it existentially and in its own dimension.

The evidence of literature suggests that the essential experience of incest is one of violation and defilement, not only of the victim but also of the perpetrator. Normal language, it seems, does not suffice for this experience. Defilement, as Ricoeur puts it, 'adheres to everything unusual, everything terrifying in the world, attractive and repellent at the same time',[3] and therefore it belongs at the level of dream, where body and consciousness fuse, expressing themselves in terms of symbol rather than of rational thought. This is perhaps why, in matters of incest or suspected incest, it is so difficult to come at the 'truth' of what happened and why the real and the imaginary seem so inextricably bound together. But it is also the reason why a study of the treatment of incest and literature may be so revealing.

The language of literature is the language of symbol. In this kind of language 'something else' is brought to bear upon, and united with, the normal socially recognised meaning of the word. Words say something other than what they seem, superficially, to be saying. The symbol puts us, so to speak, 'at the origin of the speaking being', as dream also does,[4] pointing beyond itself to its origin in experience. Hence Ricoeur's saying, 'the symbol gives rise to thought', and his gloss on that saying, 'the symbol gives, but what it gives is occasion for thought, something to think about'.[5] One thus escapes from what Wittgenstein categorises 'as the general form of propositions', the descriptive form of the social sciences which can only say 'this is how things are'. Wittgenstein argues that although 'one thinks that one is tracing the outline of the thing's nature over and over again, one is merely tracing round the frame through which we look at it'.[6] The point, in the case of an experience as complicated and profound as the experience of incest, is to get as close as we can to that experience.

When one turns to survey Australian literature for its treatment of incest, the first impression is that the subject does not exist, either in fiction or in poetry. Its absence from drama, of course, is perhaps not surprising given the social nature of drama and the nature of our society—the ancient Greeks were much less reticent, perhaps because theirs was a society preoccupied with questions of the sacred and its profanation. On reflection, however, this reticence is quite understandable, given the widespread suppression, evasion and denial evident elsewhere on the subject. In one of the novels we are about to discuss, Christina Stead's *The Man Who Loved Children*, the rage of Sam Pollit at a newspaper report of a case of incest is perhaps not atypical, although one would not necessarily want to suggest that everyone who shares his outrage, shares the inclination to incest which is the novel's main subject.

Sam's hair rose on the first evening, and suddenly flaming with temper, shouting with rage, he seized a stick and declared there and then that he would head a posse[7] of respectable fathers and citizens and go to chastise the editor of the paper. 'I am a man of peace,' cried Sam shouting with rage, 'but this is a case where vigilante law comes into being and has its function.'[8]

The reasons he gives for his rage which is first of all defence of the 'sanctity of the family' in general and of the rights of the father, attacked by some 'miserable yellow devil . . . in his own home', and, last of all, his concern for the girl herself, are also familiar.

Australian publishers are not famous for their daring in promoting works likely to cause outrage or, even worse, provoke prosecution. On the other hand, writers tend also to reflect the views and feelings of their culture, hence a general lack of interest in subjects of a genuinely erotic nature, as distinct from the sentimental. So it is not really surprising that so few have dealt with incest. Of those who have done so, however, the most notable seem to be Christina Stead, Elizabeth Harrower, Kate Grenville and Patrick White. In Patrick White's case, the relationship involved is between siblings including, for instance, Arthur and Waldo in *The Solid Mandala*. But this relationship is of such a highly symbolic and benevolent kind, being closer to Plato's myth of Eros, the soul's search for its lost other half, than to actual social experience, that it has little to contribute to our understanding here. As for Harrower, the suggestions of incest in *The Watch Tower*, powerful as they are, are not really central to the work. The issue is central, however, in two novels by Christina Stead, *For Love Alone* and *The Man Who Loved Children*, and Kate Grenville's *Lilian's Story*.

It therefore seems worth concentrating on these works, making a fairly close analysis of particular texts, rather than relying on general discussion, since what we are trying to do is to get to the heart of the experience, coming at what is otherwise unspoken and, indeed, often seems unable to be spoken. In addition, we shall look at the case of the poet Christopher Brennan, and his relationship with his daughter, Anne. This may seem a move away from the literary evidence in the direction of 'fact', as distinct from the more revealing area of fiction. But we shall be using the evidence of his poetry, on the one hand, and of Axel Clarke's biography of Brennan on the other. Biography is a form of literature to the extent that it involves a reworking and reshaping of fact. Our concern will thus be with Clarke's reworking of Brennan's symbols, aware that

Keenest danger is thinking itself. (It) must think against itself, which it can only seldom do. [9]

What we want to discuss is the experience of immediacy produced by such texts, the feeling of actually having been there when it happened, the assumption being that literature can offer the actual content of this experience, that its words are like a yield or residue which give weight and significance to the transience of experience.

We begin with the opening of the significantly named *For Love Alone*, by Christina Stead. We share the intense consciousness of the main character, Teresa, as she is aware of her father standing looking down on her and her sister Kitty as they sit sewing—a tableau of male domination and female submission.

Naked, except for a white towel rolled into a loincloth, he stood in the doorway, laughing and shouting, a tall man with powerful chest and thick hair of pale burning gold and a skin still pale under many summers' tan. He seemed to thrust back the walls with his muscular arms; thick tufts of red hair stood out from his armpits. The air was full of the stench of brown seaweed and old fish nets. Through the window you could see the water of the bay and the sand speckled with flotsam and scalloped with yellow foam, left by the last wave. The man, Andrew Hawkins, though straight and muscular, was covered with flaccid yellow-white flesh and his waist and abdomen were too broad and full. He had a broad throat and chest and from them came a clear tenor voice. [10]

The fact that the story he is telling is about a black woman nursing her baby, and that he turns his time working in the islands into erotic fantasy, underlines the sense of emotional imperialism here. [11] Women exist, for him, to be colonised, turned into obedient subjects who will admire the 'beautiful white skin' which, he complacently asserts, 'women love . . . in a man'. But this woman, Teresa, is not prepared to submit. The faint sense of perversion in his reflection that it surprises women to see him 'so much fairer in colour than they are' is much stronger in Teresa's perception. Underneath the first impression of implicitly incestuous aggression, of him laughing and shouting, and of the phallic pressure of his nearly naked body, there is also a sense of decay. The powerful body is evidently running to fat so that he is associated not only with the stench of seaweed and old fishing nets but also with the flotsam and the yellow foam left by the retreating wave.

There is no experience, as Foucault remarks, which is not also a way of thinking.[12] Despite the father's determined wilfulness, the girl senses the evolutionary logic he is so fond of invoking, aware of a power larger and more powerful than he, which is evidently beginning to wreak its revenge on him, in this sense acting as her surrogate. Asserting her own youth, her own possibilities, she is determined to contest his power, mocking his claims to control. As a scientist, he lays claim to knowledge and mastery of nature, but she sees him at odds with, even disconnected from the natural world he thinks he commands. He has missed the wave, is merely flotsam; his skin is pale still despite his 'many summers'.

There are strong echoes here of *Totem and Taboo*—Stead, as we know, had studied Freud—and of the link Freud established there between prohibitions of incest and the dominant male's desire to preserve his sexual monopoly, and the violence directed against the one who would challenge this dominance. In *The Man Who Loved Children*, Stead follows this violence to its ritual conclusion when Louie, another daughter in rebellion against a potentially incestuous and dominant father, tries to kill him. But as this first chapter of *For Love Alone* develops, the strongest note is of the father's auto-eroticism. Kitty, the younger of his two daughters, is drawn by his power. Looking up at him, she admires what even the rebellious Teresa sees as 'the marvellous hair of the man'. His response is flirtatious:

Andrew Hawkins ran his hand through it, feeling it himself. A thought seemed to strike him; he brought down his hand and looked at the back, then the palm (p. 7).

Though in her perception of him Teresa takes vengeance on this vanity, seeing his hand as 'large, pale muscular . . . an artisan's hand, hairless, diseased-looking, because streaked and spotted with fresh cement', he remains untouched.

'Not a bad hand, either,' he said. He had something on the tip of his tongue but couldn't get it out, he went on about his legs instead. 'But do you know, Kit,' he said, lowering his voice, and his eyes darkening with modesty or wonder. 'You see this hand, my good right hand, do you see it, Kit?'

Kitty laughed in her throat, a troubled, sunny laugh. 'I've felt it, too, in my time.'

He said mysteriously, lowering his voice again, 'Women have kissed this hand.' (p. 7)

Teresa may attempt to turn this aggression with her mocking comment, 'Handy Andy'. But the 'soft, unresonant voice' in which she does so points to her sense of outrage. Whether or not Hawker has actually violated his daughters physically, it is clear that he does so continually in a psychic sense and that this issues in the anger, the disillusion and the long-standing sense of homelessness and nameless desire characteristic of Teresa in this novel and of Louie in *The Man Who Loved Children*. If the father is hated, he is also somehow necessary. As Kate Grenville's Lilian expresses it, without him, the world would 'lack edges'.[13] Contesting his power becomes, in a sense, the source of their energy.

This is not to say that the effects are positive. There is a sense of displacement, almost of panic, in Teresa's story as she flings herself away from the father and on to the wider world, desperate for love, so determined to get away from it all and go to England that she all but starves herself in the process. More important, perhaps, is the feeling of dissociation of parts of the body here, the emphasis on hands, legs, hair, which gives a feeling of disintegration.

A passage from *The Man Who Loved Children* points to its possible source. Sam Pollitt, having told his daughter that her mother, his first wife who is now dead, had never understood him, claims her for himself.

Pale as a candle flame in the dusk, tallow-pale, he stalked along, holding her hand, and Louie looked up and beyond him at the enfeebled stars. Thus, for many years, she had seen her father's head, a ghostly flame against the heavens, from her little height. Sam looked down on the moon of her face; the dayshine was enough still to light the eyeballs swimming up to him (p. 159).

The parts of the body, hand, head, eyeballs, here become forms of expression, categories of the feeling of personal disintegration, the other side of the appalling logic he is trying to impose on her, trying to bind Louie to him irrevocably as the moon is bound to the sun, dependent on the one she hates for the light by which she lives.

This is a form of the fetishism which Marx, for instance, saw as typical of a society which is so preoccupied with objects that it turns people into objects. This is the kind of society Aunt Bea inveighs against in *For Love Alone*, significantly on the evening of a family wedding, mocking at people with

Nothing to wear but clothes, nothing to eat but food, nowhere to sleep but bed, nothing to marry but men, nowhere to go but home . . . Nothing to do but live (p. 54).

In such a world even the erotic becomes merely mechanical, a matter of conflict rather than delight, a matter of possession rather than of joy. Walking along the cliffs at night, Teresa, in the same novel, senses this conflict.

From every moon-red shadow came the voices of men and women; and in every bush and in the clumps of pine, upon unseen wooden seats and behind rocks, in the grass and even on open ledges, men and women groaned and

gave shuddering cries as if they were being beaten. She passed slowly, timidly, but fascinated by the strange battlefield, the bodies stretched out, contorted, with sounds of the dying under the fierce high moon (p. 61).

What is manifested outwards on to the cosmos here is what lies within her own consciousness, the fear of being conquered and painfully violated.

In such a society, in which there seems no other common bond, not even work, people must be bound together libidinally.[14] The incidence of incest, therefore, may be part of this larger erotic crisis, a general loss of self-esteem, as the personal gives way to the merely economic, making for self-abnegation in women and, in the men, impotent rage. This rage is evident in Stead's characters Andrew Hawker and Sam Pollitt, in Lilian's father in Grenville's novel and, in real life, in Chris Brennan, as Axel Clarke describes him in his later years. In turn, this evidence suggests that this kind of rage often leads to incest, the desire to possess which is a kind of compensation for loss of power, a need to establish lost authority by sexual possession.

Sam Pollitt in *The Man Who Loved Children* is perhaps the most extensive portrait of this kind of incestuous desire. True, it does not seem to lead to actual physical incest. The closest he comes to it is his fascination with Louie's approach to puberty.

He poked and pried into her life . . . stealing into her room when she was absent, noting her mottoes on the wall . . . and investigating her linen, shivering with shame when suggestive words came into her mouth (p. 340).

But this kind of curiosity also points to the source of incestuous action, the desire not merely to possess her feminity but even to enslave her to him for intimate personal reasons, reasons of his own inadequacy.

Sam is in this sense an emotional imperialist—like Andrew Hawker he has also spent time as a political coloniser, in his case in Singapore, where he glories in his role of 'civiliser'. There is little that is erotic about him—that is the province of his turbulently rebellious and passionate wife, Henny, who contests him every inch of the way. His real need is power. He does not seduce women but gathers them round him, corralling them like so many fillies, an emotional John Wayne. Nor does he seem to take pleasure in women's bodies. He lusts instead for the female power which so evidently fascinates him in Louie's adolescence, longing in his imperial way to conquer this last frontier.[15]

Significantly, he seldom ventures outside the confines of the family, as if obscurely aware that the writ of his fantasies will not run further. He dreams instead of making his family 'a little nucleus of splendid men and women to work for the future' (p. 159), that is, of a world in which he will be supreme. This is why he loves children, keeping Henny pregnant not only to increase his empire but to bind her to him. Henny realises this with appalling clarity when, catching a glimpse of 'the frost glare of the wedding ring on her left fist', she reflects on her bondage to him (p. 172). The association of 'fist' with boxing suggests the desperation of the intuition that for her 'this plain ugly link' which 'stayed with her as stayed the man she had taken it from' condemns her to 'an eyeless eternity of work and poverty and an early old age'. This is the result of her enslavement to 'this potent breadwinner' who made her 'his kitchenmaid and body servant' (p. 173).

As for Louie, Sam's eldest daughter by his first wife, the passage we have already quoted suggests that she is aware, though not quite so desperately, of his desire to make her his own possession. He wants to be the source of all light, all knowledge and information, as well as all power over her. What is at issue here, then, is not normal sexuality, which belongs, as it were, in darkness, in the accepting intimacy of personal relationships, rather than in this light, the 'ghostly earth flame against the heaven' (p. 159). Sam, in fact, is appalled by sexuality, by its bodiliness. As he kept watch over Louie's development,

he went through all the literature on adolescence, becoming more horrified every day as Satan's invisible world was revealed to him, who had been a bloodless youth living on greens and tap water. Youth was one of the

*beasts of the Revelation, the worst, and more insolent than the Sun. He
writhed within himself to think that his high soul, soberminded Louie had
to go through all that (p. 341).*

But the resolution he forms, to give Louie 'proper training',
carefully watch her and protect her from all 'bad companions' points
to the real nature of his desire. Not only does he try to keep her
from young men, he even intrudes on Louie's friendship with her
teacher, Miss Aiden. His love for her is love for himself, as this
exchange with her earlier on makes clear:

*'You will be all right, Looloo,' concluded Sam, kissing her good night. 'You
are myself; I know you cannot go astray.'*
    'I won't be like you, Dad'.
    He laughed. 'You can't help it: you are myself'.
    She sulked; she wanted to be like Eleanora Duse, not like Sam (p. 164).

It might be normal for her to look for a role model but he contests
this, wanting to absorb her into and for himself. One recalls here
Malinowski's argument that the impulse to incest has to do with
'the retrospective power of new sentiments'.[16] Sam Pollitt is
evidently inadequate as a human being. A poor boy who has managed
to marry a rich woman and become a scientist, he takes refuge from
human relationships and feelings in a world of abstraction, in the
worship of nature which he wants to impose on his children; in his
enthusiasm for science and for inventions like the radio (which he
dreams of using to propagate his own ideas); and in his dream of
a 'universal humanity' in which 'all differences of nationality, creed
and education will be . . . gradually smoothed out' (p. 84). The
nature he admires, however, is antiseptic and imaginary, very
different from real nature which includes dirt, blood and faeces,
the nature so clearly recognised by the women in this book. But
instead of coming to terms with this whole range of experience,
Sam retreats from it into what Freud calls 'retrogressive phantasy-
making',[17] protecting himself by the stories he spins to enthrall his
children, presenting himself as a kind of Messiah, someone with the

ability to solve all the world's problems even though he proves quite unable even to look after his own professional and financial affairs.

Interestingly, in *Lilian's Story*, the Father (his name is always capitalised, for obvious reasons, since it is Lilian who is telling the story) also lives in a fantasy world. Even at table, he drills his children in general knowledge, firing questions at them about the length of rivers, the population of cities and about geometry, asserting his power over them by his mastery of 'facts' and at the same time banning all newspapers from the house—he is to be the sole source of information. But it is perhaps the poetry of Christopher Brennan which points most clearly to the origins of this fantasy. It is, on the one hand, an abiding longing for perfection, for some kind of pseudo-religious absolute, for the long-lost Eden, for primal innocence; on the other, it is in an abiding fear that this dream will be profaned, that it will be threatened by reality itself. The absolute he longs for is an impossible one, the dream of himself as God, infallible lord of an undivided and monastic universe.[18] Though Sam Pollitt's religion is science, he, too, shares this dream of absolute power. So he tells his children:

'I have many wonderful thoughts during those times when I am sauntering about by myself (and when I am to the foolish or mean eyes and heads that I seem to have round me just mooning about). Take the theory of the expanding universe—I want to figure it out some day . . . Very often I have an idea and then find months, years later, that a man like our very great Woodrow Wilson or Lloyd George or Einstein has had it too' (p. 106).

Like Brennan, he fancies himself as 'set apart as single in (his) kind',[19] a veritable priestly figure for all his professed secularity. To confirm his break with the ordinary world, he devises a special language which he speaks within the family, binding the children to him, making them citizens of the country he invents, a country with its own language. Like Brennan, he is actually a shy man, preferring books to people and reducing conversation to a long monologue or to the diatribes he launches against the world, and in particular against his professional colleagues. His actual life and marriage are in evident disarray, though, of course, he holds his wife to blame, 'calling upon truth to witness that never was a more faithful, long-suffering husband than he, or a lighterheaded, vainer, more pernicious woman than this that he, good soul, had innocently joined himself to' (p. 151). The real distance between them, however, is between the world of fact and the world of fantasy. 'He called a spade the predecessor of modern agriculture, she called it a muck dig: they had no words between them intelligible' (p. 167).

So neither marriage nor parenthood can overcome his isolation but serve instead to increase it. Intimacy is beyond him. In effect, he lives permanently in a public sphere, in a world of abstractions and slogans, which lacks any real sense of awareness of others, or of responsibility to them. In Singapore, for instance, told by his servant that he had been unwise to walk down certain streets at night, he retorts, 'I was not alone: I was with my fellow man' (p. 238).

His desire for his daughter Louie, is part of his fantasy. He wants to claim from her the affection he desires from his wife and wants her to understand him as he feels Henny does not, just as Lilian's Father turns to her for solace from the limply ineffectual and evidently passionless wife who retreats from him into the misty vagueness which seems to surround her. Both men, it seems, are actually afraid and insecure with their own sexuality, more intent on procreation to prove their potency than on intimacy or even pleasure. Sam's rage, already referred to, at a report in a newspaper of the incident of incest, dramatises this anxiety. He is afraid of his unconscious, of the dark, 'always anxious for morning . . . greedy for the daylight world, because the fevers of the dark, and the creatures real to man's sixth, inward, dark sense . . . all disappeared at the dark's first fading' (p. 61).

It is possible, I think, that these are the creatures Brennan describes so vividly in 'Lilith' in a passage which Axel Clarke suggests has a good deal to do with sexual disgust and disappointment in his relations with his wife.

He shall not know her nor her gentle ways
nor rest, content, by her sufficing source,
but, under stress of the veil'd stars, shall force
her simple bloom to perilous delight
adulterate with pain, some nameless night
strain'd with miasm of flesh become a tomb. [20]

While there is little that is gentle about Henny, the corruption Sam Pollitt senses in the world all around him is a projection of something he senses within himself; the mingled disgust and attraction evident in his fascination with Louie's adolescence. The puritan primness and the system of interdiction he attempts to impose on the children is evidently a reaction against it, a suppression of what he refuses to acknowledge, 'the sensuality of his own nature' (p. 287).

This projection outwards of a personal sense of wickedness is evident also and more explicitly as a consequence of incestuous feelings and actions in *Lilian's Story*.

'Lilian,' he said as if reminding me who I was. 'Lilian, you are an example of the degeneracy of the white races . . . You are sterile and degenerate and corrupt as a snake' (p. 167).

In similar vein, his biographer tells us that Brennan was scandalised by the behaviour of the daughter he had corrupted, posing as her rescuer from the life of depravity she had chosen, no doubt as her revenge on him. But moral posturing of this kind is no defence against the ultimate dread, the fear of not being able to love any more, of becoming a dead man in a world which, for all his posturing about nature, is a world of objects and abstraction. [21] It is this dread which may be the source of the impulse to incest implicit in Sam's relations with his daughter but never made explicit.

We turn now to look more closely at the children involved: Grenville's Lilian, Stead's Teresa and Louie and at Anne Brennan. It must be said, first of all, that they all seem to be strong figures.

There is little sense of the shrinking timidity and silent misery which is often a consequence of incest. That said, however, it is clear that all of them feel somehow cut off from others, feel what is a displacement not only from paternal but also from the maternal, which should be a source of indulgence. They are all strong, too strong, sometimes even savagely so, somehow excessive, estranged from tenderness and compassion for themselves, though necessarily compassionate for others. Teresa and Louie have strongly protective feelings for their siblings, for instance, as Lilian has for her younger brother, John. Their lives seem to centre on the struggle with the father, the centre of authority, an authority which they must resist and even claim for their own. Louie even attempts to beat her father at his own game, not only inventing her own language, as he does, but writing in it, staging a play about a father who attempts to murder his daughter and triumphantly translating it for him, enjoying his bewilderment and growing rage. The denunciation is powerful.

Every day with rascally wiles you ravish my only joy, my peace of mind and now my solitude is two. A stranger is there. The name of the stranger is hate . . . I am an innocent girl that you have too much plagued. As mother says, I am rotten but with innocence. If to breath the sunlight is a sin, what can I do? I see you are determined to steal my breath, my sun, my daylight (pp. 408–9).

This passage and its sequel in which, when she threatens him, the father tries to embrace and then to kill her, vividly expresses what Rene Girard in his study of Greek tragedy calls the 'mimetic double bind', which is the product of the patricidal drive which results from incest.[22] In a strange way here the identification involved leads to a desire to be the model, seeking fulfilment by appropriating it,[23] and thus, in its turn, becoming violent, even murderous. There is nothing passive or feminine about Louie here. She has become the vengeful male which she imagines her father as her violator to be.

But there is little of the other double bind, the guilt and fear of being found out and punished, which is characteristic in real life of so many victims of incest. Elsewhere, however, one senses a vivid sense of entrapment, though, it is true, this is after she has made the attempt to kill her parents. Sam survives and so, it seems, does her sense of entrapment. It is not until the story ends that she is able to break free and leave home. The novel paints a vivid picture of this sense of entrapment:

The terror of it, and her secret complicity would seem so naked to the sky that she would break out into an icy sweat and wonder that no one could hear what was going on in her brain. She would never tell anyone, and this was a corpse sealed up in the house which she alone knew of and which would eventually moulder and leave little trace (p. 517).

The fact that she claims not to care and to believe 'that she had done the only right thing, the only fun thing' only adds to the pathos since it points to the distance between her and normality. Identification has been forced on her unknowingly; her conviction 'that Fate itself had not only justified her but saved her from the consequences' (p. 514) echoes Sam's sense of omnipotence and invulnerability. So, too, does her earlier dream of herself with a large scythe, suspended in space 'beside God, reaping together with him swinging closer to the earth and (beginning) there to mow the grass' (p. 164).

Stead's characters, then, dramatise the link between incest and murder, or at least the desire for murder. Teresa in *For Love Alone* is equally unbending, reacting to her father's attempt to flirt and tease her with ' "You offend my honour! I would kill anyone who offends my honour" ', (p. 13) though she makes no attempt at action. For all that, there is a certain pathos about this strength that claims, as Louie does, that 'Nothing hurts me if I don't want it to' (p. 391). But it is the behaviour of Anne Brennan which most vividly expresses the pathos underlying this kind of defiance.

In his memoir, *The Roaring Twenties: Literary Life in Sydney 1921–26*, Jack Lindsay has a chapter entitled 'Besty's and Brennan' which tells about Brennan's descent on Betsy's, a Bohemian restaurant which Anne frequented, in an attempt to 'rescue' her. This attempt concludes with them both living together there until she manages to escape, leaving him to fall even further into the alcoholism which was to destroy him. Lindsay's account of Brennan's first encounter with Anne gives a sense of manic desolation, an insanely displaced will to an impossible joy.

Amendola's, Ray says, will always remain in his mind as the place where he first saw that fabulous beautiful bitch Annie Brennan. 'I will never forget how, one Saturday afternoon, she came in drunk and danced among the bottles and glasses on the table. It was an old stunt of hers, but to my goggled still-adolescent eyes it was the most spectacular event I had ever seen . . . How she dominated all that crowd in those days.' [24]

Her isolation is only intensified by Lindsay's further comment, that 'everybody was in love with her . . . although everybody knew what a slut she was'.[25] Once again, there is little sense of the erotic; on Lindsay's side the defensiveness of the word 'slut' and on hers the extravagant display, the craving for power and the nihilism which is expressed in the title of Brennan's MA thesis, 'the Metaphysics of Nescience'[26]. Here, too, we see the double bind identification. As Anne has plunged into self-destruction, living as a prostitute, taunting her father's scholarship by working outside the museum and the library,[27] so Brennan 'installed himself at Betsy's, in a little room in a courtyard at the back, and drank steadily'.[28] 'Heavily turned in on himself, silent, but not unfriendly to us others',[29] he was thus bound into the same nightmare as his daughter. Conversely, she is able to accelerate his destruction because, as Lindsay shrewdly observes, 'she had as her ally his poetry, the pressure on his mind of the poetry he had once written and didn't want to understand, the poetry which accused his society, his civilization, of a total dereliction from the human path, the human dream'[30] which was, of course, his own dream of perfection, the perfection of his own power. The terror involved in this appalling alliance is evident in its consequences, the destruction of both their lives and the terrible rage at their own desolation.

Theirs is an extreme case, of course, though like all extremes, it highlights what is essential. *Lilian's Story*, however, brings us closer to this essential in a less extravagant but equally moving way. Based on the real-life figure of Bea Miles, Sydney eccentric and the terror of taxi-drivers, it is told from the point of view of the victim of abuse. At the same time, this point of view is informed by a shrewd awareness of the issues at stake, which should probably be attributed to the intelligent and sympathetic understanding of Kate Grenville. Bewilderment is the more common response of victims.

In Lilian's case, it is even clearer than with Sam Pollitt that the father cannot control the other females. His wife, who escapes from him into debility, revives amazingly when, in his turn, he has a breakdown and his sister, Lilian's dazzling Aunt Kitty, who 'lived in a house with blood-red stained-glass beside the front door', consistently defies him (p. 10). To Lilian, she is a figure of freedom fabulously vibrant but also somehow fragile, like a chandelier, part, it seems to the child, of an environment of glass, a 'tinkling and continual tiny chiming around her from so many necklaces and shivering earrings' (p. 10). To her brother, Lilian's father, however, she is a wicked woman, a permanent antagonist to his orderly factual world. Where his is a world of control, hers is Dionysian. She loves drinking and seems to be in permanent motion. 'Her hair at the back was slithering out of its combs, but her face was pink, her eyes shone, and everything made her laugh and hurry' (p. 10). For this reason, she is able to cut directly through barriers and proprieties, striking back at her brother where he is most vulnerable, challenging him, as she challenges the evasiveness of his wife, Lilian's mother, when she tries to claim her as an ally, by 'giving a laugh like a shout and going on, 'My Brother Albion services you' (p. 35).

The child, Lilian, then, is the only one Albion feels he can control. The pressure he exerts on her exists from the beginning of the story. Her earliest memories are of 'a man of moustaches, of shiny boots that squeaked when he walked. His boots on the stairs filled the house, his hands with the powerful black hairs gripping the bannister hard enough to make it tremble' (p. 5). Like Teresa's and Louie's, her first response is identification, a desire to be the model he proposes, to take over what belongs to him.

'Lilian, do not bang your feet like that,' Mother exclaimed. 'What do you think you are doing?'

I turned explaining, 'I am being Father, Mother,' but she did not hear, only said, 'A lady glides, Lilian' (p. 5).

The confusion increases when she turns to her Father for enlightenment.

When I asked him, Father said, 'Your mother is a wife and mother, and a lady and I am a gentleman'. He hoisted me up on his shoulder and from such a height the floor shone in a strange way and the ceiling made me dizzy. 'And you're a young lady whose bed-time it is' (p. 5).

The sense of disorientation here, of being snatched away into a blaze of light, we have met already in Louie Pollitt's experience. Here, too, the light defuses the sexuality. She is carried away instead into his fantasy, hoisted onto his shoulder, another object in his world of objects and facts, set apart in her own way as he feels himself set apart from others. But where he chooses this exclusion, refusing to have newspapers in the house, for instance, the child suffers from it. Even at a children's party.

The thought of our clever father preyed on me throughout our cake and jelly, throughout the singing and the blowing out of the candles . . . jelly and cake sat heavily on my stomach. There was something shameful about Father that made me frightened of this noisy room, its tables littered with bright icing. Too much was hidden (p. 38).

The sense of displacement here is as yet pre-ethical, involving a loss of identity, of being drawn into another world to which she does not properly belong.

If she were a boy, like her brother, John, she could fight back against their father in an Oedipal way. But she is not. The feeling that she is somehow different grows increasingly and devastatingly, leaving her feeling more and more powerless. Her only protection is to insist on this difference, eating compulsively and using her fat as a kind of protection. 'I had grown big and could knock people down if I took a run at them, and block doorways, and there was too much flesh now for Father' (p. 18). Her father cannot be shaken off so easily, however. Her wayward behaviour provokes him to fresh efforts to bring her into line with increasingly sadist overtones.

The brass knob of Father's study door had become familiar to me. It became warm in my hand as I stood holding it for as long as possible. It was like keeping an egg warm. 'Well, come in Lilian,' Father said. 'Do not add dawdling to your other crimes . . . ' and I would at last have to let go of the doorknob and shuffle forward . . . 'Over,' Father ordered. 'Down, and over,' and I pulled down my bloomers, held up my skirt and bent over the desk. 'It is just skin,' I whispered to myself every time. 'And there is too much flesh for him now.' The sound of mother's old belt had become very resonant against so much flesh (p. 18).

Perversion, as Freud defines it, involves sexual activities beyond the region of the body designed for sexual union.[31] So the sadism here corresponds to an aggressive component of the sexual instinct which has become independent and exaggerated and, by this displacement, has usurped the leading position.[32] Significantly, however, Lilian does not respond with the masochism which is often its concomitant, by turning the cruelty she endures back upon herself. But at this stage her resistance rather involves turning herself into an object, using her flesh as a buffer between herself and her humiliation and pain.

The pressure grows as she approaches puberty. Like Sam Pollitt, her father is increasingly jealous of the feminine mystery he senses in her, determined to have it for himself.

'You are a woman now, Lilian,' he told me, and laid an arm so suddenly along my arm that I staggered. He pressed me against him, but we had not had much practice at this and I stood in an ungainly way in his arm holding my breath. 'You must tell me Lilian, if anyone is forward with you,' he said, and gave me a final squeeze that made me gasp, before releasing me. 'The world is full of bold forward men who will try anything' (p. 101).

The menace implicit here becomes explicit as 'he ran a tongue over his teeth so that they glittered', like the wolf in the nightmare of Red Riding Hood, but also glancing over his shoulder where 'Mother sat with the ribbons of her hat trying to whip her awake' (p. 101). There is no rescue from that quarter. The girl is quite alone. The permanence of her helpless isolation is confirmed, by the conclusion, 'Father's shadow on the grass reached out towards her in a dark way and the ribbons danced and fluttered urgently. Fixated, Lilian, is the name for it' (p. 101).

'Fixated' is certainly the name to describe him. The chapter 'Penetrating Secrets', for instance, shows him preoccupied with the mysteries of fertility and generation on display at the Royal Show, the prize rams, a hen which has laid an egg of record weight and, above all, the pig's organ of generation which, he tells the children, is 'sharp as a knife' (p. 117). The sadism is evident. He takes great pleasure in making up a party for the show, telling them they must 'remember the animal in us' (p. 117). The fetishism here is significant. Bodies seem now to be disintegrating; the only part of them he is interested in is genital. But this is a sign of the general disintegration of the man for whom relations between people have turned into relations between objects. But it is equally significant that when he finally takes Lilian she is in her own room looking at herself naked in a mirror, exploring her own sexuality.

Incest, as we have argued earlier, is ultimately a matter of auto-eroticism. Lilian here is miming the Father, Narcissus, intent upon the mirror in which he sees only himself. Invading her fantasy, he attempts to possess her, draw her into his own. But his desperation, it seems, is perhaps more terrible than hers.

In every room of the house, the air that had stilled fled, and was replaced by trembling and fearful vibration. I could hear my voice, a thin reedy cry like something choking and not being rescued. Father said nothing at all, but the sound of his breathing was like a thudding machine in the silence. All around us, the house stood shocked, repelling the sounds we made. My cries carried no further than the carpet of the stairway. The silent rooms would take no part in my struggle, but swallowed the sounds indifferently.

'No!' I heard myself cry with a feeble piping sound. 'No! No!' The house gave back only silence, and the panting of the desperate machine that was Father (p. 121).

The sense of appalling isolation, of being drawn into a nightmare in which the inanimate things in the house seem more living than the violent machine the Father has become, is quite overwhelming. So, too, is the perversion. Men and women need and love one another but recognise, at the same time, their independence. There is only sameness here, and a feeling of being drawn into a cruel void, an end of humanity.

The Father's triumphant, 'It's just us now' (p. 115) as Mother goes away for a holiday, is confirmed. The knowledge Lilian now has is knowledge that cannot be spoken, her very words subsumed into the dark secret between them. Though she tries, she is unable to speak about what has happened, either to her Mother or to Aunt Kitty, although her boyfriend, Duncan, senses that she is somehow different. 'My mouth and tongue were some one else's now and even the words that rose into my mind had nothing to do with me' (p. 121). Her body has become a kind of throwaway commodity, a prison from which there is no rescue, from which she must distance herself in order to survive.

Whatever had happened, and I would not ask myself just what that had been had happened to a mass of flesh called Lilian, not to me. I cowered in that flesh, my self shrunk to the size of a pea, but still I tried to speak to Mother. Perhaps she would release me from it all, or take me over, or save me (p. 121).

But, of course, she does not, since she is herself in flight from her husband. This scene in which she refuses to hear Lilian (taking out her stop-watch and timing the silences as Lilian tries to tell her what has happened), is perhaps even more appalling than the rape. With Duncan, the young man who has become her friend, she no longer feels as if she belongs to herself. 'His hand on my knee was intolerable and his face was too close to mine' (p. 122). Intimacy was no longer possible. 'He could breathe too deeply and scatter me into many fragments. Nothing was keeping me together now' (p. 122). In effect, she has become a permanent prisoner of her father. But this prison involves a backward jolt, a kind of falling apart, a permanent exclusion from normality. 'I lost everything with Father and became a collection of cells held together in an envelope of skin, propped upright in a chair'. She avoided all claims to intimacy by doing her best 'to become stone, or sky, or anything that could go on living its silent life when everyone thought it was dead' (p. 150).

The only way out, it seems, is retreat into fantasy. So like Anne Brennan, she takes to the streets, if not as a prostitute, at least as a friend of prostitutes, looking for love not so much in real life but in films, finding there 'plenty of men with moustaches with whom I could pay to fall in love' (p. 160). But even there her father pursues her and has her committed to a mental hospital, posing, like Brennan, as his daughter's protector, though actually wanting to keep her for himself as well as to protect their guilty secret.

Unlike Anne Brennan, however, Lilian is rescued by Aunt Kitty who has guessed what has happened. She takes her away from the mental hospital and installs her in a room of her own with a guaranteed weekly income from Father.

'I have blackmailed your rotten father!' She was excited almost beyond bearing. 'My brother has been beaten'. A knocking began on the floor, as if of a broomstick being hit against the ceiling below (p. 157).

As the image of the broomstick suggests, the spell has been broken and even though Aunt Kitty dies soon afterwards, Lilian does not go back to Father. At Aunt Kitty's funeral he may rage at Lilian, calling her 'sterile and degenerate and corrupt as a snake', but his power over her is broken. He retreats further into authoritarian fantasy, joining what seems like the Australia First movement during the Depression, 'strutting in khaki and mouthing . . . empty phrases about the degeneracy of the white races' (p. 169) and dying just as World War II breaks out, just when 'in his uniform . . . and given a platoon to lead', he should have felt, Lilian reflects, 'vindicated at last' (p. 169). So, Lilian's story ends more or less happily. She becomes a well-known but benign eccentric, travelling everywhere by taxi, talking with everyone and anyone and, finally, setting up house with an ex-taxi-driver, Frank.

Nevertheless, in all this, she is still seeking, however good humouredly, for a kind of retribution. Her eccentricities can be seen as a form of revenge on the society from which she feels herself forever excluded. This is a very different kind of vengeance from Anne Brennan's, who went 'whoring'[33] about the streets, telling people she was Brennan's daughter, and even more different from that of Stead's Louie who actually tries to murder her father. But Lilian's survival has something in it, too, of Louie's defiance, the defiance she asserts against Sam when he rages against the newspaper account of incest:

She got the idea that she had run up against one of the wickednesses of the universe, an infernal middle kingdom of horror that she alone could stand. For Sam could rave and the little children could look at her queerly when she blurted out the half-formed thoughts in her mind, but she felt sure that she only felt what was going on under the ribs of the visible world (p. 388).

To conclude, then, it is clear that incest has to do with displacement and violation of a most appalling kind. But if it is true, as Foucault and others would have it, that private acts articulate the body politic, then there is an urgent need to examine the interaction between the personal and the political, between our culture and the economic, social and political structures which produce it, and the intersubjective and psychological crisis to which incest gives witness. The subordination of women and the brutal dominance of the male reach their extreme point of perversity in the act of incest. The continuance of this pattern of subordination and dominance must therefore be a matter of profound concern. Personally, I wonder whether this pattern is not bound up with an economic and social system in which might is taken to be right and money and material goods to be the measure of value. What is clear from the evidence of literature, however, is that underneath the bland surface of an apparently rational society, there exists for some an area of terror, isolation and imprisonment within the self, an area from which one escapes only by violence.

NOTES

1. Paul Ricoeur, *The Symbolism of Evil* (Beacon Press, Boston, 1969), p. 12.
2. B. Andolsen, C. Gudorf, M. Pellauer (eds), *Women's Consciousness, Women's Conscience* (Harper, San Francisco, 1987), p. xii.
3. Ricoeur, p. 12.
4. Ibid.
5. Ibid., p. 348.
6. Ludwig Wittgenstein, *Philosophical Investigations*, trans. G.E.M. Anscombe (Blackwell, Oxford, 1974) pp. 48 & 114.
7. The novel is set in Washington, DC. But it is generally accepted that the raw material is to be found in Stead's childhood experiences in Sydney.
8. Christina Stead, *The Man Who Loved Children* (Penguin, 1970), p. 387.
9. Martin Heidegger, *Poetry, Language and Thought* (Harper & Row, New York, 1971), p. 8.
10. Christina Stead, *For Love Alone* (Angus & Robertson, 1982), p. 5.
11. The erotic displacements involved in colonisation are profound and worth treatment in themselves. Cf S. Gilman, 'Black Bodies, White Bodies: Towards an Iconography of Female Sexuality in Late Nineteenth-Century Art, Medicine and Literature', in H.L. Gates (ed.), *'Race', Writing and Difference* (Chicago University Press, London, 1986), pp. 223–61.
12. P. Rabinow (ed.), *The Foucault Reader* (1987), pp. 292–300.
13. Kate Grenville, *Lilian's Story* (Allen & Unwin, Sydney, 1985), p. 170.
14. Sigmund Freud, *Group Psychology and the Analysis of the Ego* (Nova, New York, 1975), p. 157.
15. F.X. Kroncke, 'Prison, Bottoming Out, and the Mother', *Cross Currents*, 38, 1, p. 60.
16. B. Malinowski, *Sex and Repression in Savage Society* (Kegan Paul, London, 1927), p. 215.
17. Sigmund Freud, *Introductory Lectures on Psycho-Analysis* (Allen & Unwin, London, 1922), p. 282.
18. Axel Clarke, *Christopher Brennan: A Critical Biography* 1980, p. 3.
19. Ibid., p. 10.
20. Ibid., p. 119.
21. Ricoeur, p. 30.

22. R. Girard, *Violence and the Sacred*, John Hopkins University Press, (Baltimore, 1977), p. 178.
23. Ibid., p. 170.
24. Jack Lindsay, *The Roaring Twenties: Literary Life in Sydney, 1922–26* (Bodley Head, London, 1960), p. 141.
25. Clarke, p. 53.
26. Ibid.
27. Lindsay, p. 148.
28. Ibid.
29. Ibid.
30. Ibid.
31. Sigmund Freud, *Three Essays on the Theory of Sexuality* (Image, London, 1949), p. 28.
32. Ibid., p. 36.
33. Lindsay's word, *The Roaring Twenties*, p. 148.

RACISM

acism is a major cause of war and social violence. The belief, often based on religious or allegedly 'scientific' grounds, that one's own group of people is innately superior to all others, leads to intolerance, justifies aggression and makes a virtue of misunderstanding, even despising others. The United Nations has declared it 'morally repugnant and unacceptable', pointing out that such feelings of innate superiority have no justifiable basis. To say the least, racists make bad citizens at both the national and the international level since citizenship is based on mutual respect and a community of value.

It is deeply troubling to realise not only that Australia is a racist society, based on the systematic oppression of its Aboriginal inhabitants, but also that internationally it is increasingly seen in these terms. We may have forgotten the White Australia Policy but many of our Asian and African neighbours have not, and the 'Blainey debate' several years ago, with its scapegoating of Asian migrants by right-wing and neo-fascist groups, was given extensive coverage especially in Asia.

It is true, of course, that most Australians are probably tolerant, easygoing and friendly, and the fact that over a million migrants have come to Australia since World War II and have become part of our society with the minimum of racial violence witnesses to this. It could also be argued that tensions between the Anglo-Celtic majority and people from other cultures are by and large the result of socio-economic factors; jealousy of the newcomers' success, for instance, or suspicion of their close-knit communities, rather than of the ideology of 'race'.

All that may be so. But there remains the problem, or rather the offence, of our treatment of Aboriginal Australians, possibly the most imprisoned people on earth and certainly the most systematically deprived and oppressed group in Australian society. Once again, it is true that most Australians are largely unaware of the grim history of contact between the two cultures and that others are able to explain away this history and the oppression which continues by stereotyping Aboriginals as lazy, ignorant, lawless and hopelessly addicted to alcohol. Comforting as they may be to some, however, these stereotypes, like the powerlessness and poverty of Aboriginal people, confirm the view that, at least as far as Aboriginal Australians are concerned, Australia is a racist society, one in which a group of people are permanently discriminated against on account of their 'colour', culture and ethnic origin and their basic human rights impaired for that reason, all this legitimated by an 'induced and subtle value acceptance of the idea [of their inferiority] interwoven, over time, into the nation's sociocultural fabric'.[1]

Morally, this is troubling. But there may also be political and economic consequences for us, a small, predominantly Western, society in South-East Asia. Indeed it is possible that with the breakdown of apartheid in South Africa, Australia may replace that country as the archetype of the racist state. There has already been some criticism in international forums of Australia's delay in giving full ratification to the International Convention for the Elimination of Racial Discrimination which we signed in 1975. The Australian government still has reservations about Article 4(a) of the convention which states that the dissemination of ideas based on racial superiority, hatred or incitement to racial hatred, as well as acts of racial violence or incitement to racial hatred, are unlawful. The government's grounds for this reservation are the challenge this article poses to freedom of speech. But it has drawn unfavourable comment internationally, especially in view of the apparent reluctance of the states to introduce legislation making racial violence and incitement to racial hatred an offence. To date, South Australia, New South Wales and Western Australia have passed such legislation. But its implementation has been 'less than enthusiastic'.[2]

This international impression of Australia is not insignificant, of course, in a world in which the hegemony of the West is increasingly being questioned and 'white' people are becoming a diminishing minority. It becomes even more troubling in the light of the connection between Australian nationalism, the sense that we are somehow pre-eminent in the region because we are 'Western', and the ideology of imperialism which assumes the right of 'white' people to rule the world and sets 'white' over against 'black: as superior to inferior, civilised to savage and sometimes even good to evil.'[3] If in the long run racism not only has to do with power but is a form of power,[4] then that power today is increasingly under challenge by those who were formerly its victims.

For all of these reasons, the publication of the report of the Royal Commission into Aboriginal Deaths in Custody is an important event, providing as it does an opportunity to take stock of the situation. The task of the commission was to investigate Aboriginal deaths which occurred in custody. But these deaths, disproportionate to those of non-Aborigines which occurred in prison, are, it appears, symptoms of a wider problem: the fact that by reasons of their culture and history Aboriginal Australians are systematically disadvantaged and discriminated against so that, in effect, they are victims of racism at the structural and cultural, not merely the individual level. Because the problem is so general, it seems better to specify and in the first instance to concentrate on factual issues. For these reasons and because the Indian Ocean Centre for Peace Studies is located in Western Australia, we shall concentrate on the Royal Commission's Regional Report for Western Australia.

Before doing so, however, the reception of the Royal Commission's report is worth comment. Only briefly, selectively and sometimes sensationally and misleadingly reported in this country— the *West Australian's* headlines, for instance, alleged, inaccurately, that the police had been 'cleared' in the John Pat case—it was nevertheless widely reported and discussed internationally. Whether or not this indicates indifference or embarrassment on the part of the Australian media, it is another example of the gap between our perception of ourselves and of the significance of our relations with Aboriginal Australians and international perceptions of the same matters.

To come to the report itself, the overall impression is that this state is, in effect, one large prison. Aboriginal people are 'grossly' over-represented in custody.[5] Thus an Aboriginal person in Western Australia is 43 times more likely to find him/herself in police custody than a non-Aboriginal person and at least 26 times more likely to find him/herself in prison (p. 2). One-third of the total Aboriginal deaths in prison occurred in this state and the ages ranged between 20 years to 55 years, the median age being 30.12 (p. 6). Yet the Royal Commission found, the offences for which Aboriginal people were arrested and punished were generally minor offences. In 1988, for example, 48 per cent of Aboriginal people in detention were there for drunkenness—the figure for non-Aboriginal people was 7.7 per cent. A further 22 per cent of Aborigines were in custody for good order offences, many of them alcohol-related; street-drinking, for instance, fighting, abusing police, or resisting arrest (p. 187). It is perhaps significant, however, that Aboriginal people were under-represented in proportion to the rest of the community in the category of more serious offences of homicide, sexual offences, robbery, fraud, drug offences, justice procedures and other offences against property (p. 157). Despite the impression given by media stories about car thefts by young Aboriginals and subsequent high speed car chases, the fact is that they were under-represented in this area in comparison with non-Aboriginals (p. 157).

It is difficult to avoid the impression, therefore, that it is the fact that they are Aboriginals which propels many Aboriginal people into a life of conflict with the law. Certainly, this seems to have been the case with many of those whose deaths in custody were investigated by the Royal Commission. Many of them first found themselves in prison in their teens, sometimes for ridiculously small matters: stealing two blocks of chocolate, for instance (p. 55), or, aged 10, for breaking into a school to steal coloured pencils (p. 68). Another had appeared in the children's court on eight occasions and been imprisoned five times by the age of 16, all for trivial offences (p. 55). Another young woman had 30 convictions recorded against her between 1976 and the time of her death in prison in 1982, mostly for petty offences and motor vehicle offences, usually committed under the influence of alcohol (p. 57). Several of these were well-read and intelligent people and one of them, Robert Walker, who died in Fremantle Prison in a struggle with prison officers, had published a book of poems. Nearly all, however, had a history of dislocation, of being taken away from their families and placed in institutions.

As far as detention was concerned, the commission's report noted 'a general lack of care' of Aboriginal prisoners (p. 8). According to a police aide, for instance, 'We'd just pop into the lockup, count heads and keep going (p. 514). This indifference to Aboriginal prisoners in general and to the state of their physical and mental health in particular the report finds 'alarming'. The police, the commissioner notes, did not seem to understand that someone who is drunk is also ill (p. 129) and that his/her condition may become worse when locked up (p. 130). Arresting alcoholics and placing them in a police lockup, as one of the witnesses, a professor of psychiatry declared, is to concentrate 'a suicide-vulnerable population' in custody (p. 129).

Several of the deaths, it is implied, might not have occurred if officers had been in any way vigilant. One prisoner, a young woman, was 'agitated, aggressive and complaining when taken into custody', yet she was put in a cell by herself where she later committed suicide. She was 21, and had been arrested for unpaid fines (p. 48). Indifference to or ignorance of prison regulations was widespread amongst police and there appeared to be little awareness of the obligation on the part of police and prison officers to care for those in their custody. Partly, the report suggests that this was due to lack of proper training and lack of interest in Aboriginal culture. But there is also a suggestion that the importance of this training was not understood at the highest levels. In 1976, for example, 7 hours out of 13 weeks of training of police recruits were given to the study of Aboriginal culture. By 1990, however, this had been reduced to 2 hours and 40 minutes, though training had been extended to 22 weeks (p. 557). Even more troubling, in 1989 the Institute of Applied Aboriginal Studies at what was then the West Australian College of Advanced Education at Mount Lawley withdrew its staff from participation in this training in protest against the short time given to it and on account of the quality of the course offered, but also because of racist behaviour directed against the Aboriginal lecturers (p. 560).

As the report sums up, 'Most police officers, like other government officials, had little or no understanding of Aboriginal history, culture, society or life style' (p. 555). Attitudes were and still are ethnocentric and 'there was little if any attempt to work with the Aboriginal Community' (p. 555). At best, concerns were pragmatic, intent upon the matters in hand, the preservation of law and order within the community. Even in training, the police, it was found

Were not really interested in Aboriginal history and would rather get rid of units like pre-history. Their main focus was on wanting to know how to handle the person in the street (p. 561).

At worst, the relationship seemed to be conditioned by history, to be that of the conquerors to the conquered and to give rise, therefore, to 'preconceived ideas about Aboriginal people which saw [police] setting out to prove they were "boss" ' (p. 555). Not surprisingly, 'these bad attitudes [(the commission found)] resulted in prejudiced and discriminatory treatment' (p. 555). It is perhaps a further indication of such attitudes and of the often unconscious assumptions of superiority on which they are based that on the whole police believed that, despite problems, relations between them and Aboriginal people were relatively good. Most professed to be satisfied with the situation (p. 595).

Aboriginal people, however, did not agree. The report lists their complaints:

lack of understanding and ability to communicate with Aboriginal people; racism; harassment of Aboriginal peoples, especially younger people; intimi-dating police practices; abusive and racist language; rough treatment, especially of young men; the unfair treatment Aboriginals received in relation to complaints against the police or non-Aboriginal people; lack of training and knowledge of Aboriginal society and culture; and inappropriate placement of police officers in towns with significant Aboriginal populations (p. 597).

97

This is a dismal catalogue. But it is important not to lay all the blame on the police. As the report suggests, the problem is systemic: that discrimination against Aboriginal people is the product of history and of the ideology of superiority and domination on which the invasion and settlement of this country were based. Consequently, change is not easy to bring about. So the commissioner, the Honourable D.J. O'Dea writes:

In describing the state of Aboriginal/police relations I am all too aware of the volume of material that has already been written on this issue and previous recommendations that have been made. It is with some dismay that I am compelled to add my voice to that of others . . . my inquiries reveal that little has changed (p. 596).

As the report puts it:

The bitter 200 years of contact between Aboriginal and non-Aboriginal society, and in the way in which police have been used by the non-Aboriginal Community to control Aboriginal people, is a starting point in understanding Aboriginal attitudes to the police (p. 597).

According to an Aboriginal witness, a community development officer with the WA Drug and Alcohol Authority in Port Hedland:

A lot of Aboriginal people in Port Hedland don't like the police, it stems from a long time ago. I don't know of any Aboriginal people who can say that he like a policeman, whether they've been arrested or not, it's just a— the same as they don't like native welfare, because native welfare took their kids away. The police used to lock them up, it's part of your tradition that you don't like policemen (p. 597).

In this way, as the report says, quoting Commissioner Muirhead in his interim report, the police 'are likely to be regarded as the cutting edge of an uncaring white society' (p. 596). This lack of understanding and recognition of Aboriginal culture and history reflects that of the wider society.

Stereotyping of Aboriginal people as ignorant and useless, drunken and lawless and a danger to respectable society is one result of this ignorance. But the effects are as disastrous, for non-Aboriginal as for Aboriginal society. On the one hand, it leads to the aggressive policing practices commented on by the commission. There is a disproportionately strong police presence in towns with a significant Aboriginal population, for instance, and police there seem to concentrate their attention on Aboriginal people. This cannot make for understanding between Aborigines and the police. In Halls Creek and Kalgoorlie, for instance, the report notes that police constantly patrolled the drinking spots favoured by Aboriginal fringe-dwellers (p. 605). Similarly in Roebourne at the time of John Pat's death, Aboriginal people were constantly being moved from the park and the river. 'Then when they were drinking down at the river the police would come and make multiple arrests for drinking in a public place' (p. 605). It is at least possible to speculate that the anger which led to the fight between the police and the group of young Aborigines which included John Pat was fuelled by this kind of policing.

To the police, it appears, Aborigines were seen as threats to law and order. This was true even, some witnesses suggested, especially, of better educated and more prominent Aboriginal members of the community. The commission heard evidence, for example, that families actively associated with campaigning for Aboriginal rights, like the Cameron family in Geraldton, one of whose members died in police custody, were seen as 'troublemakers' and targeted for special attention, with regular patrols of their neighbourhood and spotlighting of their houses at night (p. 602).

This kind of policing may reflect the unconscious anxieties of invading people who still fear some counterattack from the people they had conquered, rather than conscious prejudice. But the Royal Commission reports a general perception among Aboriginal people that they were singled out for attention through discriminatory policing practices 'in a way that non-Aboriginal people were not' (p. 601) and that this was particularly so with Aboriginal young men. Aborigines previously convicted of some offence were, they charged, singled out afterwards for special attention especially when an offence had been committed (p. 602).

This, of course, undermines the basic notion of British law that a person is innocent until proven guilty. But, given the prejudices against Aboriginal people it is understandable. As one witness to the commission said: 'if you have a population, like the Aboriginal population, about whom there are stereotypes, behaviours which might be regarded as normal in a white Anglo-Saxon resident of Nedlands' (p. 129) may be seen very differently. If Aboriginal people are seen somehow as deviant, intractable and a threat to the good order of society, then aggressive policing policies might seem necessary. In Roebourne at the time of the John Pat affair, for instance, Aboriginal drinking was seen in this way and the police visited the hotel frequently. As one police officer told the Royal Commission, almost as if he were a colonial official in 'darkest Africa' in the nineteenth century surrounded by 'hostile natives',

The purpose of going into the hotel was to show the flag. Show the uniform. I still do the same thing today. It shows the uniform to those who are there in case there may be trouble (p. 602).

The assumption, it seems, is that Aborigines are troublemakers, not good citizens like 'the rest of us'. From the Aboriginal point of view, of course, this is not only intimidating but also outrageous. It also denies their rights as citizens. One witness from Kalgoorlie alleged, for example, that his car had been followed by the police for about 50 kilometres.

I think the police have this idea in the back of their head—they see a car driving along. They will pull the car up under any sort of explanation. They will say, 'You didn't have your indicator lights on', things like that. But the moment that car is stopped they ask everyone to get out, ask them all their names. That happened to me a couple of days ago—down at Coolgardie (p. 604).

Other Aboriginal witnesses said that 'many young Aboriginal men were scared of the police saying that they will get a "flogging up" or a "smack in the mouth" ' (p. 604). Certainly, in the case of Bernard McGrath in Kalgoorlie, the commission found that he had suffered head injuries in the police station the week before his death (p. 604). He was later released but arrested again by two police officers for breach of a community service order and was subsequently found dead in custody. One of the arresting officers knew McGrath, who had previously complained of harassment by him (p. 68).

In a similar vein, many Aboriginal people complained that police used racist and abusive language to them. They 'thought that the police would not act in this way if talking to white people' (p. 599), alleging also that they were treated differently in matters of public order. In Kalgoorlie, for example, the commission was told that 'police would pick up Aboriginals first in fights before they would touch any of the white persons involved' (p. 606).

Nevertheless, to repeat an earlier point, the police should not be made scapegoats. Society as a whole must bear the responsibility for the racism which police behaviour reflects and which seems to exist sometimes even at the highest levels. The report found, for instance, that the cooperation of the Burke government with the Royal Commission was 'less than full' (p. 37). It also noted that less had been done than was desirable to implement the recommendations of the Vincent Report set up before the Royal Commission to look at ways and means of preventing deaths in custody. For instance, Aborigines were still being arrested for drunkenness (p. 594) although the Vincent Report had recommended against this. More seriously, the Royal Commission notes that in the investigation into John Pat, for instance, some documents were 'deliberately withheld' (p. 39) by government officials. Even more remarkably, the government funded the challenge mounted by the Police Union and the WA Prison Officers Union to the Royal Commission in the Supreme Court and the Federal Court. As the commission remarks, 'this led to the remarkable situation of the State funding a challenge by a third party against the letters patent which it itself had issued' (p. 38). In an attempt to reduce the hearing time in relation to those deaths the commission asked leave for the counsel assisting the commission to appear at the coronial inquest into some of the deaths which occurred during the life of the commission. But the state government opposed the application. As the report implies the state and its officials need to be accountable, especially to a particularly disadvantaged group of its citizens. Quoting the summing up of the counsel appearing for the state government:

To sum up, Sir, in our submission this application . . . is misconceived. If successful it would have far-reaching and dangerous consequences for the administration of justice in the state insofar as it concerns the conduct of coronial inquiries insofar as it may be seen to threaten independence and autonomy in the running of coronial inquiries in this state (p. 38).

The report remarks that, 'this was a surprising attitude to take to the initiative of a joint Commonwealth/State Commission which was attempting to avoid further public cost' (p. 38). In the context of the attitudes we have been discussing, it is not so surprising; perhaps, even to be expected.

Historical attitudes are not likely to change unless they are consciously challenged and worked against. In the early days of settlement many of the settlers saw Aborigines as little better than beasts, not quite human, 'nearest of all to the monkey or orang-utang and therefore incapable of enjoying the same state of intellectual existence' as ourselves.[6] According to another, they exist 'at the very zero of civilization, constituting the connecting link between man and the monkey tribe'. While few people would use language of this kind today, 'the failure of the education system to educate young people about Aboriginal issues' (p. 555) means that such attitudes may still exist at least at the unconscious level. As the report notes, there seems to be in this state little positive understanding of their culture and continuing suspicion of the difference it represents.

Moreover, these attitudes are socially and economically entrenched. Since 1788, power in Australia has centred in Anglo-Australian groups and institutions, though more recently some other European groups and some Asians have begun to be included. But by definition, Aboriginal Australians have been written into a position of powerlessness, not merely because their refusal to abandon their culture and their claims to it calls into question the moral authority of settlement, but also because the conflict continues still in places over possession of the land in general, and sacred sites in particular. Indeed, the continuing conflict between mining companies and Aboriginal people concerned to protect their sacred sites may well be intensifying at present the tension between Aboriginal and non-Aboriginal Australians.

It remains, however, that a society which excludes and oppresses a group of its own people and refuses to recognise their right to their own culture and way of life cannot call itself tolerant or peaceful. The so-called 'Aboriginal problem' is a problem of non-Aboriginal Australians, a remnant of the imperial habit of mind, its unthinking assumption of the authority of Western culture and its absolute right to impose its ways and values on the world. Elsewhere, as formerly colonised peoples recover their own dignity and regain power over their lives and culture, this habit of mind is in retreat. The findings of the Royal Commission into Aboriginal Deaths in Custody, however, provide disturbing evidence that Australia in general, and Western Australia in particular, may represent one of the last outposts of institutionalised racism.

NOTES

1. M. Radis, 'Legislative Treatment of Vulgar Racism: The Frames of Reference for Social Reform', in *Migration Monitor* (July 1988), p. 14.
2. L. Jayasuriya, Combating Racism—The Australian Experience, unpubl. notes for an address to the United Nations Association of Australia, 21 March 1991, which he was kind enough to share with me.
3. Abdul JanMohamed, 'The Economy of Manichean Allegory: The Function of Racial Difference in Colonialist Literature', in H.L. Gates (ed.) *'Race', Writing and Difference* (Chicago University Press, London, 1986), pp. 78–106.
4. Radis, p. 14.
5. Commissioner the Hon. D.J. O'Dea, *Royal Commission into Aboriginal Deaths in Custody: Regional Report into Individual Deaths in Custody in*

Western Australia, 2 vols. (AGPS, Canberra, 1991), p. 1. Hereafter all page references will be given in the text.

6. John Dawson in 1830. Quoted in J. Harris, *One Blood: Two Hundred Years of Aboriginal Encounters with Christianity* (Albatross Books, Sydney, 1990), p. 24.
7. Ibid.

ANOTHER RELIGIOUS WAR

'We are such stuff/As dreams are made on' . . . It may seem strange to begin a discussion of the war in the Gulf with a quotation from Shakespeare. But war, as the UNESCO Charter puts it, 'begins in the hearts of men' and, I would add, women. Ideology, the 'system of meanings which installs people in a particular culture in imaginary relations to the actual situation in which they find themselves' (Althusser), is, as it always has been, a potent factor in human affairs. We may like to think of ourselves and of our society as highly secularised. But I would argue, to the contrary, that it is actually highly religious, at least if we follow Clifford Goertz's definition of religion as a 'system of symbols which act to establish powerful, pervasive and long-lasting moods and motivations . . . by formulating conceptions of a general order of existence and clothing those conceptions with such an aura of factuality that the moods and motivations seem uniquely realistic.'[1]

Since 1945 with the advent of the electronic media and, more recently, the silicon chip, we have lived through a revolution in the nature of power. It is now a matter of information and persuasion: as thinkers as diverse as Foucault, McLuhan and Habermas, to name only a few, have argued. To put it in slogan form, power today grows not only out of the barrel of a gun but out of the cathode-ray tube. Those who control the media control politicians and general public alike, and those who control information not merely dominate but actually make or break the economy. We were not only persuaded to the war in the Gulf by the media, but like Vietnam, the war was also fought on the media. This time, however, the images we saw were carefully censored so that they confirmed our belief in the justice as well as the power of the Allied cause. This may be so. What I want to propose, however, is that this case needs more careful argument than it has had so far: depending on its object, faith may be a better thing than reason, but it is no substitute for it. Let us, then, look at the nature of the issues involved and then attempt to analyse and assess them.

First of all, to interrogate those who supported the war. A proposition should be that the war in the Gulf was in fact a religious war. That is not to say that economic factors were not involved. Oil clearly makes the Gulf crucial, and therefore one over which the United States and the West generally are deeply concerned to establish dominance—for 'religious' reasons, to 'protect the American way of life' as the American president put it. It is even clearer that the war rescued an ailing American economy. It provided a showcase for a dazzling array of highly efficient and successful weaponry, ensuring orders for the armaments industry from governments throughout the world for years to come and provoking soul-searching among the Russian military and armaments manufac-turers, with the loss not only of military dominance but also losing them millions of dollars' worth of sales throughout the world. But the war was also remarkably good for the construction industry. At the beginning of the war the Kuwaiti Task Force, situated in Washington DC, was set up to allocate contracts for rebuilding Kuwait and the US Army Corps of Engineers has already been awarded a contract for $4635 million, which is being passed on to the giant companies with which it usually does business, like Brown and Root, long-term constructors of military bases, Bottel and ICE Kaiser, for instance, to rebuild what has been destroyed.

The logic is clear: the business of war nowadays is business. As one triumphant American economist remarked, 'We're feeling this peace in our wallet.' War effort produces economic profit, as a British businessman realised when he remarked plaintively even before the war ended: 'It would be foolish not to expect American companies to play a leading part in the rebuilding considering the part Americans are playing in the liberation.'

Some of us find this logic unacceptable, pointing to the human cost involved: between 85 000 to 100 000 Iraqi soldiers killed as well as an as yet unestimated number of civilians, to say nothing of the devastation of cities, roads, bridges, power and water supplies or the consequences of the typhoid and cholera epidemics which have already broken out in some areas. With more than 500 oil wells burning, environmentally it has been the most destructive conflict in the history of war. President Bush may have told the people of Iraq, and implicitly the people of the region, that you 'are not our enemy. We do not seek your destruction.' But this kind of evidence refutes him. Merely to point this out, however, is not enough. The president and the supporters of the war generally will reply that it is unfortunate but unavoidable if justice is to be achieved, 'little Kuwait' liberated and international law restored. Moreover, the president was not, I think, being hypocritical when he declared in his victory speech: 'This is a victory for the United Nations, for all mankind, for the rule of law and for what is right.' He believed it, as the overwhelming majority of Americans and British and a less overwhelming but nevertheless substantial majority of Australians do. But should we?

This brings us back to the initial point, that the central issue is ideological. Karl Popper, who cannot be accused of any penchant for religion, puts it this way:

The main troubles of our time . . . are not due to our moral wickedness, but, on the contrary, to our often misguided moral enthusiasm: to our anxiety to better the world we live in. Our wars are fundamentally religious wars; and they are wars between competing theories of how to establish a better world.[2]

Thus, although the economic motive is undoubtedly powerful and probably the decisive one as far as most decision makers are concerned, for the majority of its supporters the war was fought for what I have been calling 'religious' motives, in defence of a set of symbols to which they have given their allegiance. President Bush originally called it 'the American way of life' and subsequently 'the new world order', a dream of harmony and prosperity between nations over which the United States would rule benevolently, a dream not unlike the noble dream of Rome as giver of peace and well-being to the known world with which Virgil concluded the *Aeneid*.

So it is not coincidental that the photograph of President Bush at prayer was published worldwide just before he authorised the beginnings of the air war or that he spent the night in prayer with Billy Graham the night before issuing that authorisation—significantly, the Episcopalian Archbishop of Washington, the leader of Bush's own church, had advised him against war. He seems to have turned to Billy Graham as a coreligionist, someone whose God, like his, approved of this war. The photograph which appeared the next day of wild-eyed and long-haired antiwar protestors burning an American flag underscores this point. They were presented not only as mistaken but evil, even in a sense blasphemous, given the belief that America's cause is also God's cause. In Australia it is difficult to whip up such overtly religious feelings. But the prime minister's outburst against the ABC's report of issues and events in the Gulf and for daring to question the official line suggested the fervour of a true believer rather than a democratic politician and Master of Consensus. Many letters to the paper as well as commentators attacking the peace movement expressed a similar sense of outrage: since Australia was at war, they implied and sometimes said directly, dissent and questioning were treasonable.

The vital question, therefore, is just what God, what values, the war, in fact, served. This is not to deny the good faith of those who waged and supported it. But it is to wonder about their intelligence. To quote Karl Popper once more:

Our moral enthusiasm is often misguided, because we fail to realise that our moral principles, which are sure to be over-simple, are often difficult to apply to the complex human and political situations to which we feel bound to apply them.

It is not enough to announce as Thomas Foley, Speaker of the American House of Representatives, did at the conclusion of the war, that it was 'carried on with authority, with a constitutional mandate'. Sincerity is not enough. The question is not whether or not the Allies were convinced of the rightness of their cause but whether it was in fact right. As Barthes remarked, the function of myth is to immobilise thought and put an end to history, absolutising the status quo. In the 1930s Walter Benjamin pointed to the way in which the fascist leaders of Germany and Italy had frozen history, turning politics into aesthetics. Their praise of the state as the absolute point of history disguised the present as the future, telling the masses that there was no past greater than their present. Francis Fukuyama's recent essay on the 'end of history' is not so very different. Nor, perhaps, is Bush's myth of the 'new world order'.

Before we go on to analyse it and the beliefs which sustained and empowered the Allied cause, however, it is important to make it clear that criticism of the war in no sense implies a defence of Saddam Hussein. True, his invasion of Kuwait was by no means as whimsical as the Western media made it out to be. Kuwait had been consistently exceeding the quota for oil production assigned to it by OPEC, often drawing on resources inside Iraq which happened to surface in Kuwait. There was also an argument that Kuwait, artificially created by the West, was once part of Iraq, if Iraq is seen, as Hussein wanted to see it, as successor of the Persian and Ottoman empires. But none of this excuses the invasion, the atrocities committed against its inhabitants and destruction of the environment. Hussein is a brutal tyrant who has often turned his power against his own people, notably the Kurds. Yet what also has to be said, is that his rule was no more brutal than that of many other tyrants who are supported by the West, in general, and the United States in particular, notably in South America. Similarly, it has become almost a truism to point out that Hussein's invasion of Kuwait was not the only invasion of a smaller by a larger power in recent times—quite apart from Israel's invasion of the West Bank or the United States own invasion of Panama, Grenada and so on, we in Australia have the instance of the Indonesian invasion of East Timor on our doorstep. Iraq, however, has been the only nation punished for the excesses of its ruler.

This brings us back to the question of the war's justification.

First of all, it needs to be noted that, even in church circles, there was little talk of the theory of the just war, perhaps because, as Pope John Paul II, an exception to this general silence, remarked, conditions for a just war were lacking, namely, that the end is a just one and that the means used are proportionate to it. I will take up these points later on. For the moment, we are concerned with the war's basis in the hearts and minds of its proponents and supporters. Why, for instance, were President Bush and his allies so determined to take up arms against Saddam Hussein?

One answer has already been suggested: the vital economic and strategic interests at stake in the region. But the justification of the war was usually in other terms, increasingly in terms of the 'new world order' which is supposed to emerge from it. This phrase, as we have said earlier, echoes the dream of empire and of the end of history which has haunted the European imagination since at least the time of Augustus. Ironically, in the circumstances, this also includes the Russian imagination, which saw Moscow as the 'third Rome', successor to Rome and Constantinople as capital of the world. In the American case, this dream grows out of the myth of the United States as 'God's own country' and its people as 'God's chosen', a myth which originated with the Pilgrim Fathers, of course. Turning their back on Europe as corrupt and sinful, they went to the New World, confident in the 'manifest destiny' which put into their hands the possibilities of making a 'new heaven and earth'. But the history of American hegemony in this century suggests that this belief has lost nothing of its potency. To the contrary, it seems to have expanded so that the dream is now to impose the 'American way of life' on the rest of the world in the name of all that is good, just and true.

That is the dream and no doubt there is something admirable about it. I would argue, however, that what unfolded in the Gulf was, in fact, something very different, what Paul Virilio calls the myth of 'pure war and that war is not acceptable'.[3] According to Virilio, since World War I the world economy has been a war economy, organised according to the logic of war, according to technological production, efficiency and domination, no longer, that is, for human use and enjoyment but for competition and domination. Today, he argues, preparations for war are always in train, preparations which are no longer a matter of building ramparts or digging ditches or even tanktraps (as the Iraqis did) but of producing more and more high-tech machines and weapons. The God our culture worships, in effect, is thus the God of power and his priests are the military men and the technologists. Virilio says:

There is no political power that can regulate the multi-nationals or the armed forces, which have greater and greater autonomy. There is no power superior to theirs. Therefore, either we wait for the coming of a hypothetical universal State, with I don't know what primate at its head, or else we finally understand that what is at the center is no longer a monarch by divine right, an absolute monarch, but an absolute weapon. The centre is no longer occupied by a political power, but by a capacity for absolute destruction.

This may seem far-fetched. But consider the way, at the beginning of the war, we lived under the shadow of Hussein's chemical weapons and the nuclear power which some said he possessed but which most knew Israel surely had. Consider, too, the representation of the war on television: Allied weapons; aircraft, warships and even fighting men bathed in light or emitting rays of light, emblems of invincible technological power. Bodies turned into machines with talk of 'precision weapons' and 'surgical strikes', the emphasis being on the surgeons' white coats and gleaming instruments, not on the blood which is also involved in surgery. Significantly, with the exception of the Allied bombing of the shelter full of civilians in Baghdad, where blood did seem to flow and civilian shops and houses to be destroyed, this was caused by the Iraqis in Israel and in Kuwait. Not only were they the enemy to be defeated, it seemed, but the disease to be cured by our high-tech 'surgery'.

The nature of war, as Virilio argues, has changed. It is now less a matter of encounter between combatants than of logistics, the art of moving, quartering and delivering men, weapons and supplies nearly always at high speed. This was the burden of General Schwarzkopf's briefing to the press as the war was coming to an end. Speed and efficiency, he said, were the essence of the Allied success. But behind this success lay not so much valour as organisation, a whole flow chart which put the world economy at the service of the Allied war effort.

In the United States the Pentagon has become a state within the state, the dominant arm of government, to the extent that their logic seems to prevail over all others. In the lead-up to the war, for instance, the State Department, especially its Islamic experts, were largely ignored. Indeed, it seemed at times as if they must have been used only to coach the president in ways of becoming increasingly insulting to Saddam Hussein, ensuring that he would be unable to withdraw or compromise and that war would thus inevitably follow. The intelligence of war thus eluded not only politics but diplomacy also. The so-called 'developed' world has, in effect, according to Virilio, turned into one large machine for producing and consuming military technology. In our own small way, Australia is part of this machine, providing bases for the United States and resources as well as our very own Arms Bazaar, to be held in Canberra in November.

That is one way of putting it. It can also be said that the war in the Gulf was the continuation not only of the logic of war and of empire but also of what Edward Said has called 'Orientalism'.[4] According to the logic of empire, as a Brazilian scholar, Darcy Ribiero, puts it:

Europe . . . [thinks] of itself as owner of a universe in which the whole and each of its parts could only exist to serve it, expanding its dominions, submitting to its faith and, above all, working for its prosperity.

. . . In this way, the earth and its innumerable peoples, a great part of the human race, were converted into a colonial possession and a profitable business, and acquired a new destiny. They were no longer to exist and to belong to themselves . . . but to refashion themselves according to European dictates, defined by the profit motive.[5]

This is justified ideologically, of course, by the belief that Europe and Europeans are by definition superior. In the nineteenth century this belief generated the idea of the 'Orient'. Those parts of the world which are not Europe are defined by a similar logic in terms of the difference as necessarily inferior. What is at issue, in effect, is not so much geographical as political: the 'Orient' is a 'sign of European-Atlantic power . . . a created body of theory and practice in which for many generations there has been a considerable material investment'. As a 'distribution of geopolitical awareness', it has all kinds of consequences, which we have recently witnessed in the Gulf, where the assumption seemed to be not only that we in the West are superior but that we have a God-given right to impose our will upon the rest of the world and use its resources for our own ends. What is good for the West, it is assumed, is good for everyone else.

In turn, however, this view rests on another set of assumptions, much less consciously held and therefore more powerfully destructive, what Abdul JanMohamed calls the 'Manichean allegory' which sets white against black (or brown) as good against evil, superior to inferior, civilised to savage, associating non-Europeans not only with inferiority but also with evil.[6] So the war against Iraq took on overtones of a crusade. Saddam was presented as 'worse than Hitler', the 'Butcher of Baghdad', a malignant and malevolent force spinning schemes to destroy civilisation, if not the world itself, from his underground bunker, his desert 'heart of darkness'. As Claude Julien remarked, 'Islam does not possess a monopoly on the idea of a holy war.'[7] What a best-selling American magazine, *Desert Storm* (produced in response to the war), called 'America's awesome firepower, the most devastating war machine ever' was also seen as Godlike and those who wield it as instruments of righteousness. Numbers of combatants therefore no doubt echoed the US airman of World War II who wrote:

For me this was not a war of revenge. I was struggling to destroy an impersonal evil, not to inflict punishment. I stuck with God and prayed my way through scores of 'tight situations', repeating, 'Not my will but thine be done', over and over. If I repeated this prayer enough times, I was able to relax and enjoy the battle. I was a vestal virgin warrior, an honest soldier, dedicated to defeating God's enemy.[8]

What I am arguing, then, was that what inspired this was ultimately the notion of war itself, the triumph of technology as institutionalised violence. Morally, at least in terms of any ethic which sees the human person as sacred and power as responsible to some superior power which works for the good of all, of all living beings as well as that of the fragile and vulnerable planet, this view is indefensible. Economic values are not the only values and reasons of state, especially of those already rich and powerful, the only reasons. As the economics editor of the London *Observer*, William Keegan, observed: 'Every loss of human life is a price paid by humanity. Every item of human effort devoted to war is an item diverted from other uses.'[9] The money squandered for war might, for instance, have relieved the problem of hunger throughout the world. The human person is or ought to be the centre of value. As John Paul II declared on 17 January of this year, 'War cannot be an adequate means for completely solving problems between nations. It never has been and it never will be.' Vatican II put it even more strongly: 'Divine Providence urgently commands us to rid ourselves of the ancient slavery of war.'[10] Such considerations, however, seem to carry little weight today. In our current ideology, might, it seems, is right: the Allies' military success is its ethical guarantee. Contrariwise, the peace movement stands condemned not only for its failure to prevent war but also because, as far as the Allies were concerned, that war cost so few lives—lives of Iraqis, it seems, do not count. But this, it is said, was necessary to establish the 'new world order'. What is to be said of this argument?

The first thing is that there is no doubt that the world does indeed need, and need desperately, a new world order. Quite apart from the cost in human lives, the environmental consequences of this war have not yet been assessed. Nor perhaps can they be for some time: the effects of the burning oil wells, for instance, will continue and are as yet incalculable. Yet surely any world order, new or old, must take them into account. So, too, does the fact that war tends to increase the hunger, disease, homelessness, illiteracy and oppression which are the lot of the majority of the human race and also to increase the gap between the rich and poor, both nationally and internationally, in this case making a diminishing number of corporations, their shareholders and managers richer than ever and reducing millions more to poverty and destitution. President Bush is right: we desperately need the rule of law throughout the world. But not the law of violence. Properly understood, law rests on justice, and on the idea of some common good to which all, rich and poor, Muslim and Christian, have an equal right and in which all equally share. If what I have been arguing is correct about the logic underlying the Gulf War and the Western claim to arbitrate throughout the world, however, the law President Bush would impose is partial, the rule of the victors designed to protect and expand Western interests at the expense of the victims.

At the very least, the assumption on which this new world order rests is Eurocentric, ethnocentric even, the assumption being that what is best for the rest of the world is to become part of the Western system, and on Western terms. To those who believe, as the president genuinely seems to do, in the 'American way of life' as synonymous with 'God's way', the proper way to live as human beings, then this is entirely acceptable. Whether or not the rest of the world does, ordinary people rather than their rulers and notably the millions of displaced people, many of them Muslims who see events in the Gulf in terms of the long history of rivalry between Islam and Christendom, in which Islam has over the last two centuries been increasingly defeated and humiliated by Western economic and military power, is quite another matter, however.

An Indian newspaper, the *National Herald*, for example, reflected these feelings in its editorial of 1 March, the day after the cessation of hostilities. Headed 'Whom did the war help?', this editorial saw a new chapter of world history opening out, 'full of uncertainties in the troubled West Asian region'. 'Kuwait has to be congratulated on its liberation,' the paper said. But [also] 'the people of Iraq deserve the world's support and sympathy when its national pride has taken such a beating.' Hussein may 'have made a terrible mistake'. But it was the ordinary people, not just of Iraq but of the whole region, who had paid and would continue to pay the price. Seen through Indian eyes, the 'billions of dollars . . . spent on the unnecessary conflict, and [the] billions more . . . needed to put things back into

115

shape in the region' might have gone towards human development, to provide food, housing, education and basic tools and skill to enable people throughout the world to live in dignity and freedom. The United Nations, they suggested, had been hijacked by the United States and the new world order was only another name for American hegemony.

It is not part of my brief to discuss this view. The point to be made is rather that, to the extent that it is typical of the responses throughout the region, it suggests trouble rather than peace ahead. If wars begin in the minds of men and women, then millions of people throughout the world refuse to accept President Bush's vision, seeing it rather as the instrument of domination. A peace based on war, as this seems to be, must be a fragile peace. Already, for instance, there are signs of a return to the Cold War, apparent not only from the American but also from the Russian side, especially from the Russian military, and one suspects that, once the damage caused by the war has been repaired, builders, engineers and investors will be looking for new markets and armaments manu-facturers for new customers.

Opposition to war, then, implies criticism not just of the fact of war but of the logic which causes it. That is the real problem, since, as Virilio argues, it has perhaps become the underlying logic of Western culture, the 'intelligence of war', of speed and efficiency. It has no room for politics or diplomacy, for the discussions and compromises which can bring about understanding between peoples and which might have been used in the Gulf and averted war, if only there had been the will and the patience to do so. Today, thanks not only to the media but also to our conditioning to competition, efficiency and success, most of us, as Virilio remarks, are 'already civilian soldiers, without knowing it', and this ignorance is the problem. He goes on:

The great stroke of luck for the military class's terrorism is that no one recognizes it, people don't recognise the militarised part of their identity, of their consciousness.

To conclude, then. It is hard to believe in a new world order arising out of events in the Gulf. Peace cannot be based on force of arms alone. Nor can it rest on an economy which enriches a small part of the world at the expense of millions of human beings and, just as crucially perhaps, of an increasingly fragile environment. That is the way of fantasy. The *fact* is the one Fred Hoyle proposed in 1945 when he observed that 'once a photograph of the Earth, taken from outside, is available. Once the sheer isolation of the Earth becomes plain, a new idea as powerful as any in history will be let loose.'[11] This powerful idea is that we human beings, indeed all living beings, animals, plants, the air we breathe, the waters and the earth itself all share the one life on one very small and vulnerable planet suspended in infinite space. Once we accept that fact, then the ideology of competition and war will no longer be tenable. The first step to peace, therefore, is to look very hard at the assumptions of Western culture today.

NOTES

1. Clifford Goertz, *The Interpretation of Culture* (Basic Books, New York, 1973), p. 90.
2. Karl Popper, *Conjectures and Refutations: The Growth of Scientific Knowledge* (Harper Torchbooks, New York, 1968), p. 66.
3. Paul Virilio & Sylvia Lotringer, *Pure War*, trans. Mark Polizotti (Semiotext(e), New York, 1983).
4. Edward Said, *Orientalism* (Penguin, Melbourne, 1985).
5. Darcy Ribiero, 'The Latin American People', in *Conciluum*, 1990/6.
6. Abdul JanMohamed, 'The Economy of Manichean Allegory: The Function of Racial Difference in Colonialist Literature', in H.L. Gates (ed.), *'Race', Writing and Difference* (Chicago University Press, London, 1986), pp. 78–106.
7. Claude Julien, 'Holy Wars', in *Cross Currents,* 40, 6, (Fall 1990).
8. Quoted in Sam Keen, *Faces of the Enemy, Reflections of the Hostile Imagination: The Psychology of Emnity* (Harper & Row, San Francisco, 1986), p. 29.
9. William Keegan, 'The Cost of the War', in *The Tablet*, 245, 7856 (23 February, 1991), p. 228.
10. Vatican II Pastoral Constitution on the Church in the Modern World, *Gauduim Et Spes*, no. 81.
11. Quoted in Beatrice Bruteau, 'Global Spirituality and the Integration of East and West,' in *Cross Currents*, 35, 2 & 3 (Summer & Fall 1985), p. 190.

The Dark Mirror of Narcissus
Australian Literature,
the Self and the Land

Narcissus is a constant presence in Australian literature, either in a thematic or formal sense—language and form as self-enclosure in Peter Cowan's work, for instance. So, too, is the threat of his fate. Self in search of the other is brought up before the impossibility of finding it, bound within its own image as in a mirror. Consider, for instance, the opening of White's *Memoirs of Many in One*:

I don't know where to being what may turn out a monstrous mistake . . . who knows where the end will come and whether in a flash, or a long gnawing. In any case they will be watching, from inside the house, from the garden, the park, or most disturbingly, from above.[1]

Unable to gain access to what lies outside, the self is threatened not only with incoherence but with non-existence, the grim sense Randolph Stow expresses in the character of the Law in *Tourmaline* reflecting that there is 'nothing easier than to cease, to become a stone'.[2]

This is a characteristic enough position for writing in this century, of course. In this case, however, I want to argue that what we might call the 'matter of Australia' also has a good deal to do with it; that this sense of constriction, if not entrapment, has to do with geography as well as history, with the 'land' as it figures as a trope in our literature and thus in consciousness.

I am aware, of course, that it is fashionable to dismiss this preoccupation as mere romanticism, a mystification which detracts from the proper concerns of a highly urbanised, even postmodernist, society. But I would argue that these concerns are part of the problem, part of a secret which seems to produce various forms of social pathology—alienation, loneliness, the loss of freedom and a general sense of meaninglessness.[3] This suggests the continuing importance of archaic forms and of consciousness and of the ways in which, by ritual use of sacred symbols, people can discover some sense of community. We live by symbolic as well as by merely material actions.

Seen in this light 'Australia' becomes a proper noun in Barthes's sense, a word which is an aspect of historical process as well as of memory, an attempt at naming and thus situating oneself in the world. In turn this process derives less from matters of fact than myth, what Wilson Harris calls the 'game of genesis',[4] a set of stories and metaphors, 'sustaining unconscious elements' within which people come to dwell and which shape their thoughts, feelings and actions. If this is so then as mythmakers, writers take on a new importance, and so does the preoccupation with the land in our writing from the 1890s onwards—before that, it functioned as a trope of alienation, afterwards, of belonging. True, this belonging, as I shall be arguing, is of a peculiar kind. But the point to be made is that it is a central trope in what can be seen as a symbolic ritual of taking possession—the more problematic for the rejection of Aboriginal culture—what Eliade calls the 'transformation of chaos into cosmos'.[5] There is not time here to trace its development in detail. Instead we shall focus on its use in the present in the work of a group of writers who are particularly concerned with it, presupposing that metaphor of this kind is not just a linguistic mode but a creative means of correlating knowledge and experience,[6] in which these writers discover a way out of the predicament of Narcissus which is also the modernist and indeed post-modernist predicament.

First of all, however, one or two clarifications. The land, or what the Romantics called 'nature' is, of course, a central trope of Australian literature. As in Romanticism it figures often as a living force which both gives and receives life from human beings and it has in this way been central to 'development' in most settler attitudes; in the topos of the 'American Adam' central to the development of the United States in the nineteenth century, for instance. But it is evident also in Australia in the nineteenth century where there is a similar sense of 'a newly created totality'.[7] *The Recollections of Geoffrey Hamlyn*, for instance, enthuses over the 'new heaven and the new earth' awaiting the settlers, and Charles Harpur's 'The Creek of the Four Graves' opens in a similar mood, with space opening out before the pastoral party, as if they were entering into the Promised Land. But the end of this poem points to a crucial difference; the land, in fact, is the place of menace, even of death, and the Aborigines are its representatives, leaping out from the campfire as the explorers sleep.

> . . . . *beings in their dread inherited hate*
> *Awful, vengeful as hell's worst fiends . . . come*
> *In vengeance.*[8]

This is not the place of the new beginning, it seems, but 'death-doomed', and the poem concludes with a meditation on the four graves. This is the note which in the 1890s, Baynton, Lawson and Furphy, each in his or her own way, carry on and develop and which has sounded ever since.

The second point to be made is that this note has to do with bodily anxiety. For Whitman, the American, the spread of the land became the spread of his own body: 'Divine am I, inside and out, and I make holy whatever I touch'.[9] But Australian space seemed to threaten the body, appearing as its obdurate antithesis, as fate or necessity. There is a sense of not belonging, this is a place in which one can get lost and die—Furphy's monumental description of the dead swagman epitomises this sense. The land is also a kind of 'end of the world', named in *Tourmaline*—an end of European notions of humanity and of the humane as the Other which disables rather than enables human communication—hence perhaps the ghost-like character, the somewhat sinister sense of loneliness apparent in much of our writing but particularly so in the work of Stow, Cowan and, to a lesser extent, Malouf and White.

The other main sense of nature is as an 'essential quality or character', that which also operates in our culture, but, negatively, rather than positively. Seen in this way the land here is something actively malignant, working against human intention expressed in the poem to *The Fortunes of Richard Mahony* in the image of the land which has ethical as well as mythical connotations: the image of some kind of monstrous but also monstrously violated female form which holds them captive, 'lying stretched like some primeval monster in the sun, her breasts freely bared', waiting to take revenge on the settlers' 'loveless schemes of robbing and fleeing'.[10] This, I would argue, rather than the sentimentalities of 'I love a Sunburnt Country' or the Stockman's Hall of Fame is the more authentic sense of the land; fear and an awareness of profanation—the link here with mining is significant—Richardson is describing the Ballarat goldfields. So often seen by economic rationalists as our salvation, mining not only epitomises the violation of nature, robbing it of colour, shape and its own significance and converting it into lumps of ore to be exploited for our own purposes and fetishes, but also has to do with the underworld, the unsanctified place and abode of the dead.

My last preliminary point follows from this. Settled in the nineteenth century, Australia is the product of what Abdul JanMohamed calls the 'Manichean allegory' of colonisation in which Europe is to the rest of the world as good to evil, civilisation to savagery, superior to inferior, belief to unbelief and so on.[11] In this allegory 'nature' exists to be dominated, transformed into history in Hegel's sense and made to work for our own ends, usually economic, thus condemning us to self-enclosure, to the fate of Narcissus. The writers we are concerned with, however, offer a way out not by ignoring this situation but by exploring it. In this exploration there are two phases, confronting the situation and then transforming it.

The confrontation, first of all, has to do with the critique of instrumental rationality so evident in their work. What is at issue here becomes clearer if, once again, we recur to the point of origin, using Marcus Clarke's Preface to the poems of Adam Lindsay Gordon, perhaps the classical expression of the anxiety of the self for whom the traditional metaphor of nature as a book to be opened, pored over and then mastered no longer holds. Here one can no longer read the signs; everything seems unfamiliar, 'grotesque', 'weird', merely the 'strange scribblings of Nature learning how to write'.[12] The history on which we pride ourselves and in which we see ourselves as its culmination gives way to a different kind of history, the sense of some process, looming 'vague and gigantic' in the land itself:

The lonely horseman . . . sees vast shadows creeping across the shelterless and silent plains, hears strange noises in the primeval forest where flourishes a vegetation long dead in other lands, and feels, despite his fortune, that the trim utilitarian civilisation which bred him shrinks into insignificance.[13]

The difficulty is not just external but interior as well. If, as colonial ideology has it, following Hegel, European culture provides all the 'categories which lie at the bottom of our spiritual life',[14] these categories are overturned here. This means not only that there is no goal, but the destruction of intelligibility itself since, as Foucault points out, the metaphor of the book of nature is 'the reverse and visible side of another transference, and a much deeper one, which forces language to reside in the world, among the plants, the herbs, the stones and the animals'.[15] Where language was once branded into all of 'reality' in this way, it can now only register the observer's alienation from it.

The usual way of dealing with this problem has been to ignore it. 'If 'nature' threatens our equanimity it must be imposed upon. Paul Carter has an interesting section on this imposition in *The Road to Botany Bay*, arguing that language is an essential instrument of domination. But the process can be more simply exposed by quoting the beginning of a poem published in a Melbourne newspaper in the 1840s:

Melbourne! unclassic, anti-native name!
and yet, as by magician's spell, up spring,
thee have I chosen, subject fit for song.[16]

The mention of the song here reminds us of Adorno and

Horkheimer's reading of the story of Ulysses and the Sirens in which they equate Ulysses with European technological culture and the Sirens with the voice of the natural, sensuous world, of the feminine and of the pleasure principle. Ulysses plugs the ears of his crew, as this kind of writing does, keeping them working to his own ends while he, bound to the mast, hears it but refuses either to respond to or to take responsibility for it.[17]

There is thus no way of reconciliation with nature nor with the Aboriginal people and culture with which it is associated. But the writers we are concerned with attempt a response—in *Voss* and *A Fringe of Leaves* in White's oeuvre, for instance, *An Imaginary Life* in Malouf's, *To the Islands* and *Tourmaline* in Stow's and *The Hills of Apollo Bay* in Cowan's. First of all comes the matter of Cowan and Stow. There is a strong sense of insensitivity here, that language has lost its power of reference—one thinks of Tom Spring's words about silence in *Tourmaline*, for instance. In White's work and, to a lesser extent, Malouf's, this sense leads to a reliance on the poetic, as if language has 'nothing to do but shine in the brightness of its being' (Foucault), becoming a verbal manifestation of inward experience flashing forth and often disappearing without leaving its mark on the everyday. On the other hand, its absence in Cowan's work gives it its peculiar quality of desolation.

Nevertheless, so long as language becomes its own point of reference the dilemma remains, the world remains a prison—'my cell 'tis, lady', to quote the epigraph of Stow's *To the Islands*, the place of placeless language. The only way out is thus to go inwards and it is here, as Stow's work in particular suggests, that the trope of the land becomes so important, not just as a fact of geography but, more importantly, a presence within the self.

This is a very large subject, of course. But we may be able to focus it by referring to Vernant's discussion of the function of the Colossus, a great, and shapeless block of stone, erected in Ancient Greece and Asia Minor,[18] in its immobility an image of sheer inhuman force. According to Vernant, the Colossus is thus different from any other Greek monument. What is essential to it is fixity and shapelessness; in its sheer givenness, it stands over against everything living and moving. But in this way, he argues, it speaks of the Other, that which is beyond human control and power, the otherness of death. It is thus an image not of human mastery but of finitude, and this puts it in a different psychological and epistemological, perhaps even ontological, category.

So, too, the land in the work of Baynton, Lawson and Furphy as well as our contemporary writers, is not a 'natural' object— not as 'nature' figures in European culture. But, like the Colossus, it is not just a creation of thought either, nor is it an imitation of something else. It has an objective reality exterior to the self and beyond subjective control. At the same time there is some strange correspondence between it and the self, as if it were the other we need to mediate the self to ourselves and to others.

Voss is clearest here. Voss only finds himself by means of his encounter with the land but when he finally achieves unity with Laura and with the rest of humanity he has found himself and been found. But in Malouf's *An Imaginary Life* unity only comes from dying into the land and his *Fly Away Peter* concludes similarly, with the young soldier digging himself into the earth—a counter image to the terrible image in Chaucer's *Pardoner's Tale* of the old man unable to die, knocking with his staff on the earth, crying 'leve moder, lette me inne'. Death in this sense can be seen as a way to life. Nevertheless, this is rather too easily said, a mere literary conceit. How to ground the argument?

According to Vernant, the Colossus offers an image not so much of death as of another kind of existence, opposed to that of everyday as darkness to light. In this way it is not an image but rather a double, as death itself is the double, the other side of life.[19] Thus the image works on two different levels at once; showing itself as something present to us but also as a kind of absence, belonging elsewhere to something inaccessible to normal understanding.[20] Malouf's strange image of the great stone at the centre of the land and of the self in his poem, 'Notes on an Undiscovered Continent' expresses this sense of ambiguity:

Its exiles go their own way . . . (towards)
. . . . Silence. So absolute it fills the mind with a slow-
                                            worm's giddy
horror of distance. Our counterweight to the Himalayas.[21]

So, too, does the description of the desert which opens *Tourmaline* as the enormous and desolate landscape, which 'like an unnamed and naming ghost',[22] constitutes the law, the horizon by which we live, or ought to live. Strangely enough, the 1890s ballad, 'Where the Dead Men Lie', reflects a similar movement, from the social and the metaphysical, contrasting the world of 'Moneygrub' who,

. . . as he sips his claret
Looks with complacent eye
Down at his watch-chain, eighteen carat,

with the 'wastes of the Never Never', 'out where the dead men lie', which it invests with monumental and abiding reality.[23]

The land, then, has to do with some reality opposed not only to desire but even to thought. This sounds mystical, and in a sense it is, but not in the usual sense of the word. This trope of the land is both historical and political in its implications. It represents what Baudrillard calls 'the revenge of the crystal':

The object, the pure object, the pure event, something no longer with any precise origin or end, to which the subject would like to attribute an origin and an end even though it has none, to which today . . . begins to give an account of itself.[24]

If, as we have been arguing, non-Aboriginal Australia, symbolised, for example, by Moneygrub, is based on the pursuit of objects, the 'watch-chain, eighteen carat', then this image of the land as an object, indifferent, inert and seemingly endless, stands in direct opposition to the 'tonic and finalistic passions of the subject' in consumer society.[25] What our writers, especially Cowan and Stow, express, therefore, and figure in the land is some final state of alienation by the object, the self become object.

Far from offering an escape into pop mysticism, this image is singularly inflexible—that is its strength, its sovereignty, even. The land becomes a kind of double of the self at the point of disappearances, becomes radical objectivity, a kind of metaphysic of nothingness.[26] Most evidently in White's work, the radical understanding emerges that Thanatos, not Eros prevails. Positively, however, it also appears that subject and object are not opposed to one another but reversible.[27]

This is not as inhuman as it seems. For if one sees the double in psychological terms as the equivalent of the Jungian shadow, the negative side of the personality that is insufficiently developed, the disowned and suppressed consciousness, then the shadow also becomes a moral problem which challenges the whole personality, indeed, if we are right, the whole culture. The association of the land with the Aborigines also evident in these works thus becomes highly significant. In a key scene in *The Hills of Apollo Bay*, for instance, in which troops on a troop train halted in the midst of the Nullarbor are contrasted with a group of Aborigines come to beg from them, the Manichean allegory is reversed, the whites being seen as inferior to the blacks, who seem to embody some art of living, some intimacy with nature, lost to us. In *To the Islands* Stow makes these implications more explicit; Heriot's name is a play on his situation. He is burdened with dues as yet unpaid, perhaps unpayable, to the people he and his culture have so grievously injured. A similar realisation underlies the scene in *The Merry-go-round in the Sea* in which Rob Coram fits his hand to that of an Aboriginal boy's hand painted on the walls of a cave:

He felt the cold rock under his hand, where the dead boy's hand had once rested. Time and change had removed this child from his country, and his world was not one world, but had in it camps of the dispossessed. Above the one monument of the dead black people, the sheoaks sounded cold. Colder than rock.[28]

The Wild Child in Malouf's *An Imaginary Life* can be seen in similar terms, as something

not myself or of my own imagining, something that belongs to another order of being, and which I come out of the depths of myself to meet as at the surface of a glass.[29]

In White's work the Aborigine plays a more active and positive role, functioning in *Voss* like the Eumenidies, shadowing Voss and finally conducting him to his death in the desert, the 'Dead Heart' to us but to them, singing as Voss lies dying, 'their eyes burning . . . in the shadows', very much alive. So, too, the key point of Ellen Roxburgh's journey in *A Fringe of Leaves* comes when, as their prisoner, she eats with them the food of affliction, sharing with them in a kind of Eucharist. But the Aboriginal role is clearest, if irreverently so, in *Memoirs of Many in One* when Alex, as actress, supposed to rise up from the sands of the desert declaring herself 'the spirit of the land' shouts instead, 'I am the Resurrection and the Life', identifying herself with the Aborigine who picks her up and whirls her around his head. To become conscious of the shadow, as Jung remarks, involves recognising the dark aspects of the personality as present and real, and this act, which as a rule meets with considerable resistance, is the essential condition for any kind of self-knowledge.[30]

We return, then, to the point at which we began, the problematics of a self without direct access to the non-identical. The only way out from this is figured in the confrontation with the land as a trope for that which is other, the shadow side of the self. The traditional notion of Australia as the 'place of the new beginning' takes on a new significance. That 'new beginning' becomes, rather, an ending, the breakdown of the classical episteme of Western culture which is based on knowledge as an order of representation of the mastery of nature. But this breakdown leads to a confrontation with fate and fatedness, to the kind of fiction which is 'truer than truth itself' which Furphy, in his far-sighted way, saw as the goal of any understanding of Australia.[31] This is no small achievement. If Foucault is right that the tide of history has become slack in Western culture today, then this renewal of a sense of finitude, lost in a Promethean culture, may be invigorating. 'History exists [he writes] only insofar as [humanity] as a natural being is finite.'

A finitude that is prolonged far beyond the original limits of the species and its immediate bodily needs . . . never ceases to accompany, at least in secret, the whole development of civilisation.[32]

In this sense the crucial factor may be the writing which is 'about ways of making things appear and about surrounding them with a void, thus annihilating the whole process of cause and effect,[33] the false confidence and self-enclosure of consumer society.

NOTES

1. Patrick White, *Memoirs of Many in One* (Cape, London, 1986), p. 17.
2. Randolph Stow, *Tourmaline* (Angus & Robertson, Sydney, 1963), p. 8.
3. Arie Brand, *The Force of Reason: An Introduction to Habermas' Theory of Communicative Action* (Allen & Unwin, Sydney, 1990), pp. xii–xiii.
4. Wilson Harris, 'Metaphor and Myth', in Robert Sellick (ed.) *Myth and Metaphor,* CRNLE Essays and Monographs Series No. 1 (Adelaide, 1982), p. 1.
5. Mircea Eliade, *The Myth of the Eternal Return: Or Cosmos and History*, Bollinger Series XLVI (Princeton University Press, Princeton, 1974), p. 10.
6. See the entry on metaphor in Alex Preminger (ed.) *Encyclopaedia of Poetry and Poetics* (Princeton University Press, Princeton, 1965), pp. 490–5.
7. R.W.B. Lewis, *The American Adam: Innocence, Tragedy and Tradition in the Nineteenth Century* (University of Chicago Press, London, 1955), p. 52.
8. Charles Harpur, 'The Creek of the Four Graves', in H.P. Heseltine (ed.), *The Penguin Book of Australian Verse* (Penguin, Melbourne, 1979), p. 59.
9. Ibid., pp. 43–4.
10. Henry Handel Richardson, *The Fortunes of Richard Mahony* (Penguin, Melbourne, 1982), p. 13.
11. Abdul JanMohamed, 'The Economy of Manichean Allegory: The Function of Racial Difference in Colonialist Literature, in H.L. Gates (ed.), *'Race', Writing and Difference* (Chicago University Press, London, 1986), p. 82.

12. Michael Wilding (ed.), *Portable Australian Authors: Marcus Clarke* (Queensland University Press, Brisbane, 1976), p. 647.
13. Ibid., p. 646.
14. Quoted in James A. Snead, 'Repetition as a Figure of Black Culture', in H.L. Gates (ed.), *Black Literature and Literary Theory* (Methuen, London, 1984), p. 62.
15. Michel Foucault, *The Order of Things: An Archaeology of the Human Sciences* (Routledge, London, 1989), p. 35.
16. Richard Jordan & Peter Pierce (eds), *The Poet's Discovery: Nineteenth Century Australia in Verse* (Melbourne University Press, Melbourne, 1990), p. 277.
17. Patricia Mills, *Women, Nature and Psyche* (Yale University Press, New Haven, 1987), pp. 90–1.
18. Jean Pierre Vernant, *Mythe and Pensee Chez Les Grecs II* (Maspero, Paris, 1983), pp. 65–78.
19. Ibid., p. 67.
20. Ibid., p. 70.
21. David Malouf, *Notes on an Undiscovered Continent* (University of Queensland Press, Brisbane, 1974), p. 20.
22. Randolph Stow, *Tourmaline* (Angus & Robertson, Sydney, 1983), p. 10.
23. Heseltine, *The Penguin Book of Australian Verse*, pp. 92–4.
24. Jean Baudrillard, *The Revenge of the Crystal: Selected Writings on the Modern Object and its Destiny 1968–1983* (Pluto Press, Sydney, 1990), p. 18.
25. Ibid.
26. Ibid., p. 19.
27. Ibid., p. 26.
28. Randolph Stow, *The Merry-go-round in the Sea* (Penguin, Melbourne, 1976), p. 26.
29. David Malouf, *An Imaginary Life* (Chatto & Windus, London, 1978), p. 52.
30. Anthony Storr (ed.), *Jung: Selected Writings* (Fontana, London, 1983), p. 91.
31. John Barnes (ed.), *Portable Australian Authors: Joseph Furphy* (University of Queensland Press, Brisbane, 1981), p. 406.
32. Foucault, p. 259.
33. Baudrillard, p. 27.

3. PATRICK WHITE

Patrick White: A Tribute

Settlement in a new place is a complicated business. It may be simple enough in physical terms, especially with the technology to hand today. But settling in imaginatively, that is, spiritually, is not nearly so easy. It involves a kind of remaking of the world. We need not only to find a different order of perception of what we see and how we see it but also to readjust to it our sense of value and purpose.

This may seem all very true but also all very theoretical and therefore not much to the point at issue here. But Patrick White matters for me because he helped me to settle into the world in this deep sense, a world that is Australian, not second-hand European. I still remember my first encounter with his work: I was teaching in high school and on the night before prize day, I was helping the principal set out the prizes, mostly books, when I came upon a copy of *The Tree of Man*. I dipped and then fell into it, took it away with me and sat up with it nearly all night. I did not manage to finish it, of course. But what I read overwhelmed me. Like Dante's Paolo and Francesca, my life was, if not changed, then given a new sense of reality by a book. What it opened up to me was not so much people and places, as a kind of event—a bringing together of the visible and invisible, human beings and the earth, the physical and the spiritual, making them into a whole. But it was an event which was not merely self-referential and personal but a matter of presence, of a coming to awareness, which also had public, even political implications since it insisted on community rather than competition, on being rather than having.

Each successive book has enlarged this awareness. Reading then becomes a kind of ritual, of ceremonial taking possession of a newly discovered country which is not so much a place as a state of mind, providing me with a mythic sense which not only deepens but also makes more specific and particular what I already believe.

Religion and faith do not always go together in our society. Nor do faith and the paradoxical delight and anguish in bodily existence which one finds in White's work. What is most compelling in it for me, however, is the way it gambles on the apparently impossible possibility, that not only does God exist but that he-or-she is not what we think. The divine is not to be found only in moments of splendour but also in absurdity and incongruity, sometimes even in squalor and often in suffering. Stan Parker sees God in a gob of spittle. Hurtle Duffield meditates on him on the 'dunny' and Ellen Roxburgh meets him, at the end of her human and civilised resources, in the desperation and squalor of cannibalism. There is nothing here of the 'God' we make to our own image, the 'God' of people like Mr Bonner, who is not only a bore but guarantees their boring comfort and security. Here 'terrestrial safety is not assured'. We are swept beyond propriety, beyond good and evil, especially in later works like *Memoirs of Many in One* which brings us back to 'where all the ladders start' in 'the foul rag-and-bone shop of the heart', to play there in the 'glabrous dark' with the possibility of the death of God on the one hand, and of the God of death transfigured to life, on the other.

But if White's God is the mystery of the world he is also the mystery of the word. Few writers of our time have been more ambitious, more daringly irreverent in their encounter with language, stretching and often distorting vocabulary, defying expectations and disrupting syntax, all in the attempt to speak what is really unspeakable, what you do not know but know, to name what he understands to be beyond names and explore reaches of experience about which language, of necessity, remains silent. But he is also witty and sharply irreverent, a writer with a wicked ear for gossip and for the lively irreverences of everyday talk and an eye for the fraudulent. No one, I think, picks over the 'rag-and-bone shop' with such understanding, passion and style or finds such sharp and lucent things there.

But for all his sense of style, this satiric sense is not a snobbish one. The enemy is dishonesty, false trust in possessions and position and the lack of sympathy and emptiness of heart and dullness of imagination which are its consequences. The disdain for such people is the other side of a sheer delight in people, rich or poor, who live as they speak and act, earthily and truthfully. A warmth created characters like Ellen Hunter, Alex Gray, Hurtle Duffield, Alma Lusty and incidental characters like the shopkeepers, servants, loungers, delivery boys and eccentrics of all kinds who keep asserting their claims to life throughout his work.

All of this means that Patrick White's world is one of instant discovery, excitement and challenge. But it also means that White is for many a difficult writer; uncomfortable to those who look for the comforts of familiarity but very exciting, life-giving even, for those who like to be challenged and to join in what he himself calls 'a daily wrestling match with an opponent whose limbs never become material, a struggle from which the sweat and blood are scattered on the pages of everything the serious writer writes'—and, I would add, the serious reader reads. True, it is also an absurd and irreverent, even comic, struggle, and this precisely because it is so deadly serious. It is also risky. White has a gambler's imagination. Overturning commonsense, turning the world into language and attempting a style which defies the separation of fact and value, self and world, he walks a fine line between meaning and meaningless-ness, chaos and order, risking the fall into personal fantasy, even prejudice. So there are times when his writing seems merely wilful or sentimental, working off in words feelings which neither experience nor situation can sustain. There are other times also when personal dislike or disgust prevail and stereotyping takes over from thought. But anger can also make for passion; White like Xavier Herbert and Hal Porter, is a great master of the ancient and often honourable art of vituperation. Who, for instance, can pillory political or social hypocrisy as he can?

Kierkegaard has always been one of my heroes. Like him, White contests habit, representing inertia as not merely tyrannical but evil. *Riders in the Chariot*, for instance, implies a parallel between the emotional obtruseness and vulgarity of Sarsaparilla, embodied in Mrs Jolley and Mrs Flack, and Nazism. In this sense he is perhaps the most profound and comprehensive social critic we have to date. The choice before us as a people is the one dramatised in *Voss*; between clinging to the fringes of experience as we cling to the fringe of the continent and making a journey into the interior of the self. He was also one of the first to realise that this journey may well involve coming to terms with Aboriginal people and their culture and with our offences against them.

Voss, for example, associates them very closely with the land, making them the visible presence of the fate it embodies, the claims of physical necessity which Western technological culture in general, and the culture of settlement in particular, deny. In this way the 'weird melancholy' which Marcus Clarke identified as the dominant note of the Australian landscape, and which he saw as the result of our inability to read the Book of Nature, to decipher what seemed merely 'the scribblings of Nature learning to write', takes on a deeper significance. *A Fringe of Leaves* carries the matter further, challenging the Manichean allegory[1] which divides white from black as good from evil, civilised from savage, to suggest that the Aborigine may be the shadow side of the self, which challenges the whole personality, 'the dark aspects of the self as present and real' (Jung). Until we meet that challenge, the novel implies, we will remain alienated from ourselves, pathetically ignorant and complacent but also destructive to ourselves and others.

This may sound rather general. In fact it is very practical and specific. We talk a great deal about freedom, for instance, but many of us are remarkably unfree, emotionally timid and intellectually hidebound. White is not only vividly aware of this; he offers a way out from it in the 'passion for the possible'. Evident in novels like *A Fringe of Leaves* is the language which confronts us with strangeness and difference, refusing identification with the familiar. But nearly all his fictions are open-ended in their structure, pointing beyond commonsense to what cannot be contained in words but must be lived out. Existence here is process, not possession and the 'meaning' of these stories lies ahead of them in the reader's response.

White's work offers us freedom then in the light of hope, hope for this 'something more' which we are to realise by going inwards, confronting the fact of our moral responsibility, our contingency and our vulnerability and making out of it all masterful images, as Yeats did:

A mound of refuse or the sweepings of a street,
Old kettles, old bottles and a broken can,
Old iron, old bones, old rags, that raving slut
Who keeps the till.[2]

As a Christian, someone who rejoices in the paradox of a God who was crucified by the pious people of his day for what they judged impiety, I find this deeply sympathetic. White defies the unholy alliance between religion and social and emotional habit to break through, instead, to this ultimately comic, therefore ultimately trustful, sense of reality, of a pattern beyond our comprehension, much less our judgments about good and evil. What matters then is courage, the will to be and for being to be in all its ruthless but splendid energy. 'Life doesn't end on the kitchen floor' as one of the last stories, 'Dancing with Both Feet on the Ground' concludes, 'while there is the will to dance'. The way to cure the paralysis of will, hardness of heart and dullness of sympathy which affect so many of us, especially the virtuous, lies here, not in the heroic attempt to create value within ourselves but to join in the dance.

So White's imaginative virtuosity and insouciance are not just aesthetic matters. Flamboyance becomes a form of prayer, of letting go and letting be, paying tribute to the 'privilege and panic of mortality', to what is the 'hypocrisy and cynicism, hunger and despair'. I like to think of him, then, as Yeats's 'Malachi Stilt-Jack' affirming life in the face of death:

I through the terrible novelty of light, stalk on,
stalk on;
Those great sea-horses bear their teeth and
laugh at the dawn.[3]

NOTES

1. Abdul JanMohamed, 'The Economy of Manichean Allegory: The Function of Racial Difference in Colonialist Literature', in H.L. Gates (ed.), *'Race', Writing and Difference* (University of Chicago Press, London, 1986).
2. W.B. Yeats, 'Circus Animals' Desertion', in *Collected Poems of W.B. Yeats* (Macmillan, London, 1971) pp. 391–2.
3. Yeats, 'High Talk', ibid., pp. 385–6.

A Properly Appointed Humanism
Australian Culture and the Aborigines in Patrick White's A Fringe of Leaves

Till well into my life, houses, places, landscape meant more to me than people . . . It was landscape which made me long to return to Australia . . . As a child at Mount Wilson and Rushcutters Bay, relationships with even cherished friends were inclined to come apart when I was faced with sharing surroundings associated with my own private mysteries, some corner where moss-upholstered steps swept down beside the monstera deliciosa, a rich mattress of slater-infested humus under the custard apples, or gullies crackling with smoky silence, rocks threatening to explode, pools so cold that the breath was cut off inside your ribs as you hung suspended like the corpse of a pale frog.[1]

Patrick White's sense of himself is bound up with this sense of place, and of what might be seen as the savagery of nature. But it is also bound up with an awareness of the Aborigines, of the continuity between these feelings and the Aborigines. As a child on the mountain, he goes on:

I often flung stones at human beings I felt were invading my spiritual territory. Once I set fire to a gunyah to show that it couldn't be shared with strangers. Years later I persuaded myself that I hadn't been acting merely as a selfish child, but that an avatar of those from whom the land had been taken had invested one of the unwanted whites.[2]

This connection has not been much noticed and discussed. But it may well be crucial to White's understanding of himself as an Australian and of Australian culture in general. As this passage from his autobiography suggests, it may also point to the positive side of his notorious fascination with the process of nature, especially the process of decay. In *Voss*, for instance, the Aborigines function as emissaries of the land itself, celebrants of the sacrifice Voss must pay to its mysterious powers. In *Riders in the Chariot*, the novel which follows, the Aborigine Alf Dubbo is the one of the four visionaries who manages to express as well as to live what he sees. His element is fire, the element of triumphant creativity, and his life is an indictment of the 'Great Australian Emptiness' which surrounds him. But *A Fringe of Leaves* is the novel which shows most clearly what the Aborigines mean for White's imagination, showing on the one hand the impotence of white culture, and on the other the liberating effect of contact with the 'savage' domain which they represent and inhabit.

His choice of incident and central character is significant. Set in the nineteenth century, the story, based on the experiences of Eliza Fraser, shipwrecked off the Queensland coast and taken captive by the blacks, stresses the insecurity and vulnerability of white settlement and the squalor and hunger of the Aborigines which followed the white invasion. White Australian culture tends to value aggression, energy and material possession, but in his choice of this story and this heroine White throws the emphasis on passivity, subjection and dispossession.

The changes he makes to the original story underline human vulnerability on the one hand and the savage power of nature on the other. The original Captain Fraser was a sea captain, not the delicate, bookish and ultimately ineffectual husband White gives his Ellen Roxburgh. True, Captain Fraser made the voyage to Australia for the sake of his health, but where Austin Roxburgh is more or less impotent, Captain Fraser and his wife had three children. The changes to the story of Ellen's rescue are also significant. In the original story the rescuer, John Graham, was a far less disturbing figure than White's Jack Chance, convicted murderer and escaped convict. True, Graham also was a convict and an escapee but he had returned to white 'civilisation' and given himself up, White's Jack Chance cannot face the brutalities of the chain-gang, finding life with the blacks less savage. For White there is little difference between 'civilisation' and 'savagery'. The original John Graham, however, presented himself in the account he wrote as the champion of civilisation. Hearing news of a white woman made prisoner by the blacks, he says, he thought it his duty to 'snatch a fellow Christian from a lingering state of brutality'[3]—in fact he may also have had his eye on the pardon and the £10 which was his reward and throughout he insists that he maintained the standards of propriety even 'in the midst of the horror surrounding me, nothing but native savages, clubs and spears . . . I had my clothes on',[4] secure, he declares, in his trust in Providence which 'alone strengthened and assisted me in this virtuous act of humanity'.[5] Though in some other respects White plays down the violence of the original story—the mutterings of the crew became open mutiny in real life, for instance, and far from admiring Mrs Fraser as his equivalent admires Ellen Roxburgh, the cabin boy actually snatched a cup of water from her—nonetheless, in general his changes work to blur the distinctions between nature and culture. The glimpses of the convict system work to remind us that, as the second epigraph from Ibsen suggests, there are 'gnawing things' in the house of civilisation as well as in savage life. Even as a lady married to the cultured Austin Roxburgh, Ellen is aware of the chain-gangs and floggings in Van Diemen's Land, and shortly after her return to Moreton Bay and white civilisation, she meets a chain-gang, to be 'united in one terrible spasm with this rabble of men' (p. 370). She may have suffered and been humiliated during her time with the Aborigines but 'civilisation' has its sufferings as well.

White's view of human existence, then, is the disastrous one expressed in the scene shortly after the survivors of the shipwreck have managed to beach their boat on an island and the captain offers her a sip of rum which at first she refuses:

'Ellen,' her husband chirruped, 'you must take a sip at least, out of deference to the captain, and because,' he thought to add, 'the Almighty has brought us safely to land.'

For one blasphemous instant there arose in her mind the vision of a fish the Almighty was playing, the distended lip in which the hook was caught, her own (p. 203).

The fascination with decay which might be seen as apparent in the passage from *Flaws in the Glass* points to this sense of the power of nature and to the reasons for the choice of this story. Here on the frontier the concept of civilisation has no corroborating power. Austin Roxburgh's death dramatises the futility of the merely decent and rational man. Facing a group of armed and hostile blacks, he feels that he must do something:

[He] ran forward, to do what only God could know. Here he was, bestirring himself at least, in the manner expected of the male sex. Into action! He felt elated, as well as frightened, and full of disbelief in his undertaking. (It was not, however, an uncommon reaction to his own unlikelihood.) (p. 239)

As a man of words and books, he is helpless in this savage world and as he falls with a spear in his neck his main reaction is surprise. However, as he dies White suggests that at least he catches a glimpse of what he has missed: 'The light . . . or the brim of that . . . huge . . . country . . . *hat*. Raise it, please . . . so that I can see . . . ' (p. 240)

For White, Australia seems to be the place in which the complacencies by which people like Austin live are no longer viable; 'A country of thorns, whips, murderers, thieves, shipwrecks and adulteresses' (pp. 311–12) as it appears here, it is nevertheless the place for testing communal values and discovering the true lineaments of humanity. In this test and discovery the Aborigines play a crucial part.

It has not, I think, been remarked how closely the structuring of *A Fringe of Leaves* echoes the structure and method of Lévi-Strauss's anthropology. Ellen Roxburgh's story (in which she is successively a farm girl, the wife of the gentleman Austin Roxburgh, his brother's lover, slave of the Aborigines, mistress of her convict rescuer and, finally, is about to become the wife of the merchant, Mr Jevons),[6] illustrates Lévi-Strauss's notion that the basis of society lies in the exchange of women which in turn becomes an exchange of services. The novel also makes great use of the homologies of food and clothing (which we will discuss later), attempting as the French anthropologist does to come at some basic understanding of common humanity by a comparative study of the underlying codes of social existence. Leading Ellen through a whole gamut of experiences and of different cultures and classes, White is thus in search of that 'properly appointed humanism' which Lévi-Strauss describes which 'cannot begin of its own accord but must place the world before life, life before man, and the respect of others before self-interest'.[7] Moreover, it is clear that as he describes it, and for all its rigour, Aboriginal culture is closer to this ideal than the white society represented by people like the Merivales, the Lovells and Austin Roxburgh. Ellen can only become

The perfect Woman, nobly planned,
To warn, to comfort, and command

when she has learned from her experience after the shipwreck and with the Aborigines that, as Lévi-Strauss has it, 'man is not alone in the universe, any more than the individual is alone in the group, or any one society alone among other societies'.[8]

To look, then, at White's picture of Aboriginal life. He has been criticised for perpetuating the racist stereotype that Aboriginal culture is both degraded and degrading, and it is certainly true that the life Ellen shares is a perpetual struggle with hunger and on one occasion she is even driven to cannibalism. But this picture needs to be set against the description of the cruelties of white society. The main difference between the two cultures, the comparison suggests, is that the Aborigines acknowledge their debts to nature whereas the white people do not. Even as the story concludes, Miss Scrimshaw, typically, still lives by the delusions of grandeur Ellen has learned to see through. She longs 'to soar! . . . to reach the heights! . . . look down on everything that lies beneath [her]! Elevated, and at last free'. But Ellen has learned that the true humanity comes from acceptance and thus remains 'ineluctably earthbound':

'I was slashed and gashed too often,' she tried to explain. 'Oh no, the crags are not for me . . . A woman, as I see, is more like moss or lichen that takes to some tree or rock as she takes to her husband' (p. 402).

Merely private and individual preoccupations are dangerous, part of the illusion with which in White's view Australian culture conceals its true situation from itself. What is necessary is to learn, as Ellen does, to acknowledge our vulnerability.

In this sense while the account he gives of their way of life may not be flattering, the book as a whole endorses the Aboriginal habit of mind, the 'primitive' sense of the world as one great system of symbols. Moreover, although it could be argued that the squalor of Aboriginal society is the consequence of the white invasion and its disruption of traditional food supplies and ceremonial life, it is more to the point that what we see of this society is through Ellen's eyes and that her sojourn with them represents for her the return of the repressed self—always a painful and sometimes even a violent experience. It is only after her return to Moreton Bay that she is able to look back on this experience and claim it lovingly. Significantly, this occurs when she has taken off the clothes she has been given and stands naked before a mirror (mirrors associated symbolically with the dread of the sight):[9]

She was at first too amazed to move, but then began to caress herself while uttering little, barely audible, cries of joy and sorrow, not for her own sinuous body, but for those whose embraces had been a shared and loving delight (pp. 348–9).

Set in the pattern of scenes concerned with clothes and nakedness, this is a crucial occasion. It contrasts with the two scenes in which she appears as someone else's work of art; the one in which her husband contemplates her coming down the stairs elegantly dressed and adorned with jewels and the one in which the Aboriginal women strip her of her white woman's clothes, cut her hair and then adorn her head in their own way with feathers. Here she is her own creation, poised between the two extremes of the 'raw' and the 'cooked', nature and art, in possession of herself whether naked or clothed because she has taken possession of an essential humanity. For this reason, while she may exist in society her centre of gravity is now to be found elsewhere, and this is why she is made to appear to Mr Jevons in the last scene as if she were a kind of goddess, a 'smouldering figure in garnet silk' (p. 404), and is set beside the pregnant Mrs Lovell 'in her nest of drowsy roly-poly children'. Ellen has paid her tribute to nature and to society and is now free.

But this freedom is only possible when she has come to terms with the dark side of herself and with the dangerousness of experience. The moment at sunset in the Aboriginal camp shows her coming to understand this, learning to let go the confidences in order and rationality by which her husband has taught her to live:

Round her the blacks were proceeding with their various duties, beneath a splendid sky, beside a lake the colour of raw cobalt shot with bronze . . . Evening light coaxed nobler forms out of black bodies and introduced a visual design into what had been a dusty hugger-mugger camp. What she longed to sense in the behaviour of these human beings was evidence of a spiritual design, but that she could not, any more than she could believe in a merciful power shaping her own destiny (p. 247).

The structuring of the book as a whole, based as it is on an underlying pattern—the homologies of food, clothing and sexual relationships which Lévi-Strauss see as basic codes of all human existence—also challenges the claims of rationality. In contrast with civilisation's preoccupation with explicit meaning and verbal precision White's style is highly metaphoric and works to give voice to the natural as well as the human world as the 'primitive' consciousness does,[10] and the introductory chapter which features the Merivales and Miss Scrimshaw shows that he is aware of what he is doing. Their fear of the alien and the strange, their determination to order and explain the world and circumscribe their experience of it is set up as a clear contrast to Ellen whose destiny it is to explore the 'secret depths' (p. 20) they shrink from.

To return to our opening passage from *Flaws in the Glass*, as he imagined White has become an avatar of Aboriginal culture. His preoccupation with decay reveals its source in the sense expressed here of the sheer power of nature and of the mysteriousness of existence. Ellen's story functions as a kind of ritual of initiation, involving first of all a separation from family, friends and all that is familiar, then a time of testing in the wilderness which leads to a crucial revelation and is then followed by a ritual of re-entry, ceremonies of clothing, eating and finally of the reconciliation promised in her meeting with Mr Jevons and return to Sydney. In this way her life fulfils the mystery foreshadowed in Cornwall as a girl when she lets herself down into the dark waters of St Hya's Well 'crying for some predicament which probably no one, least of all Ellen Gluyas could have explained: no specific sin, only presentiment of an evil she would have to face sooner or later' (p. 110)—an echo, perhaps, of White's own recollections of childhood initiation, of 'hanging' suspended in a cold pool,[11] which, connected with his sense of being somehow a reincarnation of the Aborigines and thus in possession of the mysteries of the land, points to the wider significance of this scene. In turn this scene points, as baptism does to the Eucharist, to the celebration of this communion, the moment in the forest when, driven by hunger, Ellen shares the Aborigine's dreadful meal, picking up and eating a piece of cooked human flesh which has fallen from one of their overflowing dillies.

Here as elsewhere it is important not to be distracted by irrelevant concerns: by the question as to whether or not Aboriginal people ever practised cannibalism, or by the shock which follows the violation of taboo. White's concern is not with the facts but with what they signify. Our present culture with its fear of alien images, values and ideas demands the symmetry of rational meaning and thus tends to subjugate the powers of metaphor and symbol, the forces of ambiguity and multiplicity. But this novel works to release these powers, demanding that the reader lets them work, gives them mental and emotional force. In this scene especially it is necessary to cross the frontiers, leaving behind the anxieties of visualisation and moralising by 'deepened and re-visionary strategies of the word as an innovative medium' and enter into the fullness of symbolic consciousness—as Ellen does after the event:

She was less disgusted in retrospect by what she had done, than awed by the fact that she had been moved to do it. The exquisite innocence of this forest morning, its quiet broken by a single flute-note endlessly repeated, tempted her to believe she had partaken of a sacrament. But there remained what amounted to an abomination of human behaviour, a headache, and the first signs of indigestion. In the light of Christian morality she must never think of the incident again (p. 272).

On the frontier between her English inheritance and a savage and mysterious universe, she crosses over, dislodging the division between the tenderness and ferocity. Cannibalism becomes a kind of 'transubstantiation in reverse'[12] as Ellen is taken up into the life according to nature, into the community of suffering, vulnerability and oppression represented by the Aborigines. The power of this incorporation is signalled by the 'single flute-note endlessly repeated'—an image, significantly, which recalls the story of the Carib devils who consumed a ritual morsel of the enemy god, the god of the conquistadors who had invaded their world, and fashioned a flute from his bones.[13] The pressure of this moment acts as a kind of alchemy to fuse the human and, indeed, conquistadorial sense of guilt Ellen feels here into genuine creative humility and compassion. Thus, paradoxically, what she experiences is not so much loss as gain, not so much exclusion as the reconciliation she had looked for as a girl in Cornwall. Moreover, this feeling grows. Her 'civilised' self attempts to repress the memory of what she has done but in 'not remembering' she continually recalls the event, finding that it makes her 'tolerably happy', happier than her white conscience should have allowed:

[In recollection her action] seemed less unnatural, more admissible if only to herself. Just as she would never have admitted to others how she had immersed herself in the saint's pool, or that its black waters had cleansed her of morbid thoughts and sensual longings, so she could not have explained

how tasting flesh from the human thigh bone in the stillness of a forest morning had nourished not only her animal body but some darker need of the hungry spirit (pp. 273–4).

We are back here with Lévi-Strauss's notion of the 'properly appointed humanism' in which human life is related to the whole range of existence. Acknowledging the 'darker need of the hungry spirit', Ellen has become more, not less, human, testing possibilities she has only been able to glimpse as a lady, as on the occasion when out walking in Van Diemen's Land she is overcome by the savage abundance of the bush and, sitting down on a compost of decaying leaves and bark, like the young Patrick White 'celebrating [his] own private mysteries' becomes aware of 'the being her glass could not reveal, nor her powers of perception grasp, but whom she suspected must exist none the less' (p. 92).

What is revealed in these scenes is the possibility of worship, the possibility unsatisfied in white society, even on 'religious' occasions like that in church on Christmas Day in Van Diemen's Land when all that Ellen feels she is celebrating is the 'God of the winning side' who supports and justifies the system which sets her and the Roxburghs in the front pew and the wretched convicts in their misery behind them. Not that the possibility which 'savage' life opens out is comfortable. Physically, her time with the Aborigines reveals a life that is 'nasty, brutish and short'. Spiritually, however, it enables her to come at the truth of her humanity, her subjection to physical necessity, and above all to the ultimate necessity of death. Where society, represented by people like the Roxburghs, the Merivales, the Lovells and Miss Scrimshaw, wants to triumph over this subjection, she finds happiness in acceptance, the acceptance she celebrates in the moment, in the empty chapel, left unfinished by the only other survivor of the wreck, Pilcher. Here in this poor little church she sits weeping, 'reliving the betrayal of her earthly loves'. In contrast with the church dedicated to the 'Lord God of Hosts' in which she worshipped on Christmas Day in Van Diemen's Land, above the altar here the legend, 'God is Love', 'in the wretchedest lettering, in dribbled ochre' reminds her of all that she has lost. But acceptance of this loss becomes something positive:

At last she must have cried herself out: she could not have seen more clearly, down to the cracks in the wooden bench, the bird-droppings on the rudimentary altar. She did not attempt to interpret a peace of mind which had descended on her (she would not have been able to attribute it to prayer or reason) but let the silence enclose her like a beatitude (pp. 390–1).

She has learned humility as 'primitive' people do, by acknowledging her limits and finding her place in the universe. Exile, physical exploitation and oppression have been positive, not merely negative in their effects, teaching her to live with uncertainty. As Wilson Harris has remarked, the relative self-sufficiency of the traditional 'strong' character does not fit the experience of the new world, being unaware of the need for change and apt to consider as evil any alteration of his other accepted character.[14] But Ellen is ready to live in a state of flux, to confront the savage domain, finding it not so much a threat as a fructifying mystery[15] from which she returns with a new definition of good and evil: evil as the non-acceptance which excludes what is 'other' from the dialogue with the self, good the universal reverence and acceptance she celebrates in Pilcher's shabby chapel.

White's view of Australia, then, is of a kind of frontier, a place of disorientation, a place of the mind for the testing of communal values which must there be confirmed or repudiated. What is in question in the crisis which occurs here is not just personal identity but the nature of humanity itself, and in the series of comparisons that *A Fringe of Leaves* sets up civilisation seems just as demeaning as Aboriginal life. Leaving the chapel after her moment of illumination Ellen has a sense of returning to imprisonment, a sense confirmed on the voyage to Sydney when she goes up on deck for a final glimpse of 'a jewellery of stars such as [she] believed she might be seeing for the last time before a lid closed' (pp. 401–2). The cruelties of civilisation are psychic whereas 'primitive societies' are physical, but the 'country of thorns, whips, murderers, thieves, shipwreck, and adulteresses' (pp. 311–12) is the product of civilisation and its discontents. With the Aborigines, however, Ellen returns to her childhood world where 'rocks had been her altars and springwater her sacrament' (p. 248), a world in which she acknowledges that primal 'law that man does not invent' (Lévi-Strauss), the law of physical necessity. Elsewhere[16] I have discussed the importance of this law for White's work as a whole. Here, however, it is clear that he sees it as the law of life and judges societies according to their acceptance of it. So the Aboriginal culture which acknowledges its debt to nature is closer to the human truth than white colonial society which does not—the society represented by Mrs Merivale, who is 'an adept at closing her mind to awfulness' (p. 11), or by Mr Roxburgh for whom even death has become 'a literary conceit' (p. 76). They, not Ellen, are the ultimate prisoners in an illusion which must inevitably be shattered by the fact of their mortality.

What White has done in this novel, then, is to exploit the Janus-like possibilities of the frontier, suggesting that White Australian culture will be incomplete until it comes to terms with the full range of human possibility, above all with the claims of nature, honoured by Aboriginal culture and intensified by white society's rejection which has laid the whole burden on a people ill prepared to resist. Ultimately, his Australia is not unlike Naipaul's Africa, a place where the task is to survive. But it is also more positive. *Flaws in the Glass* confirms what the rest of his work intimates; that White lives by the secular myth of the writer who looks to language to initiate different modes of existence, attempting to express 'a grandeur too over-whelming to express'.[17] And *A Fringe of Leaves* comes closest, perhaps, to being explicit about the nature of this grandeur. What emerges here from 'the wrestling match with an opponent whose limbs never become material'[18] is a return to childhood, to the primitive perception, and the celebration of mysteries which are primarily mysteries of decay and therefore of liberation from the confines of the merely material and even of the merely rational. What Ellen discovers, White implies, is her proper place in the universe, and she discovers this amongst the Aborigines 'in a country designed for human torment, where even beauty flaunted a hostile radiance, and the spirits of place were not hers to conjure up' (p. 248). Her situation is only evil to those who live by the spirit of possession and desire for mastery. This experience helps her to unlearn the conceptions of the individual and society inculcated by the Rox- burghs and to return again to the awareness of herself as part of the larger scheme she knew as a child and glimpses again for the first time one night in Van Diemen's Land. As she describes it in her journal:

The moon was in its first quarter, the river a faint, silver coil in the distance. Often on such a night at Z., a country to which I belonged (more than I did to parents or family) I would find myself wishing to be united with my surroundings, not as the dead, but fully alive. Here too . . . I begin to feel closer to the country than to any human being. Reason, and the little I learned from the books I was given . . . tells me I am wrong in thinking thus, but my instincts hanker after something deeper, which I may not experience this side of death (p. 104).

A Fringe of Leaves then, stands at the opposite end of the scale to *Happy Valley*, White's first novel. There Australia represented an ultimate alienation, the land and its white inhabitants cut off from one another, towns like Happy Valley being merely 'a peculiarly tenacious scab on the skin of the brown earth'. *A Fringe of Leaves*, however, celebrates a reconciliation between the two, a renunciation of the pretensions of the enlightenment that leave one grasping still 'at any circumstantial straw which may indicate an ordered universe' (p. 405), in favour of a more 'properly appointed humanism' which takes account of the full range of existence.

NOTES

1. Patrick White, *Flaws in the Glass* (Cape, London, 1981), p. 16.
2. Ibid.
3. Robert Gittings (ed.), *John Graham (Convict), 1829: An Historical Narra- tive* (Faber, London, 1937), p. 90.
4. Ibid., p. 94.
5. Ibid., p. 81.
6. C. Lévi-Strauss, *Totemism*, trans. R. Needham (St Martin's Press, London, 1964).

7. Edmund Leach, *Lévi-Strauss* (Collins/Fontana, London, 1974), p. 36.
8. Ibid., p. 18.
9. Gilbert Durand, *Les Structures Anthropologiques des l'Imaginaire* (Bordes, Paris, 1969), p. 96.
10. C. Lévi-Strauss, *The Savage Mind* (Wiederfelt & Nicholson, London, 1966), p. 219.
11. Flaws, p. 16.
12. Wilson Harrison, *Explorations* (Dangaroo Press, Aarhus, Denmark, 1981), p. 31.
13. Ibid., p. 37.
14. Wilson Harris 'Metaphor & Myth', in Robert Sellick (ed.), *Myth & Metaphor* (Centre for Research in the New Literatures in English, Adelaide, 1982), p. 4.
15. Harold Beaver, 'The Drama of Disorientation', *Times Literary Supplement*, 24 April 1981, p. 451.
16. Veronica Brady, 'The Novelist and the Reign of Necessity: Patrick White & Simone Weil', in R. Shepherd & K. Singh (eds.), *Patrick White, a Critical Symposium* (Centre for Research in the New Literatures in English, Adelaide, 1978), pp. 108–16.
17. Flaws, p. 20.
18. Ibid.

To Be or Not to Be?
The Verbal History of Patrick White

'Ce to be or not to be est une histoire
complement verbal'
(Jacques Lacan)

Now that the excitement over David Marr's monumental biography of Patrick White has died down, it is time perhaps to assess its significance. Reviews have been almost unfailingly admiring. But very few of them, with the exception of David Tacey's, have had much to say of the significance of the biography. That is surprising, especially if you think of the possible distraction the life might provide away from the task, arduous if rewarding, of reading White's work. This, in fact, is the burden of Tacey's criticism of Marr's book:

I feel that it is certainly a major text on White's outer life, but White the creative writer and visionary artist is somehow left behind. White's larger, more abstract preoccupations as novelist are hardly touched on, much less analysed or integrated into the biographical enterprise. [1]

I do not happen to agree with this. But the point it makes is well taken. After all, it used to be an article of literary faith to separate the life from the work, to 'trust the tale rather than the teller', as Lawrence put it. More recently, Barthes's famous, if much misunderstood essay 'The Death of the Author', argued that the reader's concern ought to be not with the writer but with the text itself, its language, and the complex interweaving of cultural, historical and physiological impulses and influences the language enacts. As one of Beckett's characters puts it, 'What does it matter who is speaking?', what matters is 'what is spoken'.

Could it not be said, therefore, that Marr's biography is somehow beside the main point and a diversion from the real task of reading White's work, even perhaps an incitement to the old-fashioned 'Writer and His Work' criticism? I do not think that this is the case, and why I think so is the burden of this essay. My reasons, however, rest on a set of presuppositions about reading in general, and the kind of reading White's work in particular, seems to demand. So it is best to set them out before going any further.

In the first place, the act of reading depends upon a sharing of horizons, the reader's and the writer's, and the text constitutes the meeting point between them.[2] From the array of prevailing systems of language and literary tradition and therefore of cultural and historical thought and practice, the writer selects certain forms and foregrounds, certain norms and allusions which, lifted from their original context and put within a literary text and thus made unfamiliar, are then able to convey new kinds of implication and signification. In this way the text organises networks of reference and combines different perspectives to make a world of its own, related to that of everyday experience by reason of its origin and reception within it but not a mere copy of it. That, of course, is what makes reading so liberating, in the spirit of Vita Sackville-West's reply to the question of whether she tried to 'write about the real world', 'One of the damn things is enough.'

Not every reader would agree with this account, of course, and some will regard it as naive and want to take it much further in terms of one or another currently fashionable theoretical approaches. But for the moment it will serve, I hope, to explain why Marr's book seems to me to offer important insights into White's writing. By increasing our knowledge of his cultural and personal horizon and repertoire and giving a richer and finer sense of their sources and context, of the forces operating upon and around the writing, Marr's biography also increases the reader's horizon and repertoire. If, as I have argued, every reading involves a kind of reinvention of the text, the biography provides new material for this reinvention, taking us behind the reticulated screen of language to the sources of the writer's creativity, the crossroads between physical and psychic existence, the inner and the outer dimension, the public and the private, between belonging and the sense of alienation, all so important in White's life and work. In this sense, if writing creates a space into which the writer disappears, the biography enables us to rediscover him precisely in this space as he attempts to rework his existence there.

The law of the book, as Deleuze and Guattari remark, is the law of reflection, of the one who becomes two.[3] So, too, for the reader, the space of reading as well as of writing is a dynamic one. Since it is the space of language, it is a supplementary space, unfinished but calling for completion. As Nietzsche observed, 'The sign is not the thing it stands for, the name is not the thing, the idea is not the deed, the dream is not the action', so that the 'true' world remains 'unattainable, unprovable and unpromisable', even as it continues to call us forth to try and discover it. Yet this is not to say that reading is entirely hypothetical. On the contrary, to the extent that it defamiliarises the familiar, a literary text opens out a kind of liberated zone within it, making the familiar and everyday more significant by setting it in a framework of understanding and interpretation, even perhaps calling for decision, since the significance of any text lies ahead of it in the reader's response. In this sense a literary text interprets its interpreters, drawing us into its movement, interrogating our lives and undermining our certainties, not so much describing the world as remaking it and involving us as its readers in this process. True, it usually provides a map of the everyday, but this map points us towards performance, demanding a journey towards further experience, giving an understanding of ourselves and the world which is always in process and never concluded.

These are generalisations. But they throw light on White's work and clear away some of its difficulties. To date, I believe, criticism has not really come to terms with these difficulties, with the open-endedness and complex inconclusiveness of its form and language. Instead most critics, myself included, seem to have been concerned rather to decipher and interpret, to draw the suggestive complexities of his work back into our own systems of meaning, be it Christian, patriotic Australian, or Jungian. White himself, however, always resisted this incorporation. For him writing, he insisted, was a matter of movement towards rather than possession of identity.

I chose fiction, or rather it was chosen for me, as the means of introducing to a disbelieving audience the cast of contradictory characters of which I am composed.[4]

In this sense he, too, is a reader since this cast performs for him also, displaying his own possibilities.

In early manhood I began to see that the external world was no other than the dichotomy of light and darkness I sensed inside me. The principles instilled into me by my parents and Lizzie [his nurse] were only related to my rational self. My mentors could not have imagined any of the darker undertones (p. 34).

Writing is thus an activity, at one and the same time personal and impersonal; impersonal since writing represents a deterritorialisation and destratification of self and world,[5] yet also intensely personal, to the extent that the self from which it proceeds is transformed in the process and thus in a sense is discovered. As a means to self-discovery and self-knowledge, writing thus became for White a focus of responsibility, posing at the conscious level questions of the unconscious, the one enlarging the other in the process, and demanding responses to them which led in turn to further exploration.

Tacey's approach to White's work, to return to it, tends to ignore this two-way process, tending not only to conflate the two, the conscious and the unconscious, but also to essentialise the work's concerns, reducing their complexity, taking them back to a matrix of Jungian archetypes, important to the critic but not necessarily so to the writer, and then interpreting the texts in their light. But this is to ignore the supplementary quality of language, its essential ambiguity, and to equate the literary text with the unconscious instead of seeing it for what it is, its double, thus quantifying what is essentially unquantifiable. So Tacey complains that in the biography 'White's larger, more abstract preoccupations as a novelist are hardly touched on, much less analysed or integrated into the biographical enterprise', arguing that it is these 'larger concerns, his mythical scenarios and archetypal symbolisms' which have 'made him a great writer, and are why [sic] the world stood up and took notice'.[6] For him Marr's failure to deal with them is 'a colossal error of judgement'. But if, as I have been arguing, White's preoccupations are not abstract but very specific and personal, not already defined and given but in process of definition and even of discovery, a matter of experience rather than of a system, an exploration, of 'what you do not know (in so many words) but know' intuitively, beyond words and systems, then what matters is this process, not the discovery of 'meaning'. Marr's concern with the development of man's life and struggles with himself is therefore profoundly important, not a distraction but an illumination. What the biography suggests, then, is a reading which is not so much essentialist as provisional. In the light of the evidence it provides about its origins, White's work appears not so much an organised system as a movement, a constant and dialectical interplay between self and world and the various possibilities of the self within the problematical person called Patrick White, son of Ruth and Dick and brother of Sue whose life and circumstances Marr details for us. Tacey's contention that the biography directs attention away from the work is therefore difficult to sustain. At the same time, his insistence that it is the work, not the life, which really matters is valuable. But it is not to say that the biography does not illuminate the writer. Rather, it is, I believe, an essential source for a deeper and richer understanding of it, of the ways in which life and work fold in upon and enlarge each other, as it shows us a writer whose work is so intrinsically bound up with his life and its circumstances that they became almost synonymous. Let us see how this is so.

Marr seems to have met White first in his writing, and throughout seems intent on leading his readers back to it, having given them a better understanding of its origins, its human cost and rewards and a more judicious sense of its direction and purpose. At one and the same time, the biography thus opens out possibilities of theoretical exploration and yet rescues us from the disengagement, even apathy which is one of the negative consequences of much contemporary theory. To ignore a text's origins in a particular life and in a particular historical and cultural situation can make for an indifference about its effects. But Marr shows how this kind of indifference misconstrues the nature of White's genius, exploring the ways in which the life, his ambiguous relationships with family, society and more intimately, his own sexuality, generated the question which echoes throughout his work, the question, as White said, of some grandeur:

grandeur too overwhelming to express, a daily wrestling match with an opponent whose limbs never become material, a struggle from which the sweat and blood are scattered on the pages of anything the serious writer writes (p. 70).

Life and art in this sense were for him of a piece, the work enlarging the boundaries of what might otherwise have been a privileged and previously self-absorbed existence and the life constantly making new demands of the art. It is true, as Tacey notes, that White himself was often at pains to conceal this connection in his rare conversations with critics or scholars. But these conversations, the biography suggests, were usually defensive, the result perhaps of the repression noted in *Flaws in the Glass* that society forced upon him as a homosexual (p. 80). All his life, even from childhood, as both the biography and his own autobiography, *Flaws in the Glass*, show, White's central preoccupation and problem was with himself, with the sense of his own ambiguities and of the duplicities of self in relationship to society. But this sense drove him intellectually as well as emotionally, making his life a wrestling with questions of meaning, the discovery of identity within some larger scheme. So his autobiography opens with young Patrick White sitting in the Long Room of the house in Felpham in southern England gazing into a mirror:

at one end the garden, at the other the great gilded mirror, all blotches and dimples and ripples. I fluctuated in the watery glass; according to the light I retreated into the depths of the aquarium, or trembled in the foreground like a thread of pale-green samphire. Those who thought they knew me were ignorant of the creature I scarcely knew myself (p. 6).

Narcissus longs for non-being, obscurely aware of the inadequacy of all human desire. Yet he also longs for unity, for some coincidence between himself and the world, and with others and to belong in the world. In my view this ambiguity is the source of his writing. Since, Bakhtin has pointed out, 'language for the individual consciousness, lies on the border between oneself and the other'[7] language also becomes the means to unity. But responsibility emerges here also, responsibility not only for himself but to the Other he senses in the mirror and in the light which enables him to perceive his image. Writing becomes an act of this responsibility as he presents images of himself. The accent falls not just upon self and world but primarily upon the world between them, upon consciousness. This is evident in scenes from childhood from *Flaws in the Glass*, for example, in which we see White pondering the question of God in the garden at 'Lulworth' or the force of physical necessity facing him in the tropical decay of the bush in the Blue Mountains and realising that 'the external world was no other than the dichotomy of light and darkness sensed inside me' (p. 34). Concern for the truth of his situation, for the responsibility he senses in it, points him towards some further realm, a belief that another power responds to his responsibility, that he does not exist in an utter void.

The sense of non-coincidence, that he was never entirely himself is, of course, one of the central concerns of the biography, which gives us a vivid picture of the family and the sense of social obligation it gave White, a sense which served all his life as a counterpoise to the more personal struggle with himself. The influence of his father, it seems, may not have been as strong as that of his overpowering mother but it was an important one, unassuming but enduring. This influence may have had something to do with White's return from the safety of the United States in 1940 to enlist in the RAF for instance, and to insist on being accepted despite his chronic asthma. In the 1970s it was a similar sense of duty which led him to play a public role in protesting against the dismissal of the Whitlam government and later against nuclear and environmental destruction.

As far as the writing is concerned, this sense of obligation saved him from the fate of Narcissus, rescuing him from solipsism, the creation of a merely personal imaginary world, to recognise the social dimension, and making him one of our finest social comedians and satirists—something which critics of the psychological or the topical persuasion tend to ignore.

But the biography also points to the sources of the preoccupation with the 'grandeur too overwhelming to express', with the question of God. The book's detailed and vivid account of the family and their social milieu, the servants, the large house and garden at Rushcutters Bay which was to figure in so many of White's novels and the other house in the Blue Mountains where the boy discovered his sense of Aboriginal affinity with the land, gives a sense of the ambivalence which dominated his life and drove him so constantly in his search for some further dimension. At one and the same time, he was, it seems, an insider of a rich and complex inner world and an outsider to the world of most Australians. This sense of ambivalence, the biography suggests, was more of a burden than his homosexuality. But, to the extent that it generated the desire for the Real which exasperated both the man and the artist, it drove him to create the metaphoric means to it, the elaborate fictional world he created. Having lost the aim of satisfaction within society, desire had also lost its object within it.

The biography is particularly helpful here. On the one hand it shows us a young man constantly searching for love and on the other his equally constant disappointment. But it also shows his disillusionment with conventional religion. Marr gives a vivid description of White's sudden awareness of God one day in 1955 on the farm at Castle Hill, when slipping in the mud carrying a bucket of slops to a litter of pups, he found himself on the ground cursing a God in whom he had always said he did not believe. Against his will, he was overwhelmed by a sense of some power beyond himself to whom, or to which, he was ultimately and irrevocably responsible, with whom or which he must struggle for the rest of his life. At this moment, he wrote, 'faith began to come to me'. True, it remained a difficult and problematic faith, a matter of struggle and

continuing enquiry rather than repose. But White had an intimation
here, it seems, of the goal and object of his desire. Not that this
directed his attention away from people and things. On the contrary,
it was intensified, since all things, even the gob of spittle Stan Parker
sees at the end of *The Tree of Man*, now seemed to be charged with
this glory he was aware of.

Marr's account of this scene in White's life which links it with
the following similar one in *The Tree of Man* is a classic example
of the way life and work interrelate:

*As the rain sluiced his lands, and the fork of the lightning entered the crests
of his trees. The darkness was full of wonder. Standing there somewhat
meekly, the man could have loved something, someone, if he could have
penetrated beyond the wood, beyond the moving darkness. But he could not,
and in his confusion he prayed to God, not in specific petition, wordlessly
almost, for the sake of company. Till he began to know every corner of
the darkness, as if it were daylight, and he were in love with the heaving
world, down to the last blade of wet grass.*[8]

For the life this was a crucial moment because in it White
recognised the ultimate point of authority which he had hitherto
been unable to find in his father. In this sense it represented the
culmination of the concern with responsibility which his family had
given him and which his awareness of the anarchy and cruelty of
contemporary history had emphasised. Here, however, this concern
was endorsed and intensified, and the biography shows the difference
this made, giving the life and work a weight and seriousness they
would otherwise have lacked. It also provided a counterpoise to his
disguise of worldliness, his delight in gossip, display and eccentricity
and in theatre and vaudeville. As for the writing, it became less
introverted, antithetically set over against society, and responsive
to it, dialogical rather than monological. Response to his circumstances and expenses now was a matter of listening, even of
obedience, rather than the imposition of a style.

This sense of non-coincidence became positive, here, leading
White to commitment to something both within and beyond himself.

On the one hand, this commitment made him permanently dissatisfied with himself and with the world, the dissatisfaction which made him such a sharp and savage social ironist. Yet on the other it gave him a deep certainty, the certainty which enabled him in the works from *The Vivisector* onwards to play such dangerous games with himself. Even after the moment at Castle Hill, faith, the belief that he existed in relation to another, remained simple and obvious, ' "impossible to explain but . . . like trying to explain air" ' (p. 283). It did not make him kinder or more gentle or even more loving. Indeed, Marr says, it may even have made him more demanding. But it gave his work its satiric edge—satire depends upon the outrage of passionate belief—as well as its anguished splendour, anguish being the other side of wounded belief. Having glimpsed the grandeur he was the more deeply aware of his own limitations and betrayals. If Oscar Wilde is right that falling in love with oneself is the beginning of a lifelong romance, for White the relationship now became much more ironic, even agonistic. Hence the passage in *Flaws in the Glass* in which he asks himself:

Am I a destroyer? this face in the glass which has spent a lifetime searching for what it believes, but can never prove to be, the truth. A face consumed by wondering whether truth can be the worst destroyer of all (p. 70).

In this way the biography shows a new side of the man who was often so vituperative, quarrelsome and overbearing, showing the essential humility which accounts for the sense of loss which invested his life, for all its achievements and privilege. Meeting White for the first time, Manning Clark sensed that his was 'the face of a man who wants something he is never going to get', something indeed which 'no human being can give him'.

This sense of loss, of course, set White at odds with the simple-minded materialism of Australian culture and with its naive belief that the human mind is the measure of reality. In contrast, imperious and often overbearing, White was a great seeker, an explorer of spiritual rather than material dangers, and it was this which rescued him from the authoritarian habits of mind and heart so characteristic of our culture, the product of anxious materialism. As far as the writing is concerned, the feeling of loss led him to search for perfection in the preoccupation with form which is evident in all his work. As he wrote in the autobiography:

I saw the Parthenon as the symbol of everything I or any other solitary artist aspired to before we were brought down into the sewage and plastic of the late Twentieth Century (p. 116).

This use of form to control and order the chaos he felt around him has led some critics to call White a Modernist. But his sense of self was much less monolithic, much more problematic, than that of the great Modernists. For that reason in his work there is a much greater emphasis on heroism and the heroic, on the need for some satisfaction beyond the self to be achieved at the cost of the self. His work is more personal, even anguished, as we have said, and it is this anguish rather than any sense of intellectual possession which empowers the myths he uses to shape his work, *The Brothers Karamazov* in *The Solid Mandala*, for instance, *Antony and Cleopatra* in *The Eye of the Storm*, and so on. Similarly, the lives of his heroes, which echo his own, break into and empower the form and rhythm of the novels, giving them a significance which is at once authoritative, and deeply personal. It is for this reason that most of his novels, especially from *The Vivisector* onwards, seem unable to reach an aesthetically rounded conclusion but remain open-ended.

Once again, this points to the interweaving of life and art. For White, it becomes clear, character constitutes a form of interrelation between the self and its desires which thus helps to create the clearly defined personality he longs for.[9] Yet at the same time he is caught in a painful paradox. As a writer he can only be the bearer of an artistic formulation or completion, not its object or its hero, since as a human being he has to live in the world of messy actuality, the world which the biography describes so vividly. In turn this paradox intensifies the situation since the personal pressure makes it more and more difficult to achieve aesthetic completion in the work, so that the characters become mere aspects of the self, dispersing rather than empowering his creativity.

The biography makes clear just how extensive is this problem of the interplay between life and art. But it also gives a deeper sense of the artist's achievement. At the simplest level, it shows us how the work arose out of events and circumstances, taking us to the point of intersection between the physical and historical, the psychic and the semantic. We see how *The Aunt's Story*, for instance, arose out of the pleasures of his discovery of Greece and his love for Manoly, a discovery which made him long for a life ' "stripped bare of all superfluities . . . a life of pure being, pure spirit" '. In turn, this longing led him back to the Australian landscape as he remembered it from childhood as a 'state of silence, simplicity and humility'.[10] Similarly, to take another example, it appears that *The Eye of the Storm* grew out of the long and difficult history of his relationship with his mother and was a response to her death which Elizabeth Hunter re-enacts in exact detail. In contrast, *A Fringe of Leaves* was twenty years in the writing, originating in White's first meeting with Sidney Nolan and through him with the story of Eliza Fraser, a fact which may account for the comparative serenity and aesthetic completeness of this novel. At a simpler level, the biography also describes the circumstances of the writing, the tensions, rages, tantrums and drinking bouts, the last moments of panic just before publication and White's surprising anxiety about reviews.

We are also taken to the point of origin of many of the symbols which run through his work. Many of these, of course, have occasioned abstruse and ingenious speculation. But Marr suggests that they often arose from ordinary, even banal, experiences. He tells us, for instance, that White said to him that the fascination with the colour red, evident in his work, derives from a memory of the red hairs on the chest of the young jackeroo he shared a room with at Barwon Vale in the 1930s. His feeling for wood, the symbol for him of all that is wholesome, was associated with the childhood glimpse of an Englishman, newly arrived in Australia, making furniture for the house he was building for his family in the mountains of New South Wales working amidst ' "the sweet smell of timber" '. Similarly, the table scarred with knives, which serves for Hurtle Duffield as an image of God's patient suffering, goes back to childhood memories of the kitchen at Lulworth and the long-suffering kindness of the servants which he associated with it.

This is not to destroy the power of the symbols or the mythopoeic echoes of the narratives but to intensify them, making us aware of the way in which the most masterful images grow, as Yeats said, out of 'a mound of refuse or the sweepings of the street', out of 'the foul rag-and-bone shop of the heart'. But it also points to the ambiguities involved in the act of creation, the way in which, in it, self is divided against self. So for instance, Marr's account suggests that the aesthetic splendours and personal intensities of *The Twyborn Affair*, were touched off by a story heard before a disastrous lunch about an Australian who had lived for years in England disguised as a woman.

Equally valuable is the evidence Marr provides of White's life as a young man at Cambridge and afterwards in London, a time White himself had little to say about in the autobiography. Marr, however, gives us a vivid sense of the shy young man with his love of display and longing for love. In this way he throws light on the fascination with worldliness and eccentricity, evident throughout White's work. It also connects him with the figure of the flâneur, the Baudelairean dandy, spectator rather than participant, frivolous, delighting in the extreme and the outrageous, intent upon sensation and gossip, yet also fascinated by questions of good and evil. The biography also shows us the other side to this display, giving a vivid account of the young man's colonial diffidence, his fear of loneliness, and sense of historical and social malaise, reminding us in this way that the dandy may have something in common with the prophet, to the extent that he is interested in causing surprise in others, to interrogate the status quo in order to extract from the merely fashionable something more intense or more poignant.

It follows from this that the pose of detachment was not only a way of coping with his sense of anomie as a young Australian in England and as a homosexual but also helped him as a novelist, allowing him to draw people who might merely irritate or seem excessive in life. The Russian second-hand dealer in Ebury Street, for instance, becomes the original of General Sokolnikov in *The Aunt's Story*, and is thus drawn into his personal search for more intense experience, made into a figure of ethical and even metaphysical significance. Similarly, Marr enables us to see how the early years of life at Castle Hill after his return to Australia with his friend Manoly Lascaris provided White with his mythical suburb of Sarsparilla, a kind of permanent vaudeville act in which, of course, the writer himself also figured.

What emerges from all this is the awareness that, like Basil Hunter, in *The Eye of the Storm* Patrick White was in a sense always on show, never off stage, always performing a variety of roles, some sublime but mostly ridiculous, in the long running scenario he made of his life. Gossip, tormented artist, generous but difficult friend, monster, man of the world and man of the theatre, public figure, invalid, vulgarian, mystic and seer, he was, it appears, continually putting on masks and taking them off, making and unmaking himself in a permanent interplay between life and art. But the biography also makes clear how much this cost at the personal level. The ultimate subject of the complex elaborations of the work may be the writer himself, but the self created also becomes a kind of fiction, multiple, omnivorous, permanently in process, yet driven by an insatiable longing for truth, exploring what is humiliating and even disgusting within himself as well as in others in order to find the splendid, the luminous and the holy, living dangerously and under intense pressure. Addressing the crowd at the opening of the Henry Lawson Festival in Grenfell, New South Wales, in 1974, for instance, he told them:

Believe me, the creative artist does live under enormous stress, which drives many of us to drink or drugs in order to wring out the ultimate meaning, and I cannot see that it will be otherwise unless the arts die an unnatural death.

White was a man under pressure, then. How much this pressure has to do with White's homosexuality, however, is debatable. Tacey's review would have it that this is the biography's central concern:

Marr has his own project: to portray White as a homosexual writer and as a Sydney gay. But White's homosexuality . . . is not as central as Marr wants it to be. It does not explain White's creative achievement. In fact Marr's gay ideology sits very uneasily upon White's career (p. 7).

This, I think, is to misread the biography. According to Tacey, it is 'informed by the gay understanding that homosexuals can only fulfil themselves and be genuinely creative when they have come out of hiding and made public their sexual preference' (p. 11). In fact it does nothing of the sort. True, Marr explores White's homosexuality more fully than any one else has done. Yet the exploration is discreet, and arises out of a sense that an understanding of the man's sexuality is essential for an understanding of the artist. Its point, that is to say, is to illuminate the effect of his homosexuality on the work. As White himself observed in his autobiography, 'if we can quench our fears the perception gained through our temperament strengthens our hand as man, woman, artist, whichever it may be—or all in one' (p. 23). For the homosexual even more than others, it appears, self-understanding is a goal, never a given, and in this sense a form of self-discipline. It is also something which usually needs to be repressed. As White puts it in *Flaws in the Glass*, 'the repression society demands of homosexuals obviously reduces them to some extent as members of that society' (p. 80). The strength this repression gives is a painful one. But it has little to do with the modish 'gay ideology' of which Tacey accuses the biography. On the contrary, it makes him very vulnerable, feeling different from others, the feeling expressed, for instance, in *The Vivisector* when Hurtle Duffield watches a gang of boys of his own age running down the lane as he sits on the wall around the Courtnay's house and garden:

Unconvinced, the pack ran on, and as it became an increasing blur, there flickered through his mind the person with the bell round its neck Sid Cupples had told about: the freak tinkling after them driving the 'sane buggers' always further away.[11]

Rather than being a form of fashionable indulgence as Tacey suggests, homosexuality was for White, it appears from the evidence of the biography, a form of painful self-knowledge. From childhood, Marr tells us, White knew that he was and always would be different. 'I never went through the agonies of choosing between this or that sexual way of life' he declares in *Flaws in the Glass*, 'I was chosen'. In this it was a matter of fate, not, as Tacey implies, indulgence. Love was for him, Marr points out, something which 'would not obey the rules', 'a knotty problem'. But for that reason, it also became a means to a complex truth, which he saw as essentially painful but splendid precisely because of this painfulness. Much of his work, notably *The Twyborn Affair* and *Memoirs of Many in One*, arose of this gap between desire and its realisation, the ideal and the real, though in them he also attempts to disguise the anguish by putting on a comic mask.

Tacey's misunderstanding of these works is therefore symptomatic of his larger misunderstanding of the problematic qualities of White's writing. He dismisses *Memoirs of Many in One*, for example, as 'written in a demonstrably high camp mode, with much extravagance, mannerism and elements of vaudeville . . . a slight and impoverished work . . . a bit of a laugh if you enjoy frivolity', evidence, in his view, that 'White had lost his creative powers'.[12] Yet the biography helps us to see that the extravagance of the novel resembles the defiance of Yeats's last poems as he wrestled with questions of responsibility and betrayal with no authority but that of these questions, thanking 'the Lord that he 'Has body and its stupidity'. In similar vein, in *Memoirs of Many in One* Alex Gray interrogates the dog lying on her bed:

He lays his muzzle on his front paws, the yellow eyes investigating a situation he only half believes in. Even Dog has his belief, and I am not, I never have been, one of them (p. 70).

This novel, his last, is in fact about the endurance of this self, its endurance into death.

As I have been arguing, belief was for White a matter of openness to further questions and a commitment to the fact that there may be no answer to them—hence Alex's reflection: 'O God! I don't know why I should invoke the name of someone who probably does not exist' (p. 138). Yet truth was to be found precisely here, in doubt, in the interrogation of identity the 'gap between what humans pretend to be and what they are'. And it was dedication to this truth, the biography indicates, which made White challenge himself first of all, in the spirit of Augustine's prayer, 'take us, oh Lord, from behind our back where we are hiding', and then challenge his readers. His homosexuality and the social stigma attached to it were part of this challenge; as Marr sees it, White believed that precisely 'what we are hiding—especially from ourselves' constitutes our real character, 'the more hidden and defended our faults the more they define us when they are brought into the light'. But they were not the whole of it.

In this way, far from making him antinomian, as Tacey implies, White's homosexuality increased his preoccupation with questions of good and evil, so evident in his work. The self-mockery, especially apparent in the later work, can thus be seen as a kind of asceticism, a denial of self and of conventional morality, born of the sense that the holiness and wholeness he longs for cannot be reconciled with mere self-interest or the satisfaction that comes from society's respect. Always an explorer of spiritual danger and prepared to make a fool of himself in order to get at the truth, in the last novels he pushes this exploration to its limits, representing himself in *Memoirs of Many in One*, for example, as 'old Patrick', a minor writer and something of a bore, as he sits in Alex Gray's house munching bloater sandwiches.[13]

The fact that this self-mockery coincided with increasing physical weakness and the humiliations of old age which the biographer describes so vividly, makes the courage which inspired it even more remarkable. At the end, the biography makes clear, this heroism of the work was translated also into life. Most of his energy, had to go 'into the hard work of getting more air into his lungs'. But White 'remained entirely himself: curious, tart, demanding, very funny and alert'. Moreover, much of this strength came from love, from his lifelong companion Manoly, 'this small Greek of immense moral strength', who in White's own words, had become 'the central mandala in [his] life's hitherto messy design' (Flaws, p. 100). This love, as the image of the mandala suggests, was also part of the search for order which had inspired and sustained him throughout his life and work, and the image the biography gives us of Manoly warming White's hands in his as he lay dying is an image of an order and security finally achieved. It also explains the confidence underneath the apparent turmoil which in his later years enabled White to take the risks he did with himself and his readers.

All his life, despite his own infidelities, White had regarded fidelity as a moral touchstone. Indeed, some of his most famous quarrels were occasioned by what he saw as infidelity to another. He disapproved of broken marriages, for instance, and even more of those whose fidelity to people, principles and ideas was less than it should be. Yet Marr's account of the last stage of his life shows the source of this belief which lay in his respect for fidelity, a deep sense that since in the long run all life is directed towards death, what matters most is not reconciliation with society but with oneself. Only death, White believed, could provide the antidote to the malady of history which so afflicted him. The awareness of its presence kept him open to the feelings of strangeness and awe which were for him the way to understanding.

White's disgust with contemporary society was, then, not a matter of mere feeling but of the conviction which intensified as he grew older that life is only valuable, in Nietzsche's words, insofar as it is able 'to give everyday experience the stamp of the external'. For him, contemporary Australian culture could not do this. As he wrote in *Flaws in the Glass*, 'double values abound', and nearly everyone is self-interested and intent only on material gain. For him, however, existence was 'many-faceted' and the body 'protean', in process towards some further intensity. That is the reason, no doubt, why he so despised the ethical muddle of consumerist society which confuses the material with the ethical, confusing *faring* ill, being poor, sick, unemployed, old or unattractive, with *doing* ill, and made some of his most interesting characters out of people of this kind.

But that is also the reason why White had little time for mere rationality. Because of the personal and historical circumstances the biography describes, especially after his war service, life appeared to him as mostly violent and painful, and he was deeply conscious of the cruelty, injustice and exploitation from which so many people, Jews, Aborigines, women and misfits of all kinds, suffer today. Mere reason had little or nothing to say to this 'heart pain, world pain'. White had a great contempt for what he called the 'great Australian religion of ordinariness', with its touching belief that the world's problems can be solved by merely economic or technical means. This was to him a form of demoralisation, even of nihilism, a betrayal of the personal integrity he saw as his and everyone's obligation to seek.

Seen in this light, the intemperance of his attacks on public figures like Bob Hawke or Sir John Kerr are not merely understandable but also necessary. But as far as the writing is concerned, this concern with integrity accounts for its austere insistence on style, often at the expense of comprehension, which remains intent upon the attempt to express the inexpressible. So, too, the heroism of the struggle to find a stable and well-defined hero, as part of his struggles with himself, of the struggle for authenticity and the preoccupation with objects come from the same source, the concern with integrity. Simple things such as tables, milk, rocks and even a gob of spittle may be manifestations of the 'grandeur too overwhelming to express' he was searching for just as much as the large and splendid. Yet, insisting as it does upon the specific and the individual and on the painful ambiguities of perception, this preoccupation is anything but a form of escapism. On the contrary, it can be seen as an attack upon the 'permanent ecstasy' of contemporary culture, 'the ecstasy of the social . . . of size . . . of violence . . . of sex . . . and of information',[14] which permanently distracts us from the specific and the actual.

In the long run, then, everything in White's life and work comes back to the question of authenticity. But it is an authenticity which is dialogical not merely monological, playing back to some point outside of the self which, we have argued, is the source of his art.

This point, the biography shows, constituted the dynamic of the life. In its light, what is painful or even disgusting can be transformed. As White put it, 'it is possible to recycle shit' and aspire to the order and permanence of the Parthenon (Flaws, p. 116).

Far from being a distraction from its proper task, the biography is therefore an important source for criticism, enabling us to see the other side of the interplay between the life and the art. The search for truth which this interplay generates accounts for the difficulties of White's style, since truth was a matter of interrogation, not possession, and what he sought was beyond comprehension, though it was also the source of all meaning. Words, especially words about this meaning, did not, could not, correspond with what they signified, they were at best an echo of mysterious complexity, at worst a failure to name what was unnameable. Since there was no necessary correspondence between the human mind and 'reality', what mattered for White was the longing for what was beyond comprehension, a longing, moreover, which was a matter of the whole person, not of intelligence alone.

These are difficult, perhaps exalted thoughts. But the biography also provides a vivid picture of the man in search of them. Marr's account does not lessen his frequent unpleasantness, his angers, drinking, quarrels, snobbery and arrogance. But it does help us to understand their sources. On the other side, it also shows White's generosity, his longing for simplicity and for love, his sense of justice and his heroic dedication to his life's task, his writing. It also reveals, incidentally, that White was much more widely read than he pretended to be, an admirer of writers like Joyce, Flaubert, Balzac, Dickens and Shakespeare, thus enabling us to respond more fully to the echoes of their work in White's, further liberating us from merely personal responses to it and making us aware of its complex intertextual range. The final impression, however, is of integrity. As Marr concludes:

[White] embraced whatever he needed for his work. Nothing in himself or the world around him was off limits. People, ideas, gossip, rows, were all grist to his mill. Behind his many faces, White lived one, writer's, life. He

spoke of living his real life inside his skill; he wrote that artists only experience pure being in their art. 'My flawed self has only felt intensely alive in the fictions I create.'

In the process of describing the life, then, something new emerges, a new sense of the meaning and purpose of the art. Criticism needs to take up the challenge of this new sense and to continue to extend it. In Bakhtin's words:

Understanding fills out the text; it is active and takes on a creative character. Creative understanding continues creativity; it multiplies the creative wealth of humanity. [15]

NOTES

1. David J. Tacey, 'Patrick White Marred', in *Quadrant*, XXV, 10 (October 1991), p. 280.
2. Here I rely largely on Wolfgang Iser, *The Act of Reading: A Theory of Aesthetic Response* (Routledge & Kegan Paul, London, 1978).
3. Gilles Deleuze & Felix Guattari, *Capitalisme et Schizophrenie Mille Plateaux* (Editions de Minuit, Paris, 1980), p. 11. The translations are my own.
4. Patrick White, *Flaws in the Glass* (Cape, London, 1981), p. 20.
5. Deleuze & Guattari, pp. 9–10.
6. Robert Con Davies, 'Lacan, Poe & Narrative Repression', in Robert Con Davies (ed.), *Lacan & Narrative: The Psychoanalytic Difference in Narrative Theory* (John Hopkins University Press, London, 1983), p. 982.
7. David Patterson, 'Bakhtin on Word & Spirit: The Religiosity of Responsibility', in *Cross Currents*, 41, 1, p. 34.
8. Patrick White, *The Tree of Man* (Penguin, Ringwood, 1963), p. 151.
9. Patterson, p. 48.
10. Patrick White, 'The Prodigal Son', in *Australian Letters*, 1, 3 (April 1958), p. 39.
11. Patrick White, *The Vivisector* (Cape, London, 1970), p. 128.
12. Tacey, p. 76.
13. Patrick White, *Memoirs of Many in One* (Cape, London, 1986), p. 111.
14. Jean Baudrillard, *Revenge of the Crystal: Selected Writings on the Modern Object and Its Destiny, 1968–83* (Pluto Press, Sydney, 1990), p. 16.
15. Patterson, p. 50.

4. POETRY AND THE POETIC

What Will Suffice
Les A. Murray's
The People's Otherworld

The poem of the mind in the act of finding
What will suffice. It has not always had
To find: the scene was set; it repeated what
Was in the script.
Then the theatre was changed
To something else. Its past was a souvenir
It had to be living. To learn the speech of the place.
(*Wallace Stevens*)

Les Murray is generally taken to be our most significant poet, a poet of 'international stature', and reading *The People's Otherworld* it is at first hard to quibble with this view. These poems have a force, an energy, a belief in themselves and in the world and an extraordinary technical skill which carry the reader with them. And yet—is it possible?—that is not quite enough. It is not enough, I believe, because poetry is or ought to be a kind of theology, to represent the self 'in the act of finding/What will suffice'—and Les Murray would seem to agree with this belief:

Art's best is a standing miracle
at an uncrossable slight distance,
an anomaly, finite but inexhaustible,
unaltered after analysis as an ancient face.

That is the theory, a theory honoured in much of his earlier work but not always here in this latest collection.

What has gone wrong? Here again the answer may be in part theological: 'the Kingdom of God is not a matter of talk but of power' (1 Corinthians 4, 21), in this case the power which subverts the self, subverts the world, lets the text exist in its own kind of reality, its own otherness. Again, I think, Murray would agree. In

'The Chimes of Niegeschah', for instance, he draws a parallel between poetry and God whom he calls 'The One who is in this world and next/as poetry is in the text.' In this sense poetry's meaning, like life's, is both achievement and alienation. What matters is the price underlying and empowering it. My problem with *The People's Otherworld*, however, is that in many of its poems, there are no gaps, no surplus, no sense of potential for further implication, for more intense experience. What we have here instead is a natural theology, the triumph of reason, of a kind of God—and world—forgetfulness. What the poetry forgets is the otherness of words. It reduces them instead to the compass of our everyday understanding and discourse. There are exceptions, of course, notably the marvellous poems 'Equanimity' and 'Little Boy Impelling a Scooter'. Here, as in his earlier work, one has a sense of being released into a bountiful and meaning-laden world and word, the one echoing but not dominating the other. But in a poem like 'Bent Water in the Tasmanian Highlands' the equilibrium seems to have been upset somehow. Instead of a sense of release, this reader at least feels constriction, a kind of subjugation to the dominating presence of a world which is not different but is the world of appearances behind which stands the domineering presence of the poet—and here I mean Murray himself rather than a persona he may invent. And it is a poet who, for all the brilliance and hypnotic ebullience of his language, for all its exactitude as well as its abundance and metaphorical power, seems somehow to have lost his way.

His reliance on metaphor perhaps gives us a clue to what is happening. By definition metaphor is concerned with the truth of appearance, not of 'the thing itself'. Consider these lines from 'Bent Water':

Flashy wrists out of buttoned grass cuffs, feral
  whisky burning gravels,
jazzy knuckles ajitter on soakages, peaty
  cupfulls, soft pots overflowing

or these from the beginning of 'Equanimity':

Nests of golden porridge shattered in the silky-
    oak trees,
cobs and crusts of it, their glory box.

There is power at work here, but its purpose seems to be to display itself. For me, at least, it closes off instead of opening out possibility, uniting various aspects of material and spiritual reality normally thought of as separate not so much to generate a sense of unity and multiplicity but of the poet's ingenuity. So the use of metaphor here is antimetaphysical in its implication since the perspectives through which it interprets, for all their richness and variety, depend ultimately on the poet. His very originality, the insistence on his own quirky perception, implicitly sets aside the need for that ultimate interpreter whom Murray would—and does—call God. His chosen, often proclaimed project—the art which starts, rather than ends at the 'gist'—seems to be faltering as 'gist' gives way to the gabble of 'Bent Water' and 'The Mouthless Image of God in the Hunter-Colo Mountains', and ingenuity replaces reverence.

Of course, every poet has a right to his or her lighter moments, and play with language is of the essence of the art. At the same time the distinction remains, as Murray himself insists in 'Satis Passio', between the mere expression of sensibility and that art which he defines as

. . . . what can't be summarised:
it has joined creation from our side,
entered Nature, become a fact
and acquired presence,

and the fact that he still achieves this 'standing miracle' from time to time—in the wonderful last section of 'Machine Portraits with Pendant Spaceman', for instance—makes my concern the more urgent. I sense in *The People's Otherworld* the drift, evident in that sequence, towards taking the world at face value (its skyscrapers, spacecraft, bulldozers, coal smoke, suburbs and shops) and accepting its prejudices—against 'nuclear nuts', for instance:

The sun, that is always catching up
with night and day and month and year
blazes from its scrolled bare fact
To be solar, I must be nuclear—

against 'Danish Modern Settlers', Poetry Festivals, and so on. As in *The Boys Who Stole the Funeral*, these prejudices are directed at anything which might be said to be questioning the status quo— but Murray seldom questions his own failure to interrogate what he sees and feels. Take, for example, the complacencies of the first of 'The Sydney Highrise Variations', the 'Fuel Stoppage on Gladesville Road Bridge in the Year 1980', which begins 'So we're sitting over our sick beloved engine' and concludes after a series of rhetorical games, with the idea of the bridge, its origins and appearance, and the technology which made it:

It feels good. It feels right.
The joy of sitting high is in our judgement.
The marvellous brute-force effects of our century work.
They answer something in us. Anything in us.

Compare this with the last section of 'Machine Portraits with Pendant Spaceman', which turns on the image of a river ferry on a country road:

Not a high studded ship boiling cauliflower under
    her keel
nor a ghost in bootlaced canvas—just a length of
    country road
afloat between two shores, winding wet wire
    rope reel-to-reel,
dismissing romance sternwards. Six cars and a
    hay truck are her load
plus a thoughtful human cast which could, in
    some dramatic episode,
become a world.

'No ideas but in things'. There is a humble submission here, and an eye and a mind prepared to pay tribute to what is, rather than to dominate it. This readiness to let go, to recognise that identity is not something closed from inside itself but open and resonant, makes the force that flows through these lines matter more than individual words, and even though the last few lines move in the direction of assertive statement, the last line returns us to this energy, to the real life of the poem:

> . . . *All machines in the end join God's creation*
> *growing bygone, given, changeless—but a river*
> *ferry has its timeless mode*
> *from the grinding reedy outset; it enforces*
> *contemplation.*
> *We arrive. We traverse depth in thudding*
> *silence. We go on.*

The resonant simplicity here represents a real answer to the world of 'metal-bra and trumpet-flaring film extravaganzas' celebrated elsewhere in the poem. Delighting in them on the one hand and yet able to rest in this conclusion on the other, the poet exceeds himself and his prejudices, combining the world, language and possibility in a whole within which he is, for once, subsumed.

This, of course, is the equanimity he celebrates in 'Equanimity'. This poem is lucid and eloquent, transferring close observation into metaphor. Yet, like 'Bent Water' which it follows and with which it is connected by the parenthesis with which that poem surprisingly ends, it does not really deliver what it promises. The equanimity of the title is more talked about than realised—not really, as it claims to be, something that 'lights us from the incommensurable/we sometimes glimpse', 'Of infinite detailed extent/Like God's attention. Where nothing is diminished by perspective'.

In this poem the perspectives *do* diminish, *do* keep us within the actual world. True, this actuality is rich and complex:

the jacarandas' open violet immensities
mirrored flat on the lawns, weighted by
    sprinklers

are set against 'the haze above cattleyards', hungry birds, and the condemnation to hear

. . . the profoundly unwished
garble of a neighbours' quarrel, and see
    repeatedly
the face we saw near the sportswear shop today
in which mouth-watering and tears couldn't be
    distinguished.

If poetry is, like the act of love, transporting, then here the world has not moved: things are as they are, more weighty, more clearly and beautifully themselves perhaps, but still themselves, a world of analogy not anomaly, dominated by will rather than contemplation. So in the long run the freedom and ease enacted in the grave movement of the lines points ultimately to unfreedom. To say this is not to deny the poem's moving power, its ability to speak with the pose, clarity and joy which turns statement into something monumental:

Through the peace beneath effort
(even within effort: quiet air between the bars
    of our attention)
comes unpurchased lifelong plenishment.

But one worries about the implication in the lines which follow, the tendency to take possession of this power and use it for the poet's own ideological ends:

Christ spoke to people most often on this level
especially when they chattered about kingship
    and Romans;
all holiness speaks from it.

I know, of course, that many would disagree with me, and claim instead that the poetry of discourse has its own kind of weight and power. But my point here is that Murray's kind of discourse lacks that weight and power because the discourse is ultimately divided against itself. The force supporting the poem is ultimately the poet's will and intelligence—not, as it claims, the order of things, 'God's attention'. This division, I suggest, is evident also in the reliance at crucial points upon metonymy, upon words, usually abstract, like 'peace', 'holiness', 'kingship', which in fact stand for something else, for the wholeness that the poem is ostensibly concerned with. As Lacan points out, this use of metonymy repeats an attempt at truth under oppression, the writer's power to bypass the obstacles which his social consciousness puts before notions of divinity. Far from being at ease with his world, confident of untroubled access between the divine and the human, Murray's imagination seems to be at bay before it, trying to impose on it by sheer linguistic force on the one hand and on the other by bullying the reader into complicity with his own beliefs.

Murray has always claimed to be a lover of the world and a celebrator of his times. Yet his definition of both of them is circumscribed by tastes and, more powerfully, distastes which are quite often at odds with the kind of profession he makes in some of the essays in his *Persistence in Folly*, notably in 'Some Religious Stuff I Know About Australia'. This essay opens with the proposition that 'something like a religious dimension exists in every human being' and defines it not just in terms of human response to the beauty, horror, mystery or incongruity of the world, or to some emotional need within us, but rather as 'a response to the actuality of God's Spirit working within us at a depth usually too great for direct sensory perception'. But he then goes on to contrast what he calls 'Supermarket Spirituality' with the underlying need for the religious dimension which he argues for in 'The Common Dish', 'the vessel of common human sufferings, joys, disappointments, tragedies and bare sufficiences from which most people have to eat in order to keep faith with them'. Admirable as this is, he does not go on further to explore this notion of common experience, to find in it the paradox of the God whose presence in this experience reveals itself more as an absence, as the Crucified One living now in the mysterious activity earlier pointed to. Instead, what he argues for in the long run is 'Strine Shinto', a spirituality which arises out of the land itself:

We have come to the sense, which the Aborigines had before us, that after all human frenzies and efforts there remains the great land . . . Nothing human has yet happened in Australia which stands out above the continent itself. We know in our bones that the land is mightier than we are, and its vast indifference can drive us to frenzies of desecration and revenge.

This is fine but also revealing, pointing as it does to the problematic of argument from analogy and the natural religion to which it gives rise, the tendency to confuse God with the physical world, Being itself with words about it. What is at the heart of this sense of the world, equanimity, is ultimately stoic rather than Christian since it not merely accepts the reign of necessity but submits to it, confusing it with the divine order (in Christian belief the divine is crucified by and in physical necessity).

Perhaps the clearest example of this submission is to be found in the short poem 'Anthropomorphics' whose conclusion is imposed, as so often, by authorial presence—'I praise, nonetheless, our humane and Scythian arts' is at odds with the poem's underlying brutality, evident in the central lines:

Hunting, we know, is mostly a form of shopping
where the problem's to make the packages hold
    still;
Death's best for that, though cheetahs have been
    seen feeding
on the bulk of a gazelle while the raised head end
    still bleated.

This is 'Strine Shinto' with a vengeance, an expression of the 'frenzies of desecration and revenge' generated by the sense of the ruthlessness and force of nature which underlies so much Australian experience. At best, this sense leads to 'the quality of sprawl' celebrated in the engagingly low-key and humorous poem which begins:

Sprawl is the quality
of the man who cut down his Rolls-Royce
into a farm utility truck, and sprawl
is what the company lacked when it made
    repeated efforts
to buy the vehicle back and repair its image

For all that, however, the feeling here for the down-to-earth, for the material and the practical makes my point: 'Sprawl leans on things. It is loose-limbed in its mind'. It is essentially one-dimensional, accepting, even complacent, repeats only what is in the script, is not pressed by the need to go further. Against this, rightly or wrongly, I see the poet as frontiersman or woman, someone implicitly aware that no settlement is ever final, aware too that, touching the nerve of failure in this way, he or she ought never suffer the failure of nerve—as Murray seems to do in this poem, as elsewhere, especially in the conclusion which opens up the whole question of justice and power only to renege on exploring it:

Reprimanded and dismissed
[sprawl] listens with a grin and one boot up on the
    rail
of possibility. I may have to leave the Earth.
Being roughly Christian, it scratches the other
    cheek
and thinks it unlikely. Though people have been
    shot for sprawl.

Murray's imagination cannot explore this question of 'sprawl' because ultimately he is in complicity with what underlies it; the will to power, apparent in poems like 'Bent Water in the Tasmanian

Highlands', 'The Sydney Highrise Variations' and 'Machine Portraits with Pendant Spaceman'. Failing to differentiate between Being and being, God and nature, leads him to elevate natural forces to a kind of consciousness with which his human consciousness then identifies. In turn this leads to fascination with the less rational aspects of human experience, with energy, aggression and violence: 'The Romantic Theme of Ruins' delights in destruction; 'Time Travel' in the 'spit fire world/of the duel'; 'The Grassfire Stanzas' in the annihilating energy of fire which challenges the sun itself:

It's the sun that is touched, and dies in
   expansion, mincing,
making the round dance, foretelling its future,
   driving
the frantic lives outwards.

The cruelty here, the implicit longing for an—if not *the*—end of the world is the obverse side of natural religion, the otherwise disappointed drive to the absolute. It is true, of course, that the face of the God Murray confesses can also be monstrous, as in the Book of Job and in the story of the crucifixion, but his confession does not really acknowledge that. His God is equable:

the mystery that confers reality
and details the proud constructs away.

more like the God of the philosophers, of the religions that, as Mircea Eliade remarked, 'are the results of the vacuum left in the world by the retreat of God, his transformation into *deus otiosus*, and his disappearance from the religious scene'. What is left is the worship of energy, useful enough as a release from the lassitude and boredom of current Australian culture, but leading ultimately to the worship of the imperial self rather than of the God who is perhaps to be found at the heart of that lassitude or, better, of the void to which it is a response.

If we look at the one poem in the sequence 'Three Poems in

Memory of My Mother' which seems exempt from this self-absorption, my point becomes clearer. Here the voice is not just a matter of assertion, it speaks out of and from an experience which has been lived and suffered through. There is humility here, an acceptance of a balance between facts and desire, and the boundaries between mind and body, self and world, good and evil are no longer so firmly or arrogantly drawn. Instead, the poet is engaged in a dialogue with experience, not just a monologue imposed upon it. The event he is concerned with, his mother's death, does not happen in abstraction from the world and other humans, is not his own possession which he thrusts before the reader, but exists in a relationship with them which depends on the grave simplicity of its language as much as on its honesty of feeling:

The steel of my induction
killed my brothers and sisters;
once or twice I was readied for them

and then they were not mentioned
again, at the hospital
to me or to the visitors.
The reticence left me only.

I think, apart from this,
my parents' life was happy,
provisional, as lives are.

It is true, however, that the conclusion is marred by self-assertion, by the typical insistence on drawing a moral—a moral, moreover, which assails the current sense of things:

There is justice, there is death,
humanist: you can't have both.
Activist, you can't serve both.
You do not move in measured space.

Where another poet might point us elsewhere, to the absence which opens out from loss and to the potential of this sense of absence, Murray draws us back to himself, to a self which is opinionatedly at odds with most of his readers. If this were a self who drew us back to the humility and discipline of art, an author-creator keeping watch over, assembling, regulating the time and meaning of his representation, letting it represent him as he exists and as he thinks, then there would be no quarrel on my part. But the self one glimpses here intrudes on the reader, interrupting the sense of piety—in the Roman sense—and order built up through the poem. The vulgarity of this interruption, however, is unable to outweigh what has gone before, its gravity, its warmth and its acceptance: this, I suggest, is the true 'speech of the place', the proper words for a people subject to necessity.

In contrast, 'The Mouthless Image of God in the Hunter-Colo Mountains' takes the larrikin's way. Consciously swaggering, Boetian rather than Athenian, the poet—very clearly here Les Murray, the public figure glorying in the no-nonsense reputation he has created for himself—presents himself as a kind of parody God. If God is the name 'dog' spelt backwards the poet here is a sly dog, starting the dogs barking with his primal bark,

> barking for a lark, or to nark and miff, being
>   tough
> or dumbly meditative, starting guff, sparking
>   one dog off
> almost companionably, you work him up,
>   playing the rough riff
> of punkish mischief.

The bravado here crowds the reader out, as does the rhyme which keeps running for whole stanzas, the long, shouting, exulting lines, the rough jokes, the puns, the daring swoops of onomatopoeia. The bully-boy crowds out the poet and energy overwhelms thought, though curiously the last lines almost confess this:

For spirit is the round earth bringing our flat
  earths to bay
and we're feasted and mortified, exposed to
  those momentary heavens
which, speaking in speech on the level, we work
  for and deny.

But the denial remains, the surrender to what Foucault calls 'somocracy', as distinct from democracy, the system of power which rules most of us today and is in fact the contemporary form of tyranny, the will to pleasure which imposes itself from within, not as older forms of tyranny did from without, and rules us not by saying 'no' but saying 'yes' to our desires, thus leading to the alienation which seems to me to be also the result of reading this poem.

My problem with these poems, then, is political as well as theological—political in the sense deriving from its origin in the word 'polis', the community. Many of Murray's poems here seem to militate against this sense of community, to make rather for the arrogant individualism which is its opposite, the kind of triumph implicit in the emotional obtuseness of the last lines of the first of 'The Sydney Highrise Variations', already quoted. This recklessness, I think, yeilds ground which it seems to me to be the poet's task to defend, the union between self and others, self and world, and the fruitful division between reason and intuition. But the phase 'brute force' in these lines gives the game away. Murray's allegiances lie with conquest. With the univocal. Ambiguities and paradox are not for him.

No doubt this is why his poetry speaks to so many people today. Times of anxiety breed yearnings for simplicity and certainty, for clear structures and lucid speech, and one must be grateful for what Murray gives us; the confidence, the technical mastery, the energy and the vernacular cast of his experience and speech. Perhaps indeed it is churlish to say that this is not enough, to lament the poet who might have been, the believer who might know about unbelief, the virile, even macho poet who might know about tenderness, a theologian who might pay tribute to instead of suppressing instinct and desire. This is the poet who appears briefly in 'The New Moreton Bay', 'The Fishermen at South Head', and from time to time in 'Three Interiors', 'First Essay on Interest', 'Equanimity' and 'Satis Passio'; a poet who is able to accept the modern and modernistic world view, the sense that language exists in a state of constant self-subversion and that God, the final word, may ultimately be silence, that the final meaning may be absurd in our terms and the ultimate wisdom foolishness. This means a different sense of space, not local and limited yet railing against this limitation, as in 'The C 19–20', but open-ended, pointed beyond itself to possibility. Thinking is not a matter of power but of acceptance—as with the image he draws in 'The Fishermen at South Head':

Where they stand, atop the centuries
of strata, they don't look down much
but feel through their tackle the talus-eddying
and tidal detail of that huge simple pulse
in the rock and in their bones

This, it seems to me, is the language which will 'really suffice', the true speech of the place in which, as Murray says in 'Some Religious Stuff I Know About Australia', 'the solitary ego [is] at once as vast as the horizon and as unimportant as a straw of windblown grass'.

OVER THE FRONTIER
THE POETRY OF ROSEMARY DOBSON

Was there ever a time, since, you looked death in the face? Do you know the strange new geography death offers?—Carlos Fuentes

Rosemary Dobson is a curiously problematic writer—paradoxically, because of her work's apparently unproblematic nature, its lucidity, its monumental quality. In a time of profound anxiety, not just about ways of living and surviving, but also about language, its power and worth, she dreams still of a common language, a language which is clear, inclusive and evocative, concentric rather than eccentric, and concerned to escape from the cramp of mere subjectivity. Australian, nevertheless she invokes the

great names, to me the strange
Names of a culture still to be explored

and looks

for ways by which to understand
My origins; for ground whereon to stand
With poetry for a divining-branch
                    (The Three Fates, 28)[1]

At first glimpse, then, her work seems to fall uneasily into a book concerned with the uncertainties raised by contemporary sexual/textual politics. Yet, as Marilyn Strathern has put it, feminism is not so much a flower as a field.[2] It is a matter of goals rather than of strategies, a particular way of being in the world, ambivalently, ambiguously, somehow more or less aslant the dominant modes of discourse and being.[3] In this sense the space and time Dobson's poetry explores are feminine, since they are the space and time of the other, not just in relation to men's world but, more significantly, in relation to herself. She approaches experience obliquely, by means of mirrors, or by a series of analogies through which the self is reflected, protected, and finally securely founded in her own country of 'austerity and light'.

As she points out in the Preface to her *Selected Poems* (Sydney: Angus and Robertson, 1973), her work falls into groups: 'poems about paintings; poems arising from European myths and legends; poems about what might be termed human responsibility, and so on.' This method of writing in groups represents a kind of strategy:

Poems in series are not just substitutes for longer works that will never be written, as has been suggested. For me they provide an opportunity to arrange ideas in relation to one another, as one might arrange objects in space to construct a harmony, each expressing something by itself and something else in relation to other objects.

The resistance here to having parameters set for her is characteristic. Paradoxically, however, it springs from a reluctance to define or to assert herself—a reluctance evident also in the dismissive 'what might be termed' and 'and so on' when she comes to speak of the last group of poems in which she is at her most vulnerable and moves to declare herself most openly. But it is characteristic also of much of women's writing in general, the writing of the 'colonised'.[4] Working within male discourse—as a poet Rosemary Dobson is often bracketed with her friends A.D. Hope and David Campbell, and with Douglas Stewart and James McAuley with whom she figured in the late 40s and 50s in the *Bulletin*—her poetry nonetheless works, quietly but powerfully, to deconstruct it and to write beyond its boundaries. Comparison of her renderings with David Campbell's in the series of free translations from the Russian of poems by Anna Akhmatova and Osip Mandelstam makes this clear. As A.D. Hope notes in his preface:

David Campbell, it seems to me, descends like the eagle of Zeus on the poem he is to render, and with something of the Olympian lightning flash he carries it off and transmogrifies it; it becomes a poem in his manner . . .

Rosemary Dobson . . .works in quite another way. She flows round and over and through the poem until it is totally absorbed into her . . . personal habits of language, of rhythm, of feeling; and then, with delicate care and exquisite adjustment of detail the poem so dissolved is encouraged to re-crystallise itself in the medium of another language and another poetic personality.[5]

Implicitly here Hope points to the connection between textuality and sexuality. Campbell's writing is patriarchal. His pen is an instrument of generative power like a penis as he swoops on the original poem and takes possession of it.[6] Dobson's, by contrast, works maternally, receiving and assimilating in order to give new life. Her poetry belongs to what Hélène Cixous calls the Realm of the Gift, Campbell's to the Realm of the Proper.[7] While that of the proper is concerned with property and appropriation, putting its emphasis on self-identity, self-aggrandisement and arrogative dominance, the Realm of the Gift is essentially open, part of a circuit of giving and receiving. It lives from within, where, to use Cixous' words, woman,

the outcast, has never ceased to hear the resonance of fore-language. She lets the other language speak . . . To life she refuses nothing. Her language does not contain, it carries, it does not hold back, it makes possible.[8]

To *read* Dobson's work in the active sense is to miss the point. The task we are engaged in here is rather to cross over the frontier, to learn to listen, to catch a glimpse of that 'outline of non-existence' which 'can be held by the inner eye' ('Always moving, it assumes the shape of stillness').[9] What matters here, that is to say, in art as in life, is some quality of pure answerability. Thus what criticism of Dobson's work that exists—and there is surprisingly little for so substantial a poet—seems largely beside the point. Adrian Mitchell, for instance, is troubled by the 'limited extent of her thought', and the conclusion he reaches is that 'hers is not the poetry of systematic thought'.[10] To accept this and to be disappointed by this 'limited extent' of thought is, of course, to include her poetry in the economy she has rejected, the economy of classification, system and hierarchy which her work is in fact trying to undermine. Appealing from metonymy to metaphor, from rationality to analogy precisely because it comes from elsewhere, her poetry attempts to express what has been repressed or censored out by dominant definitions of reality and value. The task she sets herself is not so much one of transcription as of recreation. Not that it seems that a task was immediately clear to her—it was Zeus who bore Athena fully formed from his head; woman's gestation is more laborious, more of a process of attention and nurture. For this reason it is important, I think, to trace this process in Dobson's poetry from its beginnings.

The first poem in her *Selected Poems*, 'In a Convex Mirror' (the first, that is, of the poems she 'would wish to see reprinted'), already seems to represent a kind of 'return from afar, from always', though not yet from beyond culture.[11] Here, as elsewhere in her early poems, being cannot be separated from becoming. The two lovers who stand transfigured before the mirror in their own sacred and creative space

As pictured angels touching wings
Inflame a Dutch interior
Bespeaking birth, foretelling kings

are also aware of the pressures of contemporary history:

But ruined Rostov falls in flame,
Cities crumble and are gone,
Time's still waters deeply flow
Through Here and Now as Babylon.

Yet the outstanding feature of the poem is its irony, the subjective freedom the poet claims to disregard, however temporarily, the world that is governed by the clock and by the swirling flood of history, not wilfully but in order to create an alternative space and time which, precisely because they are bodily, contain within themselves the possibility of new beginnings. Not that this possibility is openly declared—there is a young poet and a young woman here, waiting her turn to speak. The language is cool, seemingly abstract, though in fact highly metaphorical and thus potentially deceptive. Metaphors of painting and reflection emphasise evasion and concealment, a retreat into silence as self is turned into an image or, better, a reflection, if not to escape then at least to control the pain of being subject to time and history, the pain of living bodily:

Shall we be fixed within the frame,
This breathing light to clear-cold glass
Until our images are selves
And words to wiser silence pass?

The best she can achieve is this question, not quite a rhetorical one but nevertheless shadowed by a sense of impossibility rather than possibility, as the poem's conclusion insists with its image of time 'Engulfing with unnumbered floods/The hidden spaces of the heart.'

One is reminded here of Simone Weil's sense of the force of necessity which is also the weight and fate of bodiliness. But, as with Weil, this sense is not merely negative. It points to something other, beyond the sphere of the usual, the intelligible and the familiar, and expresses a longing for unity on some other plane, impelled by the pressure of necessity towards a unity which in some way mysteriously this pressure also guarantees. The appeal, then, is to feelings which in a sense transcend experience.

In its own way 'In a Convex Mirror' thus offers the challenge Cixous sees implicit in woman's writing:

Because she arrives, vibrant, over and again, we are at the beginning of a new history, or rather a process of becoming in which several histories interact with one another. As subject for history woman always occurs simultaneously in several places.[12]

The interplay between body, mirror and painting, between historical time and sacred time, between public and private is not merely an aesthetic device; it has ontological and epistemological implications.

'Woman un-thinks the unifying regulating history that homogenises and channels forces, herding contradiction into a single battlefield.'[13]

Many of her early poems ('Young Girl at a Window', 'The Fire', 'Moving in Mist', 'Foreshore') rely on this tactic, embracing contradiction and ambiguity as a way of life. But there is also a certain self-consciousness about them which reflects the weight of commonsense, of the masculine interrogation which insists on categorisation, proximity and rationality, the principle of non-contradiction. To some extent at least the series of poems about paintings, notably the series from *The Ship of Ice*, 'The Devil and the Angel', respond to this interrogation by refusing battle and retreating to the merely aesthetic. If they do not quite surrender their hold on the actualities of bodily experience, these poems nevertheless encode and distance them, disguising the debates of passion, of love before death, of light before darkness, as figures in paintings or, more evasively still, as devil and angel. Convention tends to crowd feeling, irony to prevail over the longing for a new beginning on which it rests.

This widening of the distance separating her from actuality highlights the uneasiness and vacillation with which Dobson's work begins and the sense of impotence—a belief, evident in poems like 'In a Convex Mirror', in the inability of poetry to influence history—that goes with it. Not that the retreat is all loss. 'The Bystander' (*SP* p. 43), for instance, turns this distance into a gain which is ethical as well as aesthetic:

I am the one who looks the other way,
In any painting you may see me stand
Rapt at the sky, a bird, an angel's wing,
While others kneel, present the myrrh, receive
The benediction from the radiant hand.

Lacking authority or a place in the public life, the bystander here takes possession of her/his own space, her/his own perceptions. It may be impossible to grapple with vast issues like war and tyranny or belief and unbelief:

I hold the horses while the knights dismount
And draw their swords to fight the battle out

But that makes for a saving kind of innocence. The world's evils are separate from the self and its perceptions:

I hang upon the crowd, but do not mark
(Cap over eyes) the slaughtered Innocents,
Or Icarus, his downward-plunging flight.

Thus, for all its reticence, the poem's claim is finally a large one:

Once in a garden—back view only there—
How well the painter placed me, stroke on stroke,
Yet scarcely seen among the flowers and grass—
I heard a voice say, 'Eat', and would have turned—
I often wonder who it was that spoke.

The refusal to join in the world of violence, aggression and display has its rewards. But innocence is not enough, especially if the exclusion from the Fall, from evil, means exclusion from life. The poem, in fact, for all its wit and precision, has a sense of weightlessness or worldlessness—a reflection, it might be said, of the condition of woman, her exclusion, the dissolution of her identity, the 'lack' which has traditionally been associated with the feminine, but not necessarily a response to it.

It might even be argued that there is a refusal here to assume the name and the responsibility of Eve, in male discourse the bringer of evil. Yet the way to refute this attribution is not to refuse to take issue with it. The coolness, the refusal to speak in her own name, but rather to put on the disguise of 'the silly soul who looks too late, the dullard dreaming' is a familiar enough tactic on woman's part. But though it may make good poetry, it surrenders all claim to history or to the public life without taking on another life of her own. There is a similar sense of a self 'refined out of existence', though even more obliquely put, in the well-known 'Country Press', where the seeming lack of interest in woman's experience as such can be seen as the subject of the poem.

True, the mere exhibition of wounds and cries of anger are not enough either. Yet, as Xavière Gauthier remarks, 'as long as women remain silent, they will be outside the historical process. But, if they begin to speak and write *as men do*, they will enter history subdued and alienated; it is a history that, logically speaking, their speech should disrupt'.[14]

'In My End is My Beginning' (*SP* p. 38: the title evidently invoking the memory of the doomed Mary Queen of Scots) marks a change, the beginnings of a commitment to the life of the body, to speaking one's self as woman:

For blood's my argument and reason
And flesh is audible, and heart
Will know the way if these should fail,
And head will bear a steady part.

The sense here of being beleaguered, fragile and vulnerable on the 'hazardous path to Death from Birth' is made positive, and subjection to death is turned into something lyrical. The text is not merely literary, not merely historical but, in Cixous' words, the 'body—shot through with stream of song'—the body not of an 'overbearing, clutchy 'mother',' but rather of a young girl dancing, singing what is touching her and 'filling her breast' with an urge to come to language and to 'what launches [her] force':[15]

Wit's the one weapon for my fending,
Who travels farthest journeys light,
Save that the mind has faggots stored
To kindle fire on darkest night.

The rhythm here is almost impudent, the body its own circle, but it is a circle of risk rather than of protection:

Draw a circle round me thrice
Arm's radius to this piece of earth;
Here's my Tom Tiddler's Land of danger.

The game that is played here is played out of the fullness of freedom—man (or woman) only plays, as Schiller says, when in the full meaning of the word he/she is a man/woman, and he/she is only completely a man/woman when he/she plays. Here, too, the game is an end in itself:

In this small orb is compassed wonder,
Passion, despair, and state of grace.

But self is affirmed in the game which leads to the triumphant insouciance of the conclusion:

No fares for ferrying. If you will,
Saint Christopher, be with me still.

Flying, Cixous argues, is woman's gesture—'flying in language and making it fly', but also, as here, 'flying the coop', 'rearranging the order of space to suit her own body', dislocating things and structures and turning propriety upside down.[16] If darkness is to be woman's place, then it will be turned into lightness also—the return of the repressed is not always explosive, it can be joyous, if defiant.

In poems like this we glimpse the possibility of another kind of poet, ecstatic, dionysian, sweeping away limits and restrictions, re-working language, defying syntax, redefining herself and her world by defiance. But this kind of poetry can fall subject to another kind of ideology, and claim absoluteness and exclusiveness as patriarchal thought also does. Dobson's great gift, however, is for truthfulness and integrity, for remaining in contact with daily experience and thus with common language. Refusing to live by presuppositions, suspicious of prejudice and cliché, she leaves herself open in her work to honest criticism on the one hand and to the possibilities of change on the other. This is the importance of her poems about paintings.

They kept her in touch with what is already given and sensuous and thus enable her to use this as a measure of, and sometimes a judgement upon, the present. Personal space in life, irony in art, depend upon the possession of some internalised standard of this kind. Writing poetry may be the most innocent of occupations, but in this sense it is highly subversive, setting personal experience against the collective representations of things, confirming her existence in the world in her own terms—as her Breughel, in 'Painter of Antwerp' (*SP* p. 26), returning home from Italy and its splendours,

Put thumb to nose with neither pride nor envy
At Soaring wings—a Southerner's invention—
Icarus sprawling, two feet out of the sea.

Nevertheless, the reluctance to define herself, to liberate the new possibilities inherent in the image of Icarus remains. Instead, Dobson is content here and in other poems of this period with the other kind of flight, with stealing away quietly, more or less unobserved. So irony becomes a kind of diversionary tactic. Yet it is also in danger of becoming an end in itself, of making for dessication, of undue emphasis on intelligence as a substitute for feeling.

At this stage it was possible that Dobson might have become merely provident, like those women of Louise Bogan's poem who 'have no wilderness in them' but are 'content in the tight hot cell of their hearts/To eat dusty bread.'[17] In many of these poems about paintings—'Azay-Le-Rideau', for instance, or 'The Masquerade'—there is a sense of an experience that is somehow precious, separate, set apart in the narrow room of a canvas or a period of history turned into fantastic reverie. 'On a Tapestry' (*SP* p. 62) perhaps most vividly sums up this sense. Here love turns into a literary conceit, poignant in its conclusion in which life finds itself inadequate to all:

'In loving is my sum of happiness'.
'Oh, all the sadness in the world—' I cried
Who loved not, whether loved or unbeloved.

In contrast with earlier poems like 'In a Convex Mirror' in which nothing exists but what the poet knows, self is agonistic here. Personal experience has been appropriated by and excluded from public and historical discourse. True, there is something of that feminine sense Joan Didion describes of 'living one's deepest life under water' but nothing of the sense which corresponds with it of woman's 'dark involvement with blood and birth and death'.[18] But perhaps the problem that was uppermost for Dobson at this middle stage was survival—other women poets, her contemporaries (most notably Judith Wright), seem to have ceased developing in new ways at this stage of their career. With Dobson, however, it was different. Even as a spectator, or perhaps particularly because she was a spectator, she had managed, in the poems about paintings, to clear a space for herself, and to find a room of her own. Keeping to her own way, her own space, she had thus implicitly destroyed the authority of others to determine her experience—something quite crucial for a woman writer—and at the same time effectively declared her independence of their praise or blame.

In one way, of course, this sense of displacement, of confinement to a fictive, scriptive realm, reflects the loss of self characteristic of writers generally, men as well as women, in this century. But a curious quality of bodily awareness marks Dobson's work and points a way out of the disillusionment, loss of energy, and final sterility which marks literature of this kind. The poem 'Jack' (*SP* p. 103) is written from this awareness. Jack-in-the-box here is flesh and blood yet, paradoxically, an image of death:

My mortal husk is shelled at death
And shut inside a narrow box;
But he is coffined up in life:
Oh, what a bitter paradox!

The friskiness of the rhyme here only serves to highlight the poignancy of the situation. It is also a tactic to defend an artist from the panic of the perception that, in this case, art is refusing to keep its distance but is invading life or, better, being invaded by it.

The children laughed and stretched their hands
And called again for Jack, for Jack,
But with a sudden brutal thrust
I caught his head and pushed him back,

Thinking, it does not do to muse
And give to toys of stick and straw
Emotions that belong to life
Lest the conclusions that we draw

Might yet be turned upon ourselves
To show each in his narrow piece
Of flesh and blood, like Jacks of straw
Shut down, and crying for release.

Here, looking death in the face, she is also laying claim to her body and to the geography and history of the body—claims enforced on her, as on most women, by children.

In the remarkable group of poems which turn on the experience of pregnancy, birth and, most poignantly, losing a child, this claim is made most directly, most enduringly. Dobson writes herself more fully than she had done before, as woman letting her body be heard and thus releasing the sources of the unconscious, hitherto held back, unspoken and concealed. In my view, even if they are not the most accomplished poems she has written, they thus mark a turning point. If, as Heidegger has said, thought left to itself traverses everything and finally loses itself in imageless night, then thought here is suffused with the passion of the body and writing gives the poet back to herself instead of being an evasion of herself. 'The Edge' (*SP* p. 80), for instance, about 'the mazy paths that woman treads', opens up the immense and mysterious bodily territories of maternity:

Three times to the world's end I went,
Three times returned as one who brings
Tidings of light beyond the dark
But voiceless stays, still marvelling.

The woman returns here, in the words of Cixous, 'from afar, from always: from "without", from the heath where witches are kept alive; from below, from beyond culture'.[20] Having been confined within the frame of art, she emerges now to write as a woman, perhaps especially for woman. But the title 'To Meet the Child' signals also a liberation into a larger, more visionary world, the world patriarchal scientific culture would have us forget. The poem dramatises this liberation, beginning paradoxically with the woman's sense of necessity, her dependence upon the processes of birth:

I await the signal for setting forth, the journey
To be taken alone across an unmapped country,
A land now tremulous with pain and mirage,
Now bright beyond the focus of my vision,

and ending with the meeting, the birth of the child, which is also a birth of new possibility within the self:

Then shall I look upon that face with knowledge
And eyes look back at mine with recognition,
And together we shall return to our own country
With word of wonders, by another way.

The gravity of the long pentameter beat and the falling intonation of the line-endings combine authority with submission, assertion with reverence, and dramatise the 'revaluation of values' at work within the poem, a revaluation confirmed by the echoes of sacred history in 'return to own our country . . . by another way'.

As David Brooks argues, there have always been two histories, two cultures, two stories of the world, a man's and a woman's.[21] Earlier in her career, this allowed Dobson the possibility of the ironic perspective, by seeing what patriarchal culture regarded as a given as an imaginative construction. But here even that construction unravels, to use Brooks's image, 'as if a thread unravelled in a garment'. Woman takes possession of her own history and thus enters into 'the strange new geography of death', not negatively but rather to open up the full range of existence which is suppressed in a culture of mere rationality. Caught up in the process of gestation and birth, the woman comes to understand that death inhabits life, that sexuality is in a sense death's share in us—as Freud understood. Yet, importantly, this world is not merely biological, it also opens out before intuition and leads into a sense of worship, not of nature but of something that is other than nature. Thus, even as she celebrates birth and death, the refusal to worship nature—as her contemporaries, Stewart, Campbell and others tended to do—continues here.

The experience of maternity serves, in fact, to intensify the sense of duplicity, of contradiction, already prevalent in her work. But here the contradiction works as a kind of heuristic device. As in the thought of Simone Weil, a sense of contradiction leads to the discovery of mystery, something which is quite different from mystification, is not a lack of knowledge, not a blank unknown nor a puzzle to be solved, but is apprehended, according to Gabriel Marcel, by 'an essentially positive act of mind'.[22] Thus it is not an obstacle to thought but an essential part of our knowledge, enlightening not only the existential but also the rational level. For Weil, contradiction, the perception that something both is and is not what it is, points to a more inclusive and insightful way of conceiving our existence and its contradictions than a merely rational or grammatical way could do:

We can shape the world to our size but we only understand its existence as independent of our thoughts when we find that it somehow manages to go its way, despite our expectations. The mind that can accommodate shocks to its self-imposed order is therefore one that has emerged from a solipsistic dream and has begun to think in truth. Noting the opposition of 'contradiction' between our mental order of the world and the way the world goes on its own can therefore be a gateway to a fuller encounter with reality.[23]

That is to put it prosaically. Dobson puts it poetically, writing out of her experience as a woman:

Child, children, though I hold you here
A moment to my mortal heart
You go from me as rivers go,
As stars move to their destined place.
The beating wings are clamorous.
I hear the word. I let you go.

The title of this poem, 'Annunciations (*SP* p. 79), points on the one hand to the problem of reading in the sense of interpreting what our senses present to us which arises out of the experience of contradiction, and on the other to its resolution, to the acceptance of the dimension of mystery, of the sacred as Rudolf Otto defines it, as 'the wholly other, that which is quite beyond the sphere of the usual, the intelligible and the familiar . . . filling the mind with blank wonder and astonishment'.[24] So in the poem

The farthest galaxies recede
Beyond the reach of human sight
As starry rivers to that sea
Unbounded, shoreless, infinite,
From whence we come, to which we go.
In the Beginning was the Word

Dobson is not usually seen as a religious poet—prejudice might have it that she is too intelligent for that. But here is precisely the play of intelligence on the profound bodily experience of pregnancy:

Lulled by the drumming of my blood,
The distant thunder of my heart,
You slept upon the moving tide
Of darkness, sealed in mortal flesh

which leads to the perception of the sacred, a perception which reverses the direction of the earlier poetry, turning flesh into the Word. The task of religion then becomes the woman's task of articulating the sensuous and bodily, turning pain into praise, absence into a new kind of presence. Naming the gods, as Heidegger says, means that they claim us, as here, as the poet perceives and lives out in her own flesh the parallel between the divine linguistic creation of existence and her own creative power as woman and poet.

This is poetry, then, that brings us to the edge, to the foundations of existence. Yet its great achievement lies in the way in which the language refuses to be overwhelmed by this experience, even as it points beyond itself to what is unspeakable. Naming the experience, the poet is claimed by it. The result is neither speechlessness nor excess of speech, but the poise of a poem like 'Out of Winter' (*SP* p. 78), in which the words do not so much denote what they describe as take up residence in it:

Darkness shaken by the wind; winter
Beating the tree of darkness gathers
The windfall stars, unnatural harvest,
Bright bitter fruit colder than water.

The single words here, each with its dictionary meaning, are subordinate to the sentence, carried along by the flowing movement of the stanza, pointing beyond themselves to a system flowing through them which is both a system of meaning and a system of being. So the experience of bodiliness in the poem, 'The fruit of pain, the fruit of grieving', is shadowed with a sense of abstraction, of concern with a fundamental logic of existence:

. . . the anatomy of beginnings, landscapes
Bared to the bones of rocks and boulders,
The simple truths of early paintings—
Births, deaths, and belief in visions.

The definiteness of this language is important but not self-sufficient. It exists in a mode of human truthfulness which keeps knowledge from being unattainable at the one extreme or exhaustive at the other. But this experience of subjectivity also becomes an experience of the limits of subjectivity as the poem suggests that what is spoken about and experienced here is only partially available to language.[25] Yet for this reason it also becomes an experience of community—the facts and symbols here, winter as time of wind, cold and darkness and winter as symbol of loss, for instance, cannot be taken independent of the values—every human being knows about wind and cold and about loss and loneliness.

These poems, then, mark a crucial point in Rosemary Dobson's development because in them the object of desire, the body, is literally there, is spoken and given its own place. But their very success, and the unrepeatability of the experience they depend upon, pose a new problem. This problem arises out of the gap which is implicit in these poems between art and life. The vividness of memory and the intimacy of bodily experience combine to give a degree of certainty that is also potentially destructive to poetry. Concern with bodily experience can also become prescriptive. 'It is . . . dangerous', as the editors of the journal *Questions Feministes* observe, 'to place the body at the centre of a search for female identity'.[26] On the other hand it is also important not to lose the sensuous authority, the personal directness which has been obscured in, if not entirely absent from, the earlier poems about paintings.

What provides the way through to a more permanent reconciliation between all these elements is, I think, the concept of grace which Dobson writes about in her Preface to the *Selected Poems*:

there is always something that eludes one . . . the poems presented here are part of a search for something only fugitively glimpsed; a state of grace which one once knew, or imagined, or from which one was turned away.

If woman's task is dynamic, to go on seeking for herself and thus for a form of writing, of inscription, which will liberate rather than contain her, then this sense of expectation, of being in motion or, better, of being moved, can become a means to this end. In the name of the economy of the gift, it challenges the world of property, the world of simple location, of the one-dimensional perception of reality in which only one mode of occupancy, the material, is allowed. Yet the economy of the gift also points to the limitations of the body which, as we have argued, only allows us to test and interpret experience in a partial way. By remaining faithful to the quest for the 'state of grace', 'fugitively glimpsed' but always the centre of her longing, Dobson is able to transcend these limitations. But it is also important that hers is essentially written rather than spoken poetry. Where the spoken word is immersed in the immediacy of social exchange, the written word lies hidden in a book, to be opened and read at diverse times and places. It generates its own life and is thus abstracted from the insistency of present surroundings and circumstances,[27] in touch rather with tradition and the abidingness of memory.

If it is true that the proper question to ask when one is lost is not 'where am I?' but, as Whitehead says, 'where are the other places?[28] then this sense of continuity moves Dobson to begin looking for the other places in the mythical word described by Pausanias in his *Guide to Greece* and in the poetry of the Russians who also learned to live through dark times and make poetry out of them.

If she still had her body but had lost her way, these poets, above all Mandelstam, reminded her that the self is elsewhere. Mandelstam was taken away by the Secret Police to Siberia where he disappeared. He questioned the state and the state destroyed him:

the line of the type broken, the letters scattered
like cramp-irons, as he called them, pincers, staples—
like bird-marks printing the page's final hard-packed
snow-drift. The journey ended in snow and silence.[29]

It is possible to wonder what affinity Rosemary Dobson, Australian woman and poet, living quietly in Canberra, discovered with this most desolate yet also most intransigent of poets. Yet intensity is qualitative, not quantitative, and the body's geography as it had opened out before her is always shadowed with death, the final goal of birth. Although it is altogether in a lighter mode, the sense of destiny, of being subject to necessity, in this case the necessity of death, is in its own way analogous to the situation of the Russian poet waiting for his ominous visitors. True, Dobson trusts still in her writing—'I would like first to write it all down and leave the pages/On the table weighted with a stone' (*SP* p. 116)—but necessity will take her where all this will be irrelevant:

Nevertheless I have put in a basket
The coins for the ferry.

The poem which follows this in the *Selected Poems* ('Cultural Meeting') underlies this, contrasting the superficialites of the

. . . long table . . ., pencils, glasses of water,
Deliberations, reports, heated exchanges,
And thoughtful, absent glances out of windows

with the foreign writer who speaks for the writers in exile, for 'those forgotten in camps and prisons'. But it also points to ways in which a poet like Dobson may find community with them. They do not belong to a country but to a people; to 'All those forbidden the bread of their own country;/Its wells and streams, its plunging ravenous rivers.' It is not, I think, excessive to link the final image of the exiled person—sitting beside the poet at lunch, speaking little but eating 'as one whose hunger would never be filled'—with the sense of exile with which Dobson's Preface to the *Selected Poems* concludes; the sense of having been turned away from the 'state of grace' she longs for, the 'doomed but urgent wish to express the inexpressible.'

Here and in the poems in *Over the Frontier* and *The Three Fates*, taking Mandelstam's point that 'there is no "I" without a we'[30] and that it is this community and thus this identity which is most threatened in this century of mass slaughter and concentration camps, she seeks for a community across space and time—in 'Praxilla, Yuna and the Cucumbers' (*OF* p. 8), for example, with the Greek poet Praxilla of Sikyon who left behind her three lines only, and the Russian poet, Yuna, writing in 1960 and dwelling 'upon time and mortality'—but what is perhaps most powerful about these poems is the way they combine a sense of loss with a sense of fullness, a sense of distance in time with a sense of contemporaneity. If inner space is woman's space, it can all too easily become vertiginous. In these poems Dobson keeps control by means of discovery rather than by invention—and, importantly, what she discovers is not so much things as persons: Praxilla, Yuna, the Greek archaeologists, Pronomos the flute player, even Helikonian Poseidon:

Earthquakes, Pausanias says, are of three kinds.
I know the third, described in human terms,
the deadliest kind: a man's breath coming fast
convulsions shaking him.
                  Look at my hands,
here, underneath the wrists. Hands shake just so
as fever and as force betray the heart—
so force and fever speak the coming shock. [31]

Once again it is the body which leads her across the frontier, to the 'wonder of being several' (Cixous), as well as to the mystery of being vulnerable. Earlier 'The Gods' (*SP* p. 114) had projected upon an everyday domestic scene—

The mother and the father sitting still
At evening by the fire with their books
Are gods that guard the temple, cut in stone
That neither moon, nor sun, nor time has changed,
Only the thin attrition of blown sand

—an intimation that even or perhaps especially in their simplest moments our lives are not our own but echoes, in a sense, of other lives, other occasions. True, in 'The Gods' this intimation is not treated entirely seriously, and there is something constraining about its implicit suggestion that the human being may be a mythic ensemble of imaginary figures each endowed with its own force: predetermination is the enemy of freedom. But the poems of *Over the Frontier* manage to reconcile the two.

The title poem, which opens this collection, announces this reconciliation, paying tribute at one and the same time to existence and non-existence. The poem that exists echoes the poem that does not, and concludes, wittily, with an image which reflects the scholastic notion of God as pure being, pure movement, at the same time as he is the unmoved mover of all things. This image grounds the assertion upon which the poem depends, that what is seen rests upon the unseen:

The outline of non-existence
can be held by the inner eye,
always moving, it assumes the shape of stillness.
So a plate spinning on a stick
is the essence of plate, a still one,
absolute plate with a fish on it.

Characteristically unpretentious, this poem represents an act of deconstruction, treating philosophical discourse as a kind of text, a signifying production to be read with an eye to its metaphoricity, its various levels and the inbuilt contradictions it refuses to acknowledge. Like Derrida, Dobson questions a metaphysics of presence in favour of absence which, as woman, she lays claim to as her own territory—significantly, *Over the Frontier* acknowledges a debt to the Polish poet Zbigniew Herbert.

In contrast with the confidence that patriarchal thought reposes in ideas, words, images, Dobson here sets herself to undermine the act of thinking, even of writing, thus undermining the fundamental presupposition of Western Culture; the belief in meaning, in the mind's ability to read the natural world and human experience alike as if they were books. In the 'strange new geography of death' there are no interpretations, only contradictions, and no one experience is subordinate to another. Both stillness and movement exist, both being and non-existence, as in the 'Koans' of Eastern thought. This disintellectualising move is a way of making something positive out of woman's identification with 'lack', her displacement into inner space, since it represents a move to the realm of the sacred.

Paradoxically, however, the gods she meets here are not the gods of nature, projections of natural events and needs, but presences experienced as absences, myths which tend to reduce one's life to silence rather than to express it. 'Knossos' (*OF* p. 6), for instance, begins:

Impossible to build the palace again over our heads,
the painted roof-beams, the cisterns, the great granary,
impossible to think of people living simply,
going about their errands in the sunshine,
the king receiving suppliants in the throne-room

and concludes:

Do not disturb the gods, do not disturb them
asking urgent and impossible questions.
This is the birthplace of Zeus, home of the snake-charming
dangerous goddess. Remember here also
Icarus flying too close to the sun.

The moment of grace is a moment of enlightenment, but an enlightenment into mystery, into what cannot be known but only experienced, cannot be spoken but only heard. It also offers confirmation of the freedom which had earlier seemed threatened, most especially by the body's subjection to necessity.

'The Artist's Wife' (*OF* p. 4), about a meeting with a woman whose daughter has been killed at twenty-three, confronts this subjection. The freedom that is discovered here is something given, not something that originates in the self. The grieving mother writes out her grief in poetry and the poet, grieving for her grief, offers her a poem. In it she attempts if not to elucidate then at least to point the order in which their grief is contained and which exists entirely independent of them. But it is precisely this independence which justifies it just as the poetry 'shapes its movement to the love', not to the grief, and 'One sees the words aspiring for perfection':

since only the perfect is enough to give
and giving is the crown, the act, the purpose,
the meaning and the imagery of love
which makes a lesser burden of acceptance.

Woman's economy, as I have been arguing, is the economy of the gift. But it is also for this reason the economy of mystery. The grave movement of the lines belies the complexity of the thought because they point beyond themselves to 'that grave dance in which we all take part'. The notion of mystery arises out of a logical and rigorous use of intelligence which leads to an impasse, and a contradiction which is inescapable in the sense that the suppression of one term, death and grief, makes the other, the love and the poem, meaningless, and that to pose the one entails posing the other. It is then that, in the words of Simone Weil, 'like a lever, the notion of mystery carries thought beyond the impasse, to the other side of the unopenable door, beyond the domains of intelligence and above it'.[32]

All this is abstruse, though the abstruseness is carried lightly and expressed lucidly. Perhaps, after all, it is Pausanias and his *Guide to Greece* that serve to lead Dobson back to the common life that has always been her great concern. Yet, as Peter Levi notes in his Introduction to the *Guide*, Pausanias's work was undertaken

in the attempt to satisfy a deeper anxiety which had once been apprehended
in religious terms. The collapse of ancient religion or some deeper collapse
was the unspoken object of his studies.[33]

What Dobson found in him had something to do, it seems, with a similar anxiety she found in herself, the longing for 'a state of grace which one once knew, or imagined, or from which one was turned away':

This most I envy, most would emulate,
the watchful eye, the trained receptive ear,
the mind that waits illumination, waits
to see, though blind; though deaf, at last to hear.[34]

So, too, less obliquely, more conversationally, but just as surely, Dobson turns later, in *The Three Fates* ('A Letter to Lydia'), to Greece as a place of analogy, looking

> . . . *for ways by which to understand*
> *My origins; for ground whereon to stand*
> *With poetry for a divining-branch.*[35]

Here, perhaps, she is writing less as a woman than as an Australian— the analogy with Greece is very important also for writers as different as Patrick White and George Johnston. Nevertheless, if flying, as Cixous insists,[36] is woman's gesture, Dobson has always been troubled by the figure of Icarus. Besides, it is still necessary to find one's own ground for taking off and landing, especially if one takes the point of Cixous' pun on the word *voler* and sees woman also as stealing—stealing away from the given world as well as robbing it for her own needs and pleasures. Certainly 'A Letter to Lydia' makes clear that this final ground is not the world of commonsense. Rejecting fashion, the 'rejected cultures and impoverished lives' of consumer society, she looks elsewhere for a paradigm, to find it in the island of Crete, both as place and image:

> *Pulses of scent and shimmerings of sight*
> *Move ever outwards in concentric rings*
> *Circling the island.*

At this point, art in which she has trusted begins to give way before the pressure of sheer being. What saves her, however, is the woman's gesture, flight, even if her wings, like Icarus', may be fragile:

> . . . *How begin to write*
> *Unless like Ikaros my words take wings*
> *To fall from such impossible endeavour*
> *Down down, and drown in silences forever,*
> *Or to be immolated in the eye of light.*

What remains, rather, is a memory of simple, earthly things—the meal in the two roomed house past midnight when

>   . . . With a noble sense
> Of dignity the mother of the household offered
> What food there was. Raki and bread were proffered
> And ewe's milk cheese. And so we were well fed

and her walks in the mountains:

> The scent of aromatic herbs dispersed
> Like rising light from fractures in the stone.

It seems to me that the uncharacteristically expansive and unselfconscious 'A Letter to Lydia', longer than any other single poem in Dobson's oeuvre, proclaims her arrival at last in secure possession of her own space. The rest of the poems in *The Three Fates*, Dobson's prize-winning collection, are written from here. Not that this is in any sense an easy or protected place. Her affinity with the Russians Mandelstam and Akhmatova remains, and the sense of life remains tragic—the moving sequence 'The Continuance of Poetry', dedicated to David Campbell, her collaborator in those translations, grows out of his illness and death. Yet the country of death here is a fertile one, lyrical with the presences which only absence makes possible. In 'After Receiving the Book of Poems by Li Po' (*TF* p. 46), for example, subject is taken up into a larger subject. The reality of a dry river bed, the fallen needles of she-oaks and the smell of dry resin is both what it is for itself and what it is as it is taken up also into the poems of Li Po, contributing objective data for the experience of other kinds of possibilities which open out as the poem concludes:

> Not being able to find the hermit he wanted to visit
> Li Po looked deeper into the landscape.
> Like Li Po we lean against a pine-tree;
> And looking into the landscape find your poems.

What is lost continues to affect us, has assumed a function in the process of generating new meaning by the challenge it offers to language and commonsense. The exactness of language here dramatises the absence it is concerned with, evacuating all that is merely emotional or shadowy—for Rosemary Dobson, as she declares in 'A Letter to Lydia', mystery is a matter of lucidity, the 'austerity and light' which 'detain/My heart, my longing, intellect and sight.' But it also renders the integral nature of the experience, expresses its general form, divested of irrelevant detail. Even as the poem honours the world of appearances, it undermines it, being concerned, as always, with pattern and relationships.

The predominant note of these poems, then, is their intelligence, an intelligence so strong that it encompasses its own defeat at the hands of mortality and vulnerability. This, of course, represents the high point of her task as woman to speak herself as woman. It can be seen in the tense understatement of 'The Letter' (*TF* p. 24) with its beginning:

I have read the letter
And learnt about the illness.
Carefully I walk outside and stand under the grapevine
Wondering why I am there

and after refusing the cheap comfort of any analogy with the life of nature—

The grapes are unripe,
Not ready for picking.
I cut down a cluster.
No, not ready.

—concludes austerely:

Who, then? Fate? Justice?
No, there is no justice in it.

But it can also be seen in the conceit of the poem 'The Three Fates' in which the man drowning invokes the three sisters and is given his life to live over again—backwards and forwards ceaselessly. There may be no justice in it, but living subject to necessity is the only way to the order she celebrates and finds her strength in. Not that all these poems are dark. There are poems about willows, suburban mornings, waiting for the postman in a garden where

Plums fallen to the ground
Are singing with sweetness.
Bees are busy in them.

There are poems, too, about visiting friends, poems about New York which, resisting the move to sensationalism, find it a human place, poems about museums, a wonderful poem ('Folding the Sheets') about love and friendship. Nevertheless, the full possession of bodiliness here also means that a sense of loss or at least limitation prevails. Art, of course, is a matter of limitation, of the limits that make for intensity on the one hand and truthfulness on the other. 'Flute Music', for instance, like the music of the poet described in the poem playing his flute as he walked to the place of execution, dances the more lightly for the limits it works within, dramatised by the brief stanzas, the limits of being mortal. So too, in 'The Eater of the Pomegranate Seeds' (*TF* p. 13), Eurydice, dressed like a campanula,

. . . *swinging as a bell swings*
Back and away in time with her hastening, hastening,

becomes more beautiful against the darkness into which she is descending.

In contrast with other women poets who have been overborne by death, loss and the pressures of physical necessity, Rosemary Dobson's achievement here is to transform the world of death, loneliness and the fragility of innocence by means of a complex set of coherent judgements, the product of the contradictory range of her experience and of a deeper intuition of some ultimate mystery. As Northrop Frye remarks, a serious human life can hardly begin until we see an element of illusion in what is really there and something real in fantasies about what might be there instead. So, to conclude, we might take the unpretentious 'Waiting for the Postman' (*TF* p. 20). Ecstatic bees, busy about her in the fallen plums, pursue their own lives. They do not for her, as they did for Sylvia Plath, offer analogies of the self either in its terrors or its joys. She remains other, waiting for the moment of grace (it is perhaps relevant that for Plato in the *Ion* bees are associated with wisdom and with the gift of poetry). For Dobson, who has renounced the mode of Prometheus and chosen the mode of Eurydice, the wisdom lies in the waiting. But the waiting is charged with ironic self-awareness and a firm sense of her place in the world and a commitment to it. The bees are excited, expecting the arrival of a new queen whose coming they sense by some special gift, some extra-sensory perception. But for the mere poet, the human woman, there is a longer, possibly inconclusive wait; for the postman first, but finally for some other message which may or may not arrive:

For my neighbour's hive a queen
Maybe Monday, Tuesday.
For me, someday, a message.

This may seem a strange note upon which to conclude. But it is an entirely characteristic one—characteristic, moreover, of Dobson's achievement and peculiar strength, which is to let other languages, the languages of experience, speak. As I see it, her work, private and personal as it is, nevertheless explodes the notion of poetry as the expression of a merely individual gift. The dedication to her craft, the 'long loneliness' (a phrase of Mandelstam's), the austerity and discipline nevertheless enable her to speak out of a complex framework of memory, experience and relationship, as part of that great community from which both her admired Mandelstam and Akhmatova also speak, the community of the outcast and the oppressed or, less dramatically, of those who stand to one side, the bystanders. In this sense, of course, she does not speak only for women, yet her writing raises precisely those questions of sexuality and textuality, of genre and gender, of psycho-sexual identity and cultural and social authority which are central to discussions of woman's writing.[37] In this way her work is at one and the same time feminine and universal, a process which is also a goal, in the words written about the poet George Seferis by his translator Walter Kaiser, words Dobson has taken for her own: 'to know and accept who one really is, to understand one's place in history, to create poetry out of tragic times, to learn the meaning of love, to persist in the "long journey".'[38]

NOTES

1. *The Three Fates and Other Poems* (Hale & Iremonger, Sydney, 1984), p.28. This collection is henceforth cited in my text as *TF*.
2. 'Dislodging a World View: Challenge and Counter-challenge in the Relationship Between Feminism and Anthropology', *Australian Feminist Studies* 1 (Summer 1985), p. 2.
3. Elizabeth Lawson, *The Slanted View: Some Perspectives of Alienation in Modern Poetry* (Unpublished PhD thesis: University of Western Australia, 1982).
3A. Rosemary Dobson, *Selected Poems* (Angus & Robertson, Sydney, 1973).
4. Elaine Showalter, 'Feminist Criticism in the Wilderness', *Critical Inquiry* 8 (Winter 1981), p. 192.
5. David Campbell and Rosemary Dobson, *Moscow Trefoil* (Australian National University Press, Canberra, 1975), p. viii-ix.
6. c.f. Sandra M. Gilbert and Susan Gubar, *The Madwoman in the Attic: The Woman Writer and the Nineteenth Century Literary Imagination* (Yale University Press, New Haven, 1979), as quoted in Showalter, p. 187.
7. Hélène Cixous, 'The Laugh of the Medusa', *Journal of Women in Culture and Society* 1.4 (1976), p. 889.
8. Ibid.
9. Rosemary Dobson, *Over the Frontier* (Angus and Robertson, Sydney, 1978), p.3. This collection henceforth cited in my text as *OF*.
10. Adrian Mitchell, 'A Frame of Reference: Rosemary Dobson's Grace Notes for Humanity', *Australian Literary Studies* 10.1 (1985), p. 5.
11. See Cixous, p. 877.
12. Ibid, p. 882.
13. Ibid. Cixous' translator here notes '*dépense*, a neologism, formed on

the verb *penser*, hence "unthinks", but also "spends" (from *depenser*)'.

14. trans. Marilyn A. August, in *New French Feminisms*, ed. Elaine Marks and Isabelle de Courtivron (Harvester Press, Brighton, 1980), pp. 162–63, and quoted by Showalter, p.191.
15. Cixous, p.884.
16. Ibid., p.889.
17. Quoted by Showalter as the epigraph to her essay, p.179.
18. Hester Eisenstein, *Contemporary Feminist Thought* (Unwin Paperbacks, Sydney, 1984), p.4.
19. Edward Said, *Beginnings* (Basic Books, New York, 1975), p.88.
20. Cixous, p.877.
21. 'Unnatural Naturalism', *The Age Monthly Review* 5.11 (April 1986), p.7.
22. Quoted in Eric O. Springstead, 'Contradiction, Mystery and the Use of Words in Simone Weil', *Religion and Literature* 17.2 (Summer 1985), p. 1.
23. Ibid., p.3.
24. Ibid., p.1.
25. See Lyman Lundeen, *Risk and Rhetoric in Religion* (Fortress Press, Philadelphia, 1972), pp.79–80.
26. Showalter, p.189.
27. Lundeen, p.57.
28. Ibid., p.164.
29. 'Reading Mandelstam', *OF* p. 18.
30. Nadezdha Mandelstam, *Hope Abandoned: A Memoir*, trans. Max Hayward (Penguin, Harmondsworth, 1976), p.17.
31. 'Helikonian Poseidon', *OF* p. 37.
32. Springstead, p.6.
33. Pausanias, *Guide to Greece: Volume 2, Southern Greece* (Penguin, Harmondsworth, 1971), p.3.
34. 'Of Pausanias', *OF* p. 27.
35. *TF* p. 28.
36. Cixous, p.887.
37. Showalter, p.183.
38. In the Foreword to Seferis's *Three Secret Poems* (Harvard University Press, Cambridge, Mass., 1969).

CAUGHT IN THE DRAUGHT
BURNING BUSH AND BLOWING WIND

My title is meant to provoke thought. When you think of it, we are all 'caught in the draught'. The word 'draught' is a better spelling than 'draft' because it reflects its origins, being the past participle of the Old Teutonic word 'dragon', to draw. What the phrase implies, then, is that we are all, to a greater or lesser extent, drawn into the process of culture, mass-media culture, which flows around us and through us, persuading us to consume, compete and console ourselves with mostly mindless pleasures. Far from being secular, this culture is organised to the worship of the unholy trinity of Mammon (God of money), Moloch (God of struggle and violence) and Marilyn Monroe (the human sacrifice to the God of mindless pleasure). Imagination has seized power with a vengeance, ruling people from within by means of their desires. Power grows now not, as Chairman Mao said, out of the barrel of a gun but out of a cathode-ray tube.

Similarly, it could be said that the wars of this century have been religious wars, as the great scientific thinker Sir Karl Popper argued. The main troubles of our time he said, are and have been due not to our moral wickedness but to our often misguided moral enthusiasm. Our wars have generally been between competing theories of how to establish a better world, thus George Bush went to war on behalf of the 'American way of life', confident that God was on his side while Saddam Hussein for his part saw himself as the champion of Islam. The fact that on the Iraqi side the religious rhetoric was about dreams of conquest and on the American side with dreams of profit—having devastated the region Western companies are making millions of dollars building it up again—does not change the religious nature of the beliefs which sanctioned them.

All this may sound contentious, mere 'wild and whirling words'. Before we go any further, therefore, let us define 'religion', using the careful definition by the anthropologist Clifford Gertz. According to him, religion is 'a system of symbols which act to establish powerful, persuasive and long-lasting moods and motivations, by formulating conceptions of a general order of existence and clothing these conceptions with such an aura of factuality that the moods and motivations seem uniquely realistic'.

This, is where the value of scepticism on the one hand and of the arts on the other begins to emerge. A sceptic is one who questions certainties, doubting whether absolute knowledge is ever attainable. In this sense scepticism is not so much a fixed position as a starting point. Kant, for instance, associates the sceptic with the nomad who traverses a territory instead of occupying it and settling down. Nor is it a belief to be justified or attacked. Rather it is a habit of mind, something like being a reader, trying to interpret, and make sense of existence, ready all the time to revise one's position. By definition, I would argue, art, therefore, has to do with scepticism since what it does is make us aware and capable of our mortality, what Heidegger calls our 'Unshieldedness', the fact that we live in bodies, which for all their great abilities and powers are subject to pain, sickness and death as well as to fierce joys, and live nevertheless in this subjection with 'immortal longings'. Think, for example, of the vision of great tragedies like *Hamlet* or *King Lear* or, more recently, of the poignant exposure of self in a novel like Patrick White's *The Twyborn Affair*, summed up, ironically, that is, properly sceptically, in its cheeky epigraph: 'Sometimes you'll see someone with nothing on but a band-aid'. In the same vein we might think of Peter Cowan's novel, *The Hills of Apollo Bay*, in which the pain lies rather in the concealment and understatement, in the sense of loss and unknowing and bewilderment which pervades it.

Art—and here I shall limit the discussion to the art of the written word, to literature—is profoundly sceptical, then, of the claims of mere rationality and technology, and aware of the mystery of existence itself and of our position within it. Like Wittgenstein, the artist is aware that the wonder is not so much how things are, but that they are in the first place. It speaks to us not merely through our minds but in and through our bodies, making us conscious that we exist not just in our minds or within our culture but in the world as a whole, conscious, that is, of our fatedness, our mortality, but also of the richness of the common life we share with all other living creatures.

To put it in slogan form, art leads us in Patrick White's words, to 'know what we do not know', to be aware with the whole body, the evidence of all senses, not just of the mind but also with intuition, of the sense of what cannot be put into words but is experienced intensely and intimately. In this sense it has to do with faith, commitment to 'realities at present unseen' rather than with the certainties of 'religion' as we have defined it. To the extent that it generates a sense of strangeness, of otherness, to that extent it points in the direction of the holy, of that 'mysterium tremendum et fascinans', that mystery which makes us tremble yet draws us to it with intense longing, symbolised by the burning bush of Exodus, burning yet never consuming itself.

As I see it, this is what all major art is about. Patrick White put it this way, for instance, in his autobiography, *Flaws in the Glass:*

What do I believe? I am accused of not making it explicit. How to be explicit about a grandeur too overwhelming to express, a daily wrestling match with an opponent whose limbs never become material, a struggle from which the sweat and blood are scattered on the pages of anything the serious writer writes?

Another writer, the poet Vincent Buckley, refers quite specifically to the symbol of the burning bush as the centre of his art:

When the bush burns to ashes
I must touch my forehead to the ground still,
Because its radiance is in my body.

What makes a major artist, I would submit, is this sense of self and life as dialectical, not one-dimensional, open to the interplay of what is other, what cannot ever be put fully into words. Hence Rimbaud's enigmatic 'Je est un autre' (I *is* another). Hence, too, White's description of the musician Moraitis, playing the cello in

The Aunt's Story: 'he wore an expression of sleep and solitary mirrors. The sun was in his eyes, the sky has passed between his bones'. Perhaps the most vivid expression of this sense of self as somehow from time to time swooped upon, claimed by an otherness which transfigures and breaks open the ordinary, sometimes with joy and sometimes with terror, even with squalor, is Robert Adamson's 'Drawn with Light'.[1]

The poem begins with the image of an owl swooping low over the city, hooking a rat from a lane, 'owl-eyes adrift, drawn by moonlight'. But the eyes and the moonlight fuse into an image of fire, a sense of some 'silent language' beyond us in an 'age of precious mumblings', of the 'clever emblems' of advertisers and politicians, of:

Sports heroes, suspended in the air
to sell alcohol, pictures of sleek yachts
their spinnakers ablaze
with multicoloured jingocam

Beyond all this, however, beyond the 'Streets of homeless, suburbs of living dead', we are drawn to some frightening power and intensity for which the owl becomes the symbol; the power and intensity of art:

. . . Drawn with light
so that the image perfects itself
in our seeing it—Drawn out from dark
to make bright images of life in our livings
lucidity, clear fire.

What is powerful in this poem is not just what it says but what it points to, something unspeakable, a silence beyond words, what one cannot say but can only become. Wittgenstein was aware of this: 'We should not try to communicate the incommunicable', he wrote, 'that will be futile. That which is unsaid in what we have said will manifest itself by its silence'. It can perhaps only be spoken in the silence which a poem like this makes around itself, the break with and the intensification of everyday language, transforming sign into symbol.

The world thus becomes multiple, not single. Not that art is thus other-worldy. If there is another world, as Paul Eduard says, it is in this one, in its intensification. Nothing is necessarily commonplace or boring since, to quote Blake, 'everything that lives is holy', full of possible significance—as so-called 'primitive' cultures have always known. 'Cursed be he (or she),' Blake said, to whom a 'line is merely up and down'. Or, as Shakespeare's Horatio has it, 'there are more things in heaven and earth than are dreamed of' in a merely materialistic philosophy.

One result of this awareness can be the sense of exile, of living in a world from which the gods seem to have withdrawn, expressed, for example, in Shane McCauley's poem 'Delphi'.[2]

Pythian Apollo has long been evicted,
Statues taken to Constantinople and lost.
The cliff from which Aesop plunged looks
Calm enough, the sunlight clear.
Laurel trees crown the ageing marble.

A place of inscriptions and griffins, dried
Libations, green tripods, a crumbling
Stadium. Time here does not stand still,
But gathers up its fragments like memories,
Preserves names, is an enigmatic guide.

So even the most pragmatic of religions
Is consigned here to shattered rocks
And columns littering the hill, piles of
discarded Bones. We try to catch echoes on the wind.
There are none. We photograph silences.

The epigraph to McCauley's book *The Butterfly Man*, from Rainer Maria Rilke, points to the properly religious sense implicit here:

Alarmed within by the distant thunder of the god,
bewildered from without by any irresistible excess
of appearances, the object of such violent treatment
has only just room to stand on the narrow
space between two worlds, until suddenly
a neutral little event inundates his
monstrous condition with innocence.

Belief of this kind is the other side of scepticism, of disbelief in the crowding preoccupation with property, power and possessions. One begins to understand what Jesus meant when he said that unless we 'become as little children' we would not 'enter the Kingdom of Heaven'. Children know, as all art knows, that what we call 'real' is what we agree to do so, and that this 'reality' depends on the stories we believe in. As Nietzsche remarked, therefore, 'we possess art lest we perish by the truth'.

In effect, art reminds us life is stranger, more beautiful, demanding, joyous and painful than commonsense knows. Gwen Harwood's 'Bone Scan', for instance, turns the threat of serious illness and an X-ray into a kind of apocalypse.[3]

In the twinkling of an eye,
in a moment, all is changed:
on a small radiant screen
(honeydew melon green)
are my scintillating bones.
Still in my flesh I see
the God who goes with me
glowing with radioactive
isotopes. This is what he
at last allows a mortal
eye to behold: the grand
supporting frame complete
(but for the wisdom teeth),
the friend who lives beneath
appearances, alive

with light. Each glittering bone
assures me: you are known.

The seemingly irreverent identification of the X-ray with the Last Judgment is, in fact, an index not only of courage but also of the sceptical faith which affirms the full 'privilege and panic of mortality' (W.H. Auden).

In another vein Philip Salom's *The Barbecue of the Primitives*[4] presents a barbecue as a primitive ritual. Standing 'in a roughish circle: a row of backs/a muddling Stonehenge', the people here are worshipping fire, some strange potency which 'pre-empts the liquor, and perhaps the light as/the city stands fifty dry kilometres towards the coast, under the radiation of what it means to be human'. Cars and the very insects turn into living things as the poem concludes, ominously, even menacingly: 'Something is being counted off, by ones'.

The sacred is not something static but dynamic, not just a source of consolation. Some people, as the medieval mystic Eckhart said, want to love God in the same way they love a cow, for what he gives and for their own profit. But this poem introduces us to the danger of belief, the sense that the world may be other than we think. As Vincent Buckley remarked, believing is not like belonging to a football team: it involves a sharp sense of living in a universe much larger than we know, or can control, exposure to 'the radiation of what it means to be human'.

The holy, then, is mysterious. That underlies the vision of tragedy and, indeed of any good novel which gives us a glimpse into the mysteries of human relationships. It also underlies the sense of the world which arises from a poem like John Kinsella's 'Notes on Fire-Tumbles'.[5]

What this poem suggests is what the scientist knows—the ancient and complex strangeness of the earth. As a poet, however, Kinsella is able to put this into words:

> *i*
> *Fire-tumbles roll inward*
> *from a desert's edge.*

At first they appear as
Cart-wheeling spinifex,

later, flame beyond sight
takes hold, enthralled.

ii
It has been said their substance is
of lost forest—

breath of dried air
unable to take hold.

Consumed, moved in wind.
Sand.

iii
Back through shadow
they stretch sunset
to unimaginable limits:

enveloped sky,
cinnabar of abyss.

iv
Eyes harden and fall.
Fire-tumbles, seen in
vision, last an instant.

In desert the light
of fission lingers.

v
Fire tumbles are not poetry,
nor even a substitute for poetry.

228

They are things wild
whose wanderings
are without motive

But this sense of strangeness can arise out of the very familiar also, as in Rosemary Dobson's 'Folding the Sheets' in which this simple domestic chore becomes an echo of the action of the cosmos itself, the warp and woof of things—the action of weaving and unweaving, making and unmaking we glimpse also at the conclusion of Helen Garner's perfect little novel *The Children's Bach*.[6]

You and I will fold the sheets
Advancing towards each other
From Burma, from Lapland,

From India where the sheets have been washed in the river
And pounded upon stones:
Together we will match the corners.

From China where women on either side of the river
Have washed their pale cloth in the
White Stone Shallows
'Under the shining moon'.

We meet as though in the formal steps of a dance
To fold the sheets together, put them to air
In wind, in sun over bushes, or by the fire.

We stretch and pull from one side and then the other—
Your turn. Now mine.
We fold them and put them away until they are needed.

A wish for all people when they lie down in bed—
Smooth linen, cool cotton, the fragrance and stir of herbs
And the faint but perceptible scent of sweet clear water.

We need our artists, then, to remind us not only of who we are but also of what the world is. The real question for most of us, after all, is not economic or political, much less technological, but existential, the question of what Conrad calls 'the heart pain, the world pain . . . How to be?'. Put another way it is a question of value, and some are more important than others. First and least important are what he calls pleasure values, what is agreeable or disagreeable to the individual. Economic values, for example, come under this heading. Next come group values, those which promote health, vitality and social well-being. Politics is or ought to be concerned with these. For most people in our society these two sets of values are all that they know. But beyond them, we ought to be concerned with spiritual or cultural values, with whatever it is that words like 'beauty', 'justice', 'truth', 'honour' and so on point to. Most important of all, however, are the sacred values, the sense of the numinous we have been discussing, a sense of the sheer mystery of the cosmos and our existence in it. The society or culture which knows nothing of this value, he would argue, has no right to be called civilised because it knows nothing of the space, the maze within us. This maze according to David Brooks who explores it in his strange and powerful stories and poems, at once erotic and religious, is where we really dwell, and the way into it, as he says, is as important as the way out. Finding this way, however, has to do with language, with the attentiveness which is able to hear the silence within and beyond words, the reverence Vincent Buckley expresses:

I walk beside these fires because I must,
In pain and troubling sometimes thanking God
For what they give me, the few poems
That are the holy species of my life.[7]

Then, indeed, we can be 'bounded in a nut shell' and count ourselves Kings (or Queens) of infinite space, knowing that, as Shakespeare has it:

. . . We are such stuff
As dreams are made on, and our little life
Is sounded with a sleep.

We conclude, then, with another of Philip Salom's poems, 'Thinking of Rendra', thinking of all those like Rendra, an Indonesian poet imprisoned by his government, who nevertheless lives with us in this mysterious house of language.[8]

As Mahomet said, talking of location—
Spirit (and I rephrase, for writers—Language)
lives closer in you than your jugular.

In that country so attuned to music there are intervals so sensitive to spirit
the keys play silent. Jail for counterpoint.

Years before, writers had by order to juggle
a central, bastard language, because their own
was taken from them. Silence for counterpoint.

To juggle with a central or bastard conscience,
to speak at all, was knowing the sensual and the fierce
throat of utterance, locked from counterpoint.

The state is central as the lamp in shadowy wayang.
where characters are more than silhouettes,
ancient
as status quo. Where one voice is many voices.

The saron's tongues are pinched by fingers
thumbs, and bonangs stand in their brassiness like a row
of breasts, or soon more truly like a row of heads.

As the players at the centre strike down so exactly
the padded hammers, so certain they can tell
where the gongs finish and the heads begin.

The wayang plays, the gamelan plays, counterpoint
holds, and the shunned voices rattle in the night,
spit and burn like glow-worms in the throat.

NOTES

1. Robert Adamson, *The Clean Dark* (Paperback Press, Sydney, 1989), pp. 60–1.
2. Shane McCauley, *The Butterfly Man* (Fremantle Arts Centre Press, Perth, 1991) p. 55.
3. Gwen Harwood, *Bone Scan* (Angus & Robertson, Sydney, 1988), p. 8.
4. Philip Salom, *The Barbecue of the Primitives* (University of Queensland Press, Brisbane, 1989), p. 68.
5. John Kinsella, *Parrots* (Fremantle Arts Centre Press, Perth, 1989), pp. 31–2.
6. Rosemary Dobson, *The Three Fates and Other Poems* (Hale & Iremonger, Sydney, 1984), p. 23.
7. Vincent Buckley, 'Ghosts, Places, Stones, Questions', in Alexander Gray (ed) *Twelve Poets 1950–1970*. (Milton, Queensland, Jacaranda Press 1971), p. 59.
8. Salom, p. 68.

MALOUF'S AN IMAGINARY LIFE

Religion, it seems, is a scandal that refuses to go away, even in the most secular of societies. As Victor Turner observes, it cannot be dispelled by magical incantation but cannot be reduced either to nonsense by positivist or linguistic philosophy.[1] The impulse continues and must be acknowledged and lived through, especially perhaps in a secular society since it has to do with negative or midliminal experience of the kind which provoked Wittgenstein's famous aphorism, 'whereof we cannot speak, thereof we must remain silent', experiences as common to the unbeliever as to the believer.

In India, or at least in traditional India, this kind of awareness is taken for granted, perhaps necessarily so, if it is the case that religion begins with thinking about the universe. Interestingly, however, it is beginning to manifest itself also in Australian literature, as well as in our music and painting—think, for instance, of Fairweather, Boyd and, to a lesser extent, Nolan. Patrick White is probably the best known of such writers, concerned, indeed preoccupied, with the question of the divine. But so, too, are many others, Randolph Stow, David Malouf, Tim Winton, and, differently but just as intensely if more ambiguously, women writers like Beverly Farmer, Helen Garner, Jessica Anderson and, amongst the poets, Antigone Kefala. Indeed, their situation as women which sets them somewhat outside the structures of power, and with it, of what belief there is, often gives their work an affinity with Eastern as distinct from Western religious thinking. For them as women, life is full of a sense of this ambiguity; of the redoublings and reflections, of the play between self and other, loss and longing which is characteristic of Hinduism and, to a lesser extent, of Buddhism. In this essay, however, I want to look at the work of David Malouf and in particular at *An Imaginary Life*, a novella which seems to me to be closer than any other Australian work I know to Hindu thought, in particular to its non-dualistic, non-judgmental and multivalent sense of reality.

From the beginning of his career, Malouf's imagination appears to have been fascinated by religion, by the multiple possibilities of divinity, though also with their loss and, mostly, disguising this sense of loss with the pose of an ironic agnosticism. The poem 'Mythologies', for instance, opens:

In the old days it was easy:
enough to recognise
a god or two benignly
winking above the sill, barely surprise
if a bull you stroked
with blue eyes and a love curl
between his horns tried it
on or a swan came thwacking
your thighs.

But its conclusion is desolate enough:

Old charms laid out
in the sun catch nothing
but a headcold or a bad case of sunburn. For both
of which we have remedies:[2]

This desolation, ironically concealed yet perhaps therefore the more intense, arises from a sense that if the gods do not exist, then there is no real truth to be had, for it is their power which gives language its power, making words more a kind of charm than a sense of information.

Malouf's permanent concern with language springs perhaps from this intuition, from his desire to rescue words from their exile amongst abstractions and restore them to their proper relation to the living world of things as well as of people. It is because of this exile, he implies, that:

Legends nowadays are hard to get started
and the gods aren't easy
to believe in, let alone
offend (p. 88).

A world which is nameless is also speechless and the comment, 'Nature alas/leaves much to be desired' occurs, significantly therefore, in a poem entitled 'A Critique of Pure Reason' (p. 120). Mere reason cannot bring nature back to life. What is needed is a new sensitivity, an openness to the mysterious multiplicity of being, to the music of things which is celebrated, for instance, in 'Harmonica Mundi', which begins:

Here, take a tuning fork, throw it
down and hear the planet
hum: A natural. Vibrations scatter
from Mont Blanc towards
the limits, a tinkling
of ice at either pole (p. 122).

Things for Malouf demand speech, indeed signify speech. But it is the speech of what is other, not just what is familiar. This strangeness, implicit in the familiar, is what is pointed to in 'Off the Map', the speech of:

—black piers, bright water—silos
moonstruck, pointing nowhere
like saints practising stillness
in the ripple of grain.

The words which finally matter are about this kind of 'nowhere', to be found in the most ordinary places, in the mystery, for example, of:

. . . new streets that shine
in the eyes of farmboys, cities . . .

alive only a nightfall
that span a continent. Nameless. Not to be found by day on any map
(pp. 62–4).

This is the place which the poet, Ovid, is searching for in *An Imaginary Life*, 'the very edge of things, where nothing begins'.[3] Religious thought both of the West and of the East is also preoccupied with it. Indeed, it is in a sense its goal, since it is the place of encounter between self and other, the other which is not entirely outside the self yet also not entirely within it but which flows backwards and forward between the two, demanding recognition yet easily denied or ignored. Malouf is clear, however. The presences which meet us here are what we have dreamed of 'in our deepest lives and they are ourselves.' (p. 28).

As he develops it, this sense of depth is closer to Eastern than Western thought since the otherness he perceives is not absolute and self is neither separate nor fixed but caught up in the flow of being, concerned as fluid, indefinable, even illusory:

It is as if each creature had the power to dream itself out of one existence into a new one, a step higher in the ladder of things. Having conceived in our sleep the idea of a further being. Our bodies find, slowly, painfully, the physical process that will allow them to break their bonds and leap up to it (p. 29).

But, initially at least, this emphasis falls on the human side of the equation. As we shall see, *An Imaginary Life* begins sceptically, in the mind of a worldly-wise poet. But in his poetry also, the focus at first seems to be more psychological than religious. The longing is to rescue what is unconscious and unspoken in order to speak it into consciousness, but also, paradoxically, to rescue consciousness from its exile in a world in which:

We turn aside from miracles
to the plain facts of a case, having put ourselves
in service to this and that, the denominative

clowns who are double agents in an affair
more actual fabulous of is and were.

This speaking thus moves away from certainty, involving the kind of loss which the opening of the poem from which we have just quoted suggests:

The new day finds us here. We have come down
from the high lands of sleep in the company
of dreams, shy beasts whose scene is still upon us
invisibly we herd them, feel the heat of
their breath (pp 132–4).

This could, of course, be read as the secular irony of self-awareness expressed in Lacan's aphorism: 'I think where I am not because I am where I do not think, and I am where I am the plaything of my thought. I think of what I am where I do not think to live.'[4] But that, of course, also involves an awareness of loss. As Lacan also puts it, 'I am someone who has lost something'. For Malouf, it seems, this 'something', for all his agnosticism—perhaps even because of it— has to do with what he calls 'the gods', part literary conceit yet also part object of his desire. His longing is for some kind of revelation, and what is revealed is something. As Etienne Gilson writes:

It is quite impossible to come to the act-of-being by an intellectual intuition
which grasps it directly, and grasps nothing more. To think is to conceive.
But the proper object of a concept is always an essence *or something*
presenting itself to thought as an essence, in brief, an object.[5]

So Malouf continues to carry on what Sartre called 'la grande affaire', the 'scandal' of theological survival even in a secular age, the scandal evident in a writer like him, willing, in Wallace Stevens's words:

to be stripped of every fiction save one.
The fiction of an absolute.[6]

So we come to *An Imaginary Life*, the clearest but also perhaps the most lyrical expression of this 'reality hunger' in Malouf's work, at one and the same time personal and yet also strangely impersonal. It may be, as Malouf says, that it is:

Out of the dark
we bring these fictions forth to explain ourselves
before bicycles and clocks. The dynasties
are marked out on our palm (p. 134).

But it is also the case that for him, as we have seen, self is also somehow other, in Lacan's sense, in the sense of Rimbaud's famous 'Je est un autre'. His main character, Ovid, is a poet, as he is, though dead, it is true, 2000 years ago, also living in exile,[7] a self and not-self, caught up in the endless process of transformation and transmigration which the original Ovid described in his *Metamorphoses* and which the novel clearly argues for also. Dead yet in a fictional sense still alive, fictional and non-fictional, speaking in equivocal language which has been composed for him by another, this character addresses the reader as someone living in another century, which is, of course, our century, writing a letter, which he says he will never send but, which is sent for him by the text, writing:

to you, unknown friend, who do not exist at the time of my writing and whose face, whose form even, I cannot imagine. Can one imagine the form of a god? For that surely is what you must be at your great distance from us—the god who has begun to stir in our depths, to gather his being out of us, and will, at the other end of the great cycle that has rocked our world with its quakings, have evolved at last and come into being (p. 18).

Most Western readers find this fascinating but puzzling, bound, as we are, into unitary notions of time, space and self and into the logic of non-contradiction. But the sense of self as multiple, as process rather than entity 'like smoke/drifting up at dawn', as Malouf puts it in the poem 'A Poet Among Others', (p. 176) is familiar to Eastern thought in general, and to the Hindu tradition in particular. The very notion central to that tradition, 'That Thou Art', the identification of the divine and the soul—the elision of subject-object absorbed into some larger reality, is implicit here, though it is true, in a highly ambiguous way. But Vedantic thought is no stranger, of course, to ambiguity. Revelation is always also conceal-ment as Krishna's words in the *Gita* imply:

Foolish people despise me
When taking a human body
They ignore my high being
As the great Lord of beings (Gita, 9, 11).

What is revealed at the end of *An Imaginary Life* is similarly ambivalent, different in kind from the clarity of the Judaeo-Christian and Islamic tradition. Not that the goal is purely subjective, and is not so even in the *Upanishads*. The solitary self is lost, led astray by illusion—as Ovid is initially. Rather, the goal is oneness, unity with the all-pervadingness of being, the unity, which Malouf finely expresses in the poem 'A Poet Among Others':

. . . holding
to the isness of
things: a blade of rye, a moment spiralling
up from the stubble field on a lark's wing . . .
to enter the whole day's blue, a waterdrop filled with the light of conscious
(p. 178).

At the beginning, then, Ovid is in exile, banished by the emperor to the frontiers of the Roman empire, the fringes of the known world, and exiled from all that he, sophisticated, an acclaimed and witty writer, and a nobleman and heir to his father's estates, regards as civilisation. But as the story unfolds, it is clear that his real exile is something else, more profound yet also more remediable. Even at home in Rome he was in exile, alienated from being itself, 'distracted from distraction by distraction', a prey to illusion. Not that he understood it then. Rather he rejoiced in his situation, rejoicing in a 'sophisticated impudence' which seemed to him 'an enlightenment so great that there was no longer any need for belief' (p. 25). True, he was even then faintly troubled by the sense of divinity: 'the gods are not quite dead was my news from the universe' (p. 25) Mostly, however, he turned that news to his own sceptical ends:

But they too have ceased to be serious. They have entered the age of play. They have abandoned the holy places and taken up residence in fables that require only our amused detachment from disbelief. They would be embarrassed by anything so glum and humourless as our grandfathers' piety. We are free at last to believe in ourselves (p. 26).

This is the classic stage of enslavement to illusion, of course. But the novella's action moves away from it towards liberation and moves, significantly, by means of grace. The bliss Ovid finally achieves is revealed, not achieved by his own efforts, though, as in classic Hindu teaching this revelation is highly ambiguous, as much discovery of the divinity within himself as of that which is.

In order to make this discovery, however, he has to make a journey within himself, as in the classic way of Sankara, and to discover there another mode of being, another language, the language of the universe, of being itself. The stages are quite clear. First of all, on the frontier, living amongst the 'barbarians', Ovid is taken away from his own certainties and from the power which his skill with language gives him. As he reflects, his exile also means loneliness, isolation from language:

They are not uncivil. But no one in Tomis speaks my tongue, and for nearly a year now I have heard no word of my own language. I am rendered dumb (p. 17).

Life is thus stripped to its simplest terms. But in the silence he begins to listen to others and to the world and learn another language, that of objects, not only because he is only able to communicate with others by their means, using them as signs, but also because he begins to be aware of them as fellow creatures:

I never had much contact with the creatures before this, not even with dogs or cats. Now I find something oddly companionable about them. Like me, they too cannot speak. They move about in the cracks, in the gaps in our lives, and are harmless. Even the spiders, poor creatures. Do they have a language of their own. I wonder, if so I might try to learn it (p. 20).

He is beginning here to see that what formerly gave him so much pride, so much self-assurance, was and is in fact a kind of loss. Then he was unable to speak this larger range of being which he is discovering here and in sleep, in:

what the simple daylight blinds me that the dark side of every object here, and even more, the landscape itself when night shadows flow over it, is a vast page whose tongue I am unable to decipher, whose message to me I am unable to interpret (p. 17).

But now he is beginning to learn what Malouf calls in one of his poems 'the body's syntax' (p. 134) and to listen to 'a new style of preaching' which tells him that:

there's another . . .
world to be grasped,
if only for dizzy seconds, of jumping
free of the 'not yet proved'. (p. 120)

Nevertheless, it is not yet a language he can use. It remains somehow separate even from his own body which tags along, 'to see what goes/what goes in time' (p. 60). What he is groping towards at this stage only seems to increase this alienation from himself and from others. The language he knows and even the language he is learning seems also part of this separation since it is a repressive gesture. 'Latin is a language for distinction, every ending defines and divides' (p. 98). What he is seeking is one rather 'whose every syllable is a gesture of reconciliation' (p. 98).

It is here that the figure of the Child, introduced at the very beginning of the story becomes crucial, becoming in effect, a kind of avatar, a 'down coming' or manifestation which draws him out of the impasse of self, leading him from illusion to enlightenment.

This is not a common reading of the Child, and his function, of course. To the extent that any attempt is made to decipher it, *An Imaginary Life* is usually read psychologically, mostly in terms of a development from Lacan's 'Mirror Stage' towards the Symbolic. Descriptions of the Child's appearance, apparently out of the depth of the self, like the one early on in the story, lend credence to this kind of reading:

And something came out of the depths of my sleep towards the point where we stood facing one another, like a reflection rising to the surface of a mirror. It was there, outside me, a stranger and something in me that was its reflection had come up to meet it (pp. 24–5).

But to anyone familiar with the Hindu doctrine of the Avatar this might also be read as the beginning of the divine manifestation which is to call Ovid from illusion to liberation, from darkness to light. As Geoffrey Parrinder summarises the various aspects of this doctrine, the Avatar represents a visible and fleshly descent of the divine to the animal or human plane. The intimacy of this encounter with a presence which seems to come out of the depths of the self is described in Ramaniya's commentary on the lines in the *Gita* in which the devotee is exhorted to show love to God. God, he says, needs his worshipper as the devotee also needs him:

Who approaches me as his ultimate goal cannot maintain himself in existence without me, so I too cannot maintain myself without him. Thus he is my very soul . . . Unable to endure separation from him, I cause him to possess me.[8]

Those of us brought up within the Christian tradition have no doubt missed this implication of Ovid's encounter with this figure from the depths of himself; because our theology emphasises the others of divinity and the dialectical nature of grace. But the apparition here, is not of this kind, being non-dualistic. In a sense it might even be seen as an illusion, as Sankara does in his commentary on Bhavage Bhavage Bhavage the crucial passage in the *Gita* (4, 6–8) which deals with the coming of the Avatar:

Though I am unborn, though by nature my power of vision is undecaying, yet ruling over by nature, the maya of Vishnu . . . by which deluded the whole world knows not Vasudeva, its own self—I appear to be born and embodied, through my own maya, and not, in reality, unlike others.[9]

But he comes, for purposes of enlightenment, for the 'preservation of earthly Brahman of spiritual life upon earth'.[10] Even at this stage of the action, there is at least a hint of this in Ovid's encounter which precedes this scene with the strange centaur-like creatures which precedes his dream:

One of those creatures, out of the shadowy forces that blocked out the whole horizon above me, came slowly, putting its hooves down gently in the dust, towards me, and halted just a foot away, so that I felt its breath, its warmth, and thought I heard on the flow of its breath a sound whose syllables I could interpret (p. 59).

An Entrance–Avatar of this kind, according to the commentators, can be produced in human or animal forms. Here, this, it seems, is a 'power-entrance' rather than the 'Own Form Entrance' of the subsequent dream which we have been discussing in which the Avatar takes human form, even the form of the self. According to Ramanuja, the Lord often manifests himself out of compassion, taking the form, as it seems he does here, which will best make him understandable:

This essential form of his most compassionate Lord by his mere will individualises as a shape human or divine or otherwise, so as to render it suitable to the apprehension of the devotee and thus satisfy him.[11]

True, here it is not so much a matter of satisfaction as of disturbance, but this disturbance is the first step toward the enlightenment, to the discovery of the paradoxical unity Ramanuja describes when he writes: 'the Brahman to be reached by the meditating devotee must be something different from him'.[12] God, soul and world form a unity; soul and word are the body of God but they are real also even though they depend on God and are nothing apart from him.

In the novella, in the strange and savage presence of the horses here Ovid recognises an aspect of himself, hearing a 'sound whose syllables I could interpret'. What he recognises is music, more rhythm than words. Moreover, this insight comes out of the detachment forced on him; 'having no language of my own now, I had begun to listen for another meaning' (p. 24). In traditional teaching, the Avatar comes with work to do, and the Child's task here is clearly to lead Ovid to salvation, to the enlightenment of the final moments of his story. True, at this stage he is not sufficiently detached to go further. But Ovid understands at least that this meaning and the further glimpse he is given of his goal in the dream from which he awakens crying out, uttering a word in a language he did not understand, is the goal of his existence:

I have since tried to remember that word, but the sound has sunk back into my sleep. If I could recall that sound, and speak that word again, I think I would know what it is that I have named, what it is that I have encountered, what it is out there that is waiting to receive me (p. 25).

The action thus moves towards this reality, away from the fragmentation of his former life towards unity, towards the open flow of life.

The first stage is negative, unmasking the culturally defined illusions, the actions, institutions, words and poses which have separated him from this flow. He realises that where he has lived, Italy, is 'a created place'. Even its gods have been made and shaped by human hand and are the creation of human need. But here he must confront 'what earth was in its original bleakness' (p. 28).

'a place of utter desolation, the beginning' (p. 30). In its sheer unmade and unmaking force this power is embodied in Hindu thought in the figure of Kali. Yet as in Hindu thought, this is a necessary stage. Existence is cyclical and must pass through the darkness if it is to come to the light. *An Imaginary Life* also envisages time in this cyclical fashion. Ovid introduces himself, for instance, as someone who lives 'between two cycles of time, the millenium of the old gods, that shudders to its ends, and a new era that will come to its crisis at some far point in the future' (p. 19). The Child's coming, too, is part of this process. Appearing first to Ovid when he is a child, he is bound, Ovid realises, to come again. As Parrinder remarks:

The Avatars do not just drop into the human 'scene' . . . without roots in anything that came before or relationship to what comes after. Each Avatar . . . appears 'whenever there is a decline of righteousness'. He maintains harmony. He is in a succession, of those who have gone before. He is in turn succeeded, and since early days there has been a looking forward to the Avatar to come.[13]

Beginning with this belief, Ovid's story concludes, as we shall see, with a return which is also a going away—Avatars finally die, as Krishna did, fatally wounded by an arrow, or as Rama walked into a river, both dying when their purpose was accomplished:

The end of the mortal episode must be completed, for if it is real it is only occasional. God is not always visible though he constantly maintains the world by his power.[14]

Hence, there is an elegiac as well as a triumphant note to the story's conclusion. If, as the *Gita* puts it, all the beings spring from the Lord and all the universe is strung upon him like jewels upon a thread, then at the end of an age all things will pass back into the Lord's material nature:

By applying my own nature
I send out again and again
All this helpless host of beings (Gita, 9, 8).

Nevertheless, this cycle is ultimately benign, as Ovid realises early on in his desolation:

and yet even here [in the frozen landscape of winter] there are stirrings of new life. The first seeds are there to be separated and nurtured, and led on their long path to perfection (p. 30).

Someone familiar with the *Gita* might hear an echo here of Krishna's words to Arjuna that he is Lord of all, and seed of all that is (*Gita*, 10, 20–42). She might also find it significant that Ovid's movement towards enlightenment begins amongst simple shepherd people as Krishna's does. Here, too, Ovid lives amongst simple people and learns from them a sense of wonder. Glimpsing in their presence the unity of human life with the life of all other creatures, he then recognises the frivolity and uselessness of his former life. Whatever else they may do, these people remind him of his own situation as a luminary, in passage away from a life based on social and cultural distinctions, cognitively defined, logically articulated and endowed with legal rights and obligations[15] towards another kind of reality. Living in community with them therefore marks an important step towards liberation, towards the awareness of the cosmos not as organised hierarchically but rather as the common life which exists beyond all categories of manifestation or explanation, transcending divisible time and space and beyond words, a life in which people, objects and relationships are endlessly transformed into one another.[16]

The key to this liberation, however, lies, as it always has done—Ovid first glimpsed him in his own childhood with the Child. The central episode of this section is thus the search for the Child, in the guise of the wild boy brought up by wolves who has been glimpsed by hunters in the forest. An Avatar, of course, can manifest himself in any form and, as we have seen, usually chooses the form best suited to people's understanding. The form here is therefore at first a savage one, corresponding to the 'wolf man' within, who lives 'secretly among us' whom Ovid recognises in the Child, captured from the wilds and brought in to be adapted to the ways of man (p. 10), and in himself. Just as important, however, is the sense of wonder his presence generates:

Where does the boy come from? Who were his parents? How did he get here? How can he have survived, naked in all seasons, with no one to feed him or nurse him? (p. 48).

One is reminded here of Ramanuja's commentary on Arjuna's question to Krishna in *Gita* (4), 'How can I understand that it was you who taught this yoga in the beginning?' This question, Ramanuja argues, was put purposely to evoke or provoke thought about the Avatars; whether they were real or imaginary, under what circumstances they might manifest themselves, what the nature of the body they assumed might be and so on.[17]

Evidently, the Child here is something of a miracle. His gaze, Ovid reflects:

is something I could not have imagined. I have seen nothing like it before, except from the eyes of my Child, so many years ago. I have invented nothing like it in my poems, that were full of strange creatures caught between man and some higher or lower creature, in a moment of painful transformation. It exceeds my imagination (p. 50).

Nor is it clear where he had come from—the times of the Avatars are not fixed in classic teaching but 'whensoever night declines' then the Lord manifests himself.[18] His gaze here suggests the power he brings to bear on the need he perceives:

Whatever conception they choose to seek me, I manifest myself to them in that mode . . . I suit myself in such a manner that I am to them not only a visible demonstration, but that they may enjoy me by every one of their sense faculties, and in all diverse ways.[19]

So the poet of the *Metamorphoses* who has figured forth so many strange beings encounters here a presence beyond his comprehension, terrible as well as compelling. The Child, then, has to do with the holy, with the 'mysterium tremendum et fascinans' which exceeds human comprehension. In his presence, Ovid is at times afraid, therefore glimpsing:

Some animal presence we do not know and have never seen. What if he were in communion with that, or had the power of assuming the form of a creature whose shape, whose horror, we can only imagine, and have no magic to placate? (p. 66).

At other times, the Child calls upon 'a tenderness' within him, 'an immense pity, a need to free him into some clearer body, that is [Ovid says] like a pain in my own' (p. 77). But the Child is in no sense a projection of need, much less of desire. Godlike, he creates both the kindness and the terror he calls forth and threatens at times, like the wolf in Ovid's earlier dream, 'to consume the whole pool of my being' (p. 77).

But the fear this threat occasions is, in effect, a holy fear. Creator, preserver and destroyer, the Avatar is self and not self, but also the central goal of the self. As one of the Vedas puts it:

There is no equality in experience between the Lord and the self; for the Lord is all-knowing, all powerful and absolute; while the self is of little understanding, of little power and absolutely dependent.[20]

What matters is knowledge, knowledge of this truth which is manifest here, of the eternal nature of the soul and its identification with the divine.[21] This, for Hindu belief, is worth far more than cult or morality.

So, too, here. The final stage of *An Imaginary Life* is taken up with this search for truth, a search which arises, characteristically, out of Ovid's preoccupation with language. Having captured the Child, he decides to teach him his language. But the Child is not to be coopted in this way. The Avatar's task is instruction, to teach *dharma* for this life. Instead of bringing comfort, he begins disturbance, exposing illusion. He catches a fever, for instance, threatening the whole village with infection and death, testing their attitude to immortality in terms of the search for truth. But the threat he poses to Ovid's self-assurance is more important. Teaching the Child to speak his language, he gradually comes to realise that it is he who is the learner and the Child the teacher:

When I try to articulate what I know, I stumble suddenly on what, till that moment, I did not know. There are times when it comes strangely that he is the teacher, and that whatever comes new to the occasion is being led, slowly, painfully, out of me (p. 95).

How all this had begun to happen, he reflects, is a mystery. But if one sees the Child as the Avatar, the manifestation of the divine in human form, it is not—provided, of course, one believes in the divine. The central question, to which Ovid implicitly gives a positive answer, is whether or not one is prepared to accept within the self the presence of another who may in fact seem to be an alien, someone who, as the Child, dies here. Self is no longer something accidental, a mask to put on or a part to be acted out. It is rather a matter of deadly earnest, of entering the dimensions of self in which truth at last is to be brought to birth.

Nevertheless, this process of learning does not begin immediately with the Child's capture—there is too much self-will perhaps in that. It begins rather when the poet begins to sense 'some process of reaching up out of himself' (p. 79) and when, untying the bonds by which he has secured the Child's presence, realising that they are no longer necessary, he also understands that his life is now inexorably tied to the Child's, to that 'timeless place' within him from which the Child is also coming to him (p. 82). But here, he recognises what he has long lost or forgotten in himself, an old simplicity but also the old cruelty which made him leave home to go his own way, killing his brother and his father, in wish if not in deed.

To know oneself is to know evil as well as good. As in the *Gita*

Krishna declares his teaching and exposes evil, so here, Ovid is led to self-knowledge and then, beyond this, to know how much he does not know. Now with the Child, he begins to understand that he does not know 'who he is or what his fate is to be' (p. 89). 'The unmanifested goal (as Krishna tells Arjuna) is hard to reach for embodied beings' since it is 'not this, not this' nothing which can be put into words. The way to it, however, leads through practical knowledge, the experience deeper than any theory which is now leading him to the discovery of 'things [which] happen, deep in our lives', usually not spoken of and hidden even from ourselves but which 'do not leave us' (p. 88), remaining to become the occasion of true self-knowledge.

This, as the *Gita* teaches, demands demotion, the gift of oneself. So Ovid gives what he most values, his language, devoting himself to teaching it to the Child. But devotion brings its reward:

If one gives me with devotion
Leaf or flower, fruit or water,
From that earnest soul I relish
Such an offering of devotion (Gita, 9, 26).

Ovid in the past had been a master of words. But now becoming their servant, learning to listen as well as to speak, he learns a deeper and richer language. Earlier, he had glimpsed this possibility, stopped in his tracks out walking one day by 'a little puff of scarlet amongst the wild corn' (p. 30). Revelation comes in many forms and here it comes in the form of 'a little wild poppy, of a red so sudden it made my blood stop' (p. 31). But what it brought with it is the wonder of the earth, of being itself, in its colour, energy and fertility, putting him in touch with a spring within himself, and giving him access to a kind of password 'that would release me from my own life' (p. 32). To reach it, however, he had to learn to be silent, to let the gods name him. That happened years ago. Only now with the Child does he begin to discover its true meaning, to comprehend the real message of the words he wrote then, 'You will be separated from yourself and yet be alive' (p. 33). Now, however, he understands that it means: 'I too must be transformed' (p. 33).

According to the *Gita*, the revelation of the Lord brings divine speech to human beings. The task of the devotee is to respond, to give himself to this revelation. Ovid's dedication to the Child becomes a matter of listening to him rather than to himself, tasting the new life he has to offer, in the spirit of Krishna's words to his disciples:

Abandoning all duties
Come to me for refuge,
From every evil I will save you, do not sorrow (Gita, *18, 60*).

In this case the evil is the possession of one's own gifts. So Ovid begins to realise that language is not his own but given to him out of the gracious compassing of the gods in order to lead him to enlightenment:

This . . . is how it is done. We give the gods a name and they quicken in us, they rise in their glory and power out of minds, they move forth and act in the world beyond, changing us and it. So it is that the beings we are in process of becoming will be drawn out of us. We have only to find the name and let its illumination fill us (p. 32).

Pious repetition of 'the Name' is true religion for some branches of Hinduism. There are two forms of the Absolute, Tulasi taught, the personal and the impersonal, but the Name is greater than both, for it makes them both known. Although the Absolute, the Lord, dwells in all hearts, people are sad. It is only when his Name is uttered that he becomes manifest and they are able to rejoice. But, for this, here Ovid's task is to listen and gradually to learn the Name. So he must learn to submit to instruction:

We are moving in opposite directions, I and the Child, though on the same path. He has not yet captured his individual soul out of the universe about him. His self is outside him his energy distributed among the beasts and buds whose life he shares, among leaves, water, grasses, clouds, thunder—

whose existence he can be at home in because they hold, each of them, some particle of his spirit (p. 96).

He has been enclosed himself, but the Child leads him into the fullness of being.

The fact that the one who knows all manifests himself as a Child is important here, because it keeps alive the great paradox that that which *Is* is also that which *Is Not*. As the *Rig-Veda* declares:

Purusha is all this, that has been and will be . . .
A quarter of him in all beings,
Three quarters are the immortal in heaven . . .
With three quarters Purusha rose upward
One quarter came to be here again.[22]

The Lord's presence in this hidden form is the 'greatest secret/Of them all, the highest message' of which the *Gita* speaks, the message that 'by me you are much beloved' (*Gita*, 18, 64) The task, Ovid begins to understand, is thus to learn to accept, to let enlightenment come upon him, to give up writing and let himself be written:

. . . this is the way. Slowly I begin the final metamorphosis. I must drive out my old self and let the universe in. The creatures will come creeping back . . . re-entering their old lives, deep in our consciousness and, after them, the plants, also themselves then we shall begin to take back into ourselves the lakes, the rivers, the oceans of the earth, its plains, its forested crags with their leaps of snow. Then little by little, the firmament. The spirit of things will migrate back into us. We shall be whole (p. 96).

Physical incidents like the Child's illness, the crisis in the village that follows during the long winter when the headman's son also falls ill, no longer seem to matter. Everything in the story is now moving towards its culmination; the springtime in which Ovid follows the Child across the frontier into a 'life that stretched beyond the limits of measurable time . . . a space that has no physical dimensions' (p. 144). At the same time, the novel insists on the sheer reality of what is happening. 'No more dreams. We have passed beyond them into the last reality' (p. 141). Those who would cling to matter-of-fact, to the mere evidence of the senses, are the ones who are deluded. What is glimpsed here is fullness. As Ovid watches, the Child is finally transfigured before him. It is, the poet realises, his own nature as a god that 'his body is straining towards' (p. 150). But he also draws the watcher with him, to become one with him, paradoxically, at the moment which he seems to move away into this godhead. 'Some new energy is in him. He is lighter. He moves faster over the earth' (p. 118).

Language begins to give way here. The reality being revealed is continuous, while language, and the systems of thought that depend upon it, are discontinuous. As so often, the revelation arrives[23] here with blinding force which disables reason and the senses. The description is full of images of light, of dazzle and glitter, of light shining on pebbles and of flowing movement and of flowing stream. But there is a certain terror as well. This is a new birth, and a new, more powerful manifestation of being. The springtime of the earth also marks perhaps the beginning of some possibly more terrible, certainly more intense, being:

A membrane strains and strains, growing transparent, till the creature who is stirring and waking in there is visible in all its parts, forcing its own envelope of being towards the breaking point till with its folded wings already secure in the knowledge of flight, and of all the motions of the air, it flutters free (p. 147).

When Krishna revealed his supreme form to Duryodhana, he, too, was terrible and terrified all the assembled kings, making the earth tremble. But afterwards, he withdrew that wonderful form and went out arm in arm with his friends. So here, Ovid, drawn into the experience of rebirth, feeling the breaking that is going on around him as if it were 'occurring at the very end of [his] nerves' (p. 141), also feels a new intimacy with the Child. Even as he moves away from him, he is also 'feeding me now out of his world as I once fed him out of ours' (p. 148).

Thus he has been brought at the last to the 'place I dreamed of so often, back there in Tomis, but could never find in all my wanderings in sleep—the point on the earth's surface where I disappear' (p. 150). Here letting go of himself, he discovers his true self 'ascend[ing], of lower[ing] myself, grain by grain, into the hands of the gods' (p. 150), discovering the godhead in himself which is one with all things as the Child goes before him, 'his whole body strain[ing] towards some distance that I cannot grasp' (p. 140), drawing him into 'some life that I have not taken into account and which he will be free to enter only when our journey together is done' (pp. 149–50).

The gods come out of their compassion to rescue human beings from evil and illusion. But they withdraw their presence when they have enabled their devotees to realise the divinity within them. It is only when the Child moves away, that Ovid finally achieves illumination. The last glimpse of the Child is a kind of hierophany:

He is walking on the water's light and as I watch, he takes the first step off it, moving slowly away now into the deepest distance, above the earth, above the water, on air (p. 152).

Distinctions of here and there, like those between this and that, give way. But so, too, do distinctions between human and divine, himself and the Child:

The fullness is in [his] moving away from me, in his stepping so lightly, so joyfully, naked, into his own distance at last as he fades in and out of the dazzle of light off the water (p. 152).

This fullness is now also his own: 'the Child is there' (p. 151). But so, too, at the end Ovid is able equally to say, 'I am there' (p. 152). Time is now no longer operative either: 'I am three years old. I am sixty, I am six' (p. 152). 'Put your thoughts on me', the *Gita* commands and 'be absorbed in Me'.[24] So now the poet is merged into divinity, into the supreme bliss of eternity. 'It is summer. It is spring. I am immeasurably, unbearably happy' (p. 152).

This may seem a strange novel, then, to come from an Australian writer. But its strangeness has made it very attractive to many readers. The important thing about any work is surely that it wins the adherence of consciousness, touches upon that impulse to transcendence which, so religious belief would have it, each of us has to find and fulfil within ourselves. Whether or not they will be able to perceive the ways in which *An Imaginary Life* accords with traditional Hindu teaching, of course, is another, and probably less important, matter. Nevertheless, Indian readers may find it significant that, written by a Westerner, this novel lends itself to the kind of interpretation we have been giving it. Ramanuja's conclusion to his commentary or the Vedanta Sutra sums up this interpretation:

We know from Scripture that there is a Supreme Person whose nature is absolute bliss and goodness, who is fundamentally antagonistic to all evil, who is the cause of the origination, sustenation and dissolution of the world; who differs in nature from all other beings, who is all-knowing, who by his mere thought and will accomplishes all his purposes; who is an ocean of kindness as it were for all who depend on him; who is all merciful; who is immeasurably raised above all possibility of anyone being equal or superior to him; whose name is the Highest Brahman.[25]

The Child is, I have been arguing, the Avatar of this Supreme Person, manifesting himself in order to reveal to Ovid the illusion in which he has been living and open out to him the full range of divinity, its terror as well as its bliss, within him. In this way, as Ramanuja comments, the Lord 'frees [him] from the influence of Nescience . . . and allows [him] to attain to that supreme bliss which consists in the direct intuition of his own true nature'.[26] The revelation which came to him first in dream as another 'like a reflection rising to the surface of a mirror' (p. 24) proves itself finally as the fullness of his own truth. Nor is it all the Lords's gift. Ovid has responded also according to his own gift, his dharma, forgetting his own purposes, moving simply for the joy of his discovery. He has 'given the gods a name' and they have quickened him rising 'in their glory and power and majesty' out of his mind, going forth from there 'to act in the world beyond, changing us and it' (p. 32). The conclusion, as Ramanuja says, is liberation:

We need not fear that the Supreme Lord, when once having taken to himself the devotee whom he greatly loves, will turn him back to samsare (transmigration). For he himself has said, 'To the wise man I am very dear, and he is dear to me.'[27]

Western scepticism may find this a hard saying, but, as we said initially, the religious impulse continues, even in sceptical Australia. What else, Ovid asks as his story nears its conclusion, should our lives be but, troubled by this impulse, 'a continual series of beginnings, of painful settings out into the unknown, pushing off from the edges of consciousness into the mystery of what we have not yet become?' (p. 135). As he comes to understand, 'We have only to find the name and let its illumination find us' (p. 32). *An Imaginary Life*, then, represents an attempt to find this name and let this illumination find us. The 'scandal' remains.

NOTES

1. Victor Turner, *Revelation and Divination in Adembu Ritual* (Cornell University Press, Ithaca, 1975), p. 15.
2. Pietro Spinucci, *Un Poeta Australiano, David Malouf* (Bulzoni, 1983), p. 100.
3. David Malouf, *An Imaginary Life* (Chatto & Windus, London, 1978), p. 27.
4. Jacques Lacan, quoted in Sherry Turkle, 'Why Are You Here?', in *London Review of Books*, 5 January 1989, p. 3.
5. Turner, p. 18.
6. Quoted in John Dominic Crossan, *In Parables*.
7. Malouf at that stage spent most of his time in Italy, living in a village in Tuscany, not in Australia.
8. Geoffrey Parrinder, *Avatar and Incarnation: A Comparison of Indian and Christian Belief*.
9. Ibid., p. 50.
10. Ibid., p. 51.
11. Ibid., p. 54.
12. Ibid.
13. Ibid., p. 123.

14. Ibid., p. 122.
15. Turner, p. 22.
16. Ibid.
17. Parrinder, p. 56.
18. Ibid.
19. Ibid., p. 58.
20. Ibid., p. 53.
21. Ibid., p. 67.
22. Ibid., p. 16.
23. Turner, p. 19.
24. Parrinder, p. 41.
25. Ibid., p. 35.
26. Ibid.
27. Ibid.

5. QUESTIONS OF BELIEF

EMERGING FROM THE SHADOW

Theology is necessarily dialectical, necessarily suspended between divine revelation and human experience, since it meditates upon the God who shows himself in human form. *Kenosis*, the shedding of the fullness of divinity, stresses the significance of our humanity, involving God in human history and culture where he goes on speaking to us. The great question is thus to find where he may be speaking today and to respond in the depth of our human and historical experience.[1]

We Australians like to think of 'our Country' as the 'place of the new beginning'. In fact, however, it was founded—for us: it is different for the Aboriginal Australians—under the law of 'Ananke', of revenge. Colonisation was often, usually perhaps, a violent and often brutal process. It was especially so here. Australia originated as a penal colony and subsequent expansion into the interior and development of the land and its resources entailed a long, if undeclared, war against the original inhabitants, their dispossession from their land as well as the killing, rape and psychological violence which are the concomitants of war, especially of wars of conquest. In some places, notably in Tasmania, there were systematic attempts at genocide. Elsewhere massacres of Aboriginal people continued in isolated parts of the country into the twentieth century. To this day our Aboriginal people are amongst the most highly imprisoned people in the world.

But the first settlers were also victims of this law of revenge. Many of them poor, dispossessed or persecuted, were the victims of power. The origins of what we Australians like to call the 'Lucky Country', are thus bound up with an 'original sin', with a kind of captivity, a social situation, with alienation. As Paul Ricoeur puts it, theologically, 'the sinner is thus "in" the sin as the Hebrew was "in" bondage, and sin is thus an evil "in which" man is caught.[2] The situation is both personal and communal, known only to God in its reality and truth, an imprisonment which hardens us and holds us captive. But it is this experience of captivity, to the extent that we acknowledge it, which makes Australia perhaps the place of a 'new beginning' for Christendom, because the society and culture which we have made since 1788 are the product of Europe—they have nothing to do with the Aboriginal culture, a subtle, complex and profoundly religious culture which has developed over at least 40 000 years.

Christendom, however, has not been very ready to acknowledge this problem of origins and this may be one of the profoundest problems facing us as Christians today—I write this at the time of confrontation with Islam in the Middle East. But Australia today, as in the past, exemplifies this problem, the complicity of Christendom with the European conquest of the rest of the world, a conquest which rests on the perversion of Christianity in which white is set against black as good against evil, believer to unbeliever, civilised to savage, superior to inferior.[3]

This means, however, that our society depends in some measure at least on pseudo-theological justification, the identification of Christianity with Europe and of white people with God's chosen people.

At the same time, the actual story, the human reality of settlement, was very different. The first European settlers were either convicts or their unwilling guards, victims also of the law of retribution. The free settlers who followed were not very different. Most of them also, like many if not most migrants even today, obliged to leave their own countries by force of circumstance, were also, in a sense, disinherited. Henry Kingsley expresses this vividly in *The Recollections of Geoffrey Hamlyn*:

And then came the disturbance of the household gods and the rupture of life-old associations . . .

Only those who have done so know how much effort it takes to say, 'I will go away to a land where none know me or care for me, and leave forever all that I know and love'. And few know the feeling that comes upon all men after it is done—the feeling of isolation, almost of terror, at having gone so far out of the bounds of ordinary life; the feeling of self-distrust and cowardice at being alone and friendless in the world, like a child in the dark. [4]

The sense of disinheritance here is poignant. But this poignancy points also to another possibility. If the 'household gods' have been disturbed, the possibility arises that they might be replaced.

By and large, however, this has not happened, though the reasons why it has not are understandable. The frontier is by definition a place of exposure. Here, bereft of the protection of culture, tradition and habit, one is open to the sheer pressure of physical necessity, brought up short before questions of survival so that preoccupation with material prosperity, the preoccupation of the poor, follows. [5] This preoccupation in turn, however, often becomes a way of practical atheism, to the extent that value is defined in terms of money, consumption becomes a virtue and money the way of it. As a result, life loses its dimension of mystery and other people and the environment turn into objects for manipulation. So:

. . . The ultimate men arrive
Whose boast is not 'we live' but 'we survive',
A type who will inhabit the dying earth. [6]

This is the shadow. Nevertheless, the possibility remains of emerging from it, and this is our subject. Europe and Western culture generally may still hold to some residual belief in the Enlightenment, in its trust in human reason and perfectibility, and America (which includes Canada) may still seem to confirm this belief. But the Australian experience disallows it, for a variety of reasons, historical and geographical. Historically, as we have seen, our convict origins and our subsequent treatment of the Aborigines makes fairly clear that the Enlightenment's dream of reason may in fact in the long run produce monstrous results. Geographically, in Australia the strangeness of the environment interrogates reason, pointing beyond it, challenging the myth of control. In both ways, therefore, Australia may question the alliance between Christendom and the cultural, social and political order, the alliance which thinkers as varied as Marx, Nietzsche and Freud have also interrogated.

This challenge, however, is important theologically—God's coming is best seen as an interruption. The strangeness, the sense of exile, many of us still experience here is in Christian terms an occasion of grace, since, as Schillebeeckx puts it, the 'hermeneutical principle for the disclosure of reality is not the self-evident, but the scandal, the stumbling-block of the refractoriness of reality'.[7] Australia then, may be the place in which Europe, Christian Europe, may emerge from the shadow of the God who may be its projection.

First of all, the sheer strangeness of the geography challenges our technological complacency. The Hebrew–Christian vision, born in the desert, must take the desert as its point of reference. European Christianity, however, still clings to the Enlightenment, to the God who can be defined in terms of human reason, who blesses human culture generally, and Western culture in particular. In the desert such certainties tend to fall away and God reveals himself more as a question or series of questions than an answer. So José Faur has argued that:

Ultimately, the whole issue as to whether there is a Creator or whether the universe simply is revolves on whether one wishes to regard this world in the Greek or in the Hebrew fashion.[8]

In contrast with the Greek world view in which human beings are in charge of their world and of their existence, for the Hebrews, God is sole Lord and master. His will and his ways, mysterious as they are, are foremost and ultimately meaningful, not ours.

The important point here, in contradistinction to the Enlightenment thinking which has tended to govern Christian and especially Catholic thinking, is the notion of the mysteriousness of God, the God beyond gods. It is to this notion that Nietzsche points with his proposition that 'God is dead', a proposition which many Christians have found deeply troubling. As Ricoeur points out, however, it may in fact be liberating, may overthrow our false ideas of God. What we need, he writes:

. . . is to know, first of all, which god is dead; then, who has killed him (if it is true that this death is a murder); and finally, what sort of authority belongs to the announcement of this death.[9]

In a secular society like Australia, it is fairly clear that the cultural God of Christendom is, if not dead, at least in a terminal state, poisoned initially perhaps by the association with authority in the penal beginnings, with unjust power. What killed him was the failure of religious imagination involved. Instead of being on the side of the poor and oppressed, the official Church, the Anglican Church in particular, blessed the status quo. Announcing the death of this God of the status quo thus means announcing the possibilities of the living God of Christianity who was the friend of the oppressed.

This may seem a bleak announcement. Nevertheless, it speaks to the colonial experience, and the way forward thus lies in exploring this experience, especially as it so clearly fits with the scriptural paradigms of Exodus and Exile. It is perhaps not accidental, therefore, that our unofficial national anthem, the folk song 'Waltzing Matilda', is a song about an exile and a wanderer who chooses to die rather than surrender his freedom, or that the poet Christopher Brennan writes of 'Man the wanderer on the way to the self'.[10] In turn, in the story of Israel, the desert experience leads to the encounter with Yahweh, and this is implicit in our experience also.

For non-Aboriginal Australians, the land has figured not so much as fertile and abundant but as the antagonist, as other. In *Voss*, the novelist Patrick White explores the land in this sense, contrasting those who refuse to move into the interior, clinging to the fringes of themselves as to the fringes of the continent, with those who 'dare to go further', to confront the mystery of the desert or, in *A Fringe of Leaves*, of the wilderness within them. The nineteenth-century writer Marcus Clarke (who was, incidentally, a school friend of Gerard Manley Hopkins and kept up a correspondence with him), expresses a similar intuition. For him, the dominant note of Australian scenery was a 'weird melancholy', a melancholy which came from the sense of displacement we have been discussing. But he also sees it as a preliminary to some further encounter:

*Australia has rightly been named the Land of the Dawning. Wrapped in
the mystery of early morning, her history looms vague and gigantic. The
lonely horseman riding between the moonlight and the day . . . hears strange
noises in the primeval forest where flourishes a vegetation long dead in other
lands, and feels, despite his fortune, that the trim utilitarian civilisation
which bred him shrinks into insignificance.*[11]

Human mastery gives way here as, like the Israelites in the desert,
he confronts the reality of danger, hardship and death, of subjection
to physical necessity. Human beings are no longer lords of creation;
the Book of Nature in which we imagine ourselves the central
referent seems closed. Instead, Clarke sees only 'the scribblings of
Nature learning to write',[12] drawn back to origins in which we seem
to have no part, brought up before the mystery of creation.

No doubt there are echoes here of the shock Darwin's thought
posed so powerfully in the nineteenth century. But this is surely
an important moment for Christian faith also, to the extent that
it points beyond culture, beyond the idols we are all too ready to
make for ourselves, the projections of emotional and social need,
to the God of Sinai and of the Burning Bush, the God who was
crucified. If the Book of Nature is closed, then we are driven to
the Book of God in his creation to find his hand in what may appear
to be mere scribblings.

This question of God is, of course, the central problematic
of faith. With the triumph of Christendom, it has been increasingly
clear that what many of us call 'God' may be our own production,
the justification of our needs. Marx, Nietzsche and Freud have
all underscored this point, and the worldwide renewal of Islam,
with its insistence on the sheer otherness of God, makes the question
even more urgent today. But here in Australia, at what may be
one of the extremes of Western Christendom, this experience
of the desert reopens the question—if we are prepared to take
it. The God of the desert is the God who shows himself in this
mysterious landscape beyond anything we can conceive of or control,

who goes before us calling us into his mystery, challenging all words and thoughts about him. 'Whether He is Being or the master of Beings, God Himself is, and appears as what He is, within difference, that is to say, as difference and within dissimulation.'[13] If creation appears to us inscrutable here, it nevertheless remains the book of God's creation, writing which is living and active, constantly creating new possibilities in those of us who try to read it, drawing us into the mystery of a God 'whose being is' in his coming, who 'makes himself accessible in that he goes on ways to himself'.[14]

By definition this God stands over against and confronts the 'cheap grace' of a merely cultural Christianity. This is so not merely because the difficulty of the environment itself contests the complacencies of a materialist and consumerist culture but also because, as we learn to read what has been written in the land, we also come to discern the story of the first inhabitants, whose sense of reverence, of the holiness of God's creation and whose ability to read God's story there contrasts with our profanation, and whose fate puts to the question our history and our sense of ourselves.

Questioning, however, is the beginning of renewal. As it was the Fall which precipitated the journey to the Promised Land and the desert wanderings take on their true meaning only in relation to the imprisonment in Egypt, so it is only when we really know our need of God, when we have reached the end of our human resources, that we are properly open to the liberation grace brings. True, this emphasis may not be popular today when the stress seems to fall rather on 'original blessing'. But history cannot be denied, nor the fact that colonisation was often justified on theological grounds, in the Manichean allegory which set white against black as good against evil, godly against ungodly, civilised against savage, superior against inferior.[15] This may well be one of the reasons why the God of European Christianity seems to many increasingly ungodly.

This is not the place to detail the consequences of this heresy; the offences it entailed against the original inhabitants of Australia. The point here is rather that the God we made to our own image who justified those offences is not the God who gave himself to us in Jesus, in whom there is no division of race, class or gender but who calls us all to carry on his work of love, recognising and serving him not only in his creation but in others, especially in the 'least of his brothers and sisters'.

The mystery of the desert thus begins to expand, revealing that other desert, the desolation which lies at the heart of our aggressive, competitive and materialist Western culture. In this sense, it becomes the desert of Ezechiel's vision[16] of the valley of dried bones—and one of our ballads characterises the interior as 'the place where the dead men lie'.[17] But in that vision, of course, God breathes new life into these bones, and the desert, the place of desolation, becomes the source of new life. Significantly, our writers also point in this direction. We have already referred to Patrick White. In *A Fringe of Leaves*, a later reworking of *Voss* which explores the journey into the desert, he links this renewal even more explicitly with the Aborigines. His central character, Ellen Roxburgh, finds who she truly is through her encounter with them, enduring with them the hunger, humiliation and physical hardship which are the consequences of our invasion and discovering there the God who is not the conquerors' 'God of the winning side' but the crucified One whose power is weakness in the world's eyes and whose dignity is worldly indignity.

Put in more general terms, the Aborigine may function for us, as oppressed people throughout the world may for Western culture generally, as the Suffering Servant, the living embodiment of the consequences of our idolatry, 'wounded for our iniquities, bruised for our sins',[18] and thus open the way to the mystery of the sacred, the glory. If we and Western Christendom very badly need to recover a sense of the sacred, of the *mysterium tremendum et fascinans*, then we may find it here, in the mysterious survival and continuing hope of these suffering people. Secular society tends to be one-dimensional and its religion to be oriented away from the dimension of mystery, defending us from rather than opening us out to the challenge of chaos, evil and death. But here they confront us, bringing us up before the mystery of crucifixion and the strange logic it proclaims, that God's power is like powerlessness, God's riches like poverty and God's way of life an offence.

Seen in this light, our painful beginnings point to the possibilities of a new affinity with those whom we in our turn have persecuted. 'In the "godless" death of the Son of God, outcasts are accepted, the unrighteous are made righteous and justice is secured for those without rights.'[19]

In one of his novels, *To the Island*, another Australian writer, Randolph Stow, explores the possibilities of reconciliation implicit here. His main character, Heriot, overburdened with guilt for what he has done to the Aborigines and disillusioned with the Christianity which has justified it, journeys out into the interior, wanting to die there. But on the way coming upon an Aboriginal camp, he sits down with them, sitting down beside an old Aboriginal woman who is also blind:

In that way, they sat for what seemed a long time in that timeless place, naked brown woman by naked white man, and he stroked the loose skin of her back with tenderness, wanting to laugh, wanting to weep.[20]

Similarly, in David Malouf's *An Imaginary Life*, the highly sophisticated Ovid, in exile at the edge of the known world, finds what he has always been longing for, the lost child within him, in the 'savage' child he encounters in the wilderness. Thinking first of all to teach the child his language he learns finally from him the 'language of the earth', the language of worship and praise.

Evidently, today, the whole world is at a turning point. But this is especially so for the West and for Christendom. The old paradigm by which we lived for so long will no longer do, the paradigm of exploitation and control. Instead, we must perhaps learn to 'let go, let be', learn once again from people we despised, the mystery of 'silence, simplicity and humility', which is the mystery of the God of Israel who came to us in Jesus of Nazareth. In God's logic, therefore, the crisis we face may be the moment of liberation. The pilgrim people must move on, away from their certainties and complacencies, as we respond to the God who is always ahead of us, whose being is in his coming.

Here in Australia we have this opportunity in a special way, since on the one hand the emptiness of Western materialism, undiluted by memories from the past of other ways of living, is most clearly and poignantly revealed here, and on the other we see in the suffering of Aboriginal Australians its human cost. But their culture which we have despised as 'godless' may also offer an alternative to ours and different, more 'godly', definitions of 'reality' and 'value'. In Aboriginal culture mind and world are no longer separate. What is 'real' and valuable is not necessarily what can be seen, touched, tasted and measured. They do not live by surfaces. Reality and value for them lie rather in the unexpected, in the distances of the sacred. Space and time, similarly, are open to infinite possibility. Space is not an empty container, to be filled with goods or made to produce them, and time is not linear but the circular time of myth, in which what matters lies at the 'still point of the turning world', the hub of the wheel, the Great Time, the Dreaming in which the stories told in scripture lay down the shape and purpose of our lives. In this view, to return to the point made earlier about the choice between the Greek and the Hebraic world view, creation is in fact God's work of art, God's poem, and we in our turn, 'such stuff as dreams are made on', stuff, that is to say, in process of shaping and being shaped.

There is no space here to develop the implications of this world view, though the theologian and anthropologist Eugene Stockton has written significantly about the contribution Aboriginal culture may have to make: about its generosity, joyfulness, sense of humble dependence, and, above all, its deep sense of prayerful stillness.[21] In many ways, their culture thus seems closer to the gospel than the culture which calls itself Christian. Perhaps the time has come for the conquering Church to become the humble Church, to yet learn from them and in their place what is concealed from the rich, the wise and the powerful but revealed to the 'little ones'.

True, there is a way to go before this happens. But it is only by passing through the shadow that we may be able to emerge from it. Then, sitting down together in mutual forgiveness, compassion and love, we may emerge into new possibility, begin to discover that state of 'silence, humanity and simplicity' which is the only proper state for Christians as well as for human beings generally.

NOTES

1. John Chryssavgis 'Patristic Christology: Through the Looking Glass of the Heretics', in *Pacifica* 3 2 (June 1990), p. 187.
2. Paul Ricoeur, *The Symbol of Evil* (Beacon Press, Boston, 1969), p. 93.
3. Abdul JanMohamed, 'The Economy of Manichean Allegory: The Function of Racial Difference in Colonialist Literature', in H.E. Gates (ed.), *'Race', Writing and Difference* (Chicago University Press, London, 1986), pp. 78–106.
4. S. Mellick (ed), *The Portable Henry Kingsley* (Queensland University Press, Brisbane, 1982), pp. 134–5.
5. Hannah Arendt, *On Revolution* (Penguin, London, 1973), p. 190.
6. A.D. Hope, 'Australia', in H.P. Heseltine (ed.), *The Penguin Book of Australian Verse* (Penguin, Melbourne, 1979), p. 190.
7. Schillebeeckx, *Christ: The Christian Experience in the Modern World* (SCM Press, London, 1982), p. 33.
8. José Faur, 'God as a Writer: Omnipresence and the Art of Dissimilation', in *Religion and Intellectual Life* VI, 3/4 (Spring/Summer 1989), p. 36.
9. Paul Ricoeur, *The Conflict of Interpretations* (North Western University, Evanston, 1974), p. 445.
10. A.R. Chisholm & J.J. Quinn (eds), *The Prose of Christopher Brennan* (Angus & Robertson, Sydney, 1965), p. 45.
11. Michael Wilding, (ed.), *The Portable Marcus Clarke* (University of Queensland Press, Brisbane, 1976), p. 417.
12. Ibid.
13. Kevin Hart, *The Trespass of the Sign* (Cambridge University Press, Melbourne, 1989), p. 47.
14. Eberhard Jüngel, *God as the Mystery of the World* (William B. Erdmans, Grand Rapids, Michigan, 1979), p. 159.
15. JanMohamed, p. 84.
16. Ezechiel 37.
17. Barcroft Boake, 'Where the Dead Men Lie', in H.P. Heseltine (ed), *The Penguin Book of Australian Verse*.
18. Isaiah 53.
19. Jürgen Moltmann, *The Church in the Power of the Spirit* (SCM Press, London, 1985), p. 88.
20. Randolph Stow, *To the Islands* (Penguin, Melbourne, 1974), p. 128.
21. Eugene Stockton 'Sacred Story—Sacred Land', in *Compass*, 1/25 (1990), pp. 5–14.

Intellectual Belief and Freedom

'**G**od is dead, anyway,' one of Patrick White's characters remarks. 'Anyway—thank God—in Australia.'[1] Patrick White himself would not have agreed. But one could safely say that most Australian intellectuals, those who make their living by the life of the mind, would agree. As A.G. Stephens asserted in 1904, Australian society is characteristically 'secular and sceptical' and, if *Meanjin* is anything to go by, intellectuals tend to be more sceptical than most.

This, I think, is not just a matter of cultural complicity. The first settlers, as Stephens says, brought with them religious habits as 'they brought other habits of elder nations in older lands'. But, once here, something seized on these habits, 'modifying, altering . . . or altogether destroying them'.[2] Stephens put this down to 'the spirit of Australia, that undefined, undefinable resultant of earth, air and conditions of climate and life'. We might have difficulty with this, being more inclined to look to economic, sociological or ideological explanations. But the point remains, that there is in Australian culture 'a sceptical and utilitarian spirit that values the present hour and refuses to sacrifice the present for any visionary future lacking a national guarantee'. By and large, belief in any reality beyond the evidence of the senses or the calculation of economists is left to the few whose profession it is—to faintly comical figures like clergymen, and mavericks like Patrick White or Manning Clark— or to 'good churchgoers', who are often suspected of having it both ways, running with the religious hares and hunting with the secular hounds. However unsophisticated Stephens's analysis seems, it is difficult to disagree with it.

This scepticism is probably more pronounced among those concerned with freedom. A libertarian strain has run through Australian culture and intellectual life, and one of its targets has tended to be institutional religion—though the Roman Catholic church, with its own particular corner on the sufferings of the Irish, was until recently an exception. But from the beginning of settlement, religion was generally connected with the Establishment. Anglican ministers blessed the convict system, and some even helped to administer it, while dissenters rapidly rose to wealth and power, blessing them too. The Roman Catholic church, initially the church of the poor and the persecuted, has shown a similar willingness to establish networks of power and patronage as its congregations become more affluent. The churches have also supported numerous excursions into war—Catholic opposition to conscription in World War I came as much from Irish dislike of the British Empire as from a passion for peace and justice.

In general, then, the churches have been enthusiastic apologists for propriety, property and appropriation, and enemies of radical thought, especially as far as sexuality or women's rights are concerned. Although politicians have not yet had themselves photographed at prayer, as George Bush did before unleashing the land war in the Gulf, most progressive intellectuals tend to see religion as the ally of the status quo, its 'spiritualistic point d'honneur', as Marx put it, its 'moral sanction . . . its solemn complement [and] general ground of consolation and sanctification'. The Catholic bishops' dismissal some years ago of their Commission for Justice and Peace and the strenuous opposition within the Anglican church to the ordination of women seem to confirm those dark suspicions.

All this, it would seem, should allow conservative intellectuals to assume the religious mantle. But institutions such as the Institute for Public Affairs seldom play the religious card. Their values seem to be as secular as the left's—even more so, perhaps, if you think of their preoccupation with economics. Neo-Darwinism and a weakly adulterated neo-Benthamism seem to be their equivalent of religion.

In general, then, religious belief seems to be peripheral to intellectual life in this country, especially to concerns about freedom. In the nineteenth century, bigotry threatened to wreck the education system, which was preserved, most would argue, by becoming secular as well as free and compulsory. I think a great deal was lost by this exclusion of religion. The decision of the churches in general, and the Catholic church in particular, to go it alone and set up a separate system was not very helpful either, since it tended to marginalise religion still further, separating it off into its own particular paddock from which, as in Lindsay's *Magic Pudding*, church people could fling insults at passersby. No Australian public university has a faculty of theology and only a few, mostly the newer ones, teach religious studies of any kind. In general the consensus seems to be that if intelligent people wish also to be religious believers, then that is something they do when off duty from thought. Religion is at best a harmless recreation, like gardening or collecting stamps, and at worst a perversion of intelligence.

Inevitable as it may have been in the past, this situation seems to me to be a loss to intellectual life in general, and to the concern for freedom in particular. There are two points here: first, that a culture or society that takes no account of the religious dimension, of a 'level of reality beyond the observable world known to science, to which are ascribed meanings and purposes completing and transcending those of the purely human realm',[3] is thereby impoverished; and secondly that acceptance of this dimension, together with careful and sustained thought about it, may be necessary to preserve whatever it is that we mean by 'freedom'.

According to Clifford Geertz, culture can be defined as a 'historically transmitted pattern of meanings embodied in symbols, a system of inherited conceptions expressed in symbolic forms by means of which men communicate, perpetuate and develop their knowledge about and attitudes to life'.[4] The pattern of meanings in our culture, however, being determinedly secular, has tended to turn its symbols into signs, limiting their implications to those dictated by journalists, politicians and economists. Thinking beyond these economic and pragmatic premises is thus regarded with suspicion, as somehow non-intellectual, certainly not hard-headed. In this sense Patrick White was right to insist that he was not an 'intellectual'. He was not, on these terms. But the fact that he thought long, hard and carefully—if also passionately—about ideas as well as about society, surely makes him an intellectual, in the proper sense of someone concerned with the life of the mind; his disclaimer points to the loss involved. So, too, does the hostility directed at White's work by critics of a positivist persuasion, such as Kylie Tennant, whose remark that 'when Patrick White gets mystical, I creep out the door' expresses colloquially the feelings of more highly placed and influential critics. Taste is not the same thing as thought, however. It can be another name for prejudice.

We come, then, to the proposition that thinking about the dimension that Tennant dismisses as the 'mystical' may be important for freedom. But first we need to clarify what we are talking about. 'Freedom' is one of those words easier to use than to define. We like to think of ourselves as a 'free people' and are quite prepared to go to war to defend freedom against those who seem to threaten it, whether it be a Hitler or Saddam Hussein abroad, or criminals or (in the past) 'Commos' at home. Both left and right rely on the magic word, the right especially proposing 'free enterprise' as our best defence against 'the tyranny of socialism'. Essentially, however, freedom has to do with a habit of mind rather than with institutions, since it describes an ability to make choices for oneself. It is this ability that is at risk in our society today, where, to draw on Habermas's analysis, System tends to dominate Life-world. It would seem, therefore, that domination ought to be the concern of intellectuals who believe in freedom.

The fact that it is not may seem surprising at first. But I would argue that the materialist base from which the left tends to argue does not grasp the full force and devastating effects of ideological conditioning. Even a left-wing intellectual such as John Docker castigates those who criticise commercial TV as if they were depriving the poor of their simple pleasures. But if one sees the issue as one of values—which, interestingly enough, the early Marx did— then it is a very different matter. Abundance and endless consumption may be, as Hannah Arendt remarks, the ideals of the poor, but they are ideals that can become tyrannical. True, as she goes on, 'freedom can only come to those whose needs have been fulfilled'. But it is equally true that this freedom 'will escape those who are bent upon living for their desires'.[5] The 'dream of great wealth got without exertion' has destroyed many people, but it is a dream that is difficult to challenge on pragmatic grounds, or even in terms of a merely materialist marxist critique.

That challenge is rather the work of what Paul Ricoeur calls a 'hermeneutic of suspicion', one that makes a connection between intellectuals, belief and freedom, though it is true that in the first place the suspicion needs to be directed against what many people call 'belief'. But there is an Enlightenment belief, still anachronistically strong on the left as well as the right, that human nature is a simple thing and that political, social and economic problems are the ones that matter and can be solved simply, if only we are properly rational in dealing with them. On the right the assumption seems to be that all that is needed is to remove controls and let the market have its head, so that, like a good dog, it will find its way home to the free and prosperous society we are all supposed to dream of. The left is rather less optimistic these days. But there, too, a general sense prevails that all will be well if only we can be more rational. Even women, who ought to know better, often fail to see that the problem is systemic, that patriarchy's power is essentially ideological, and fall into the same trap, confirming what they ought to contest.

This is the trap that Wittgenstein famously described:

'The general form of propositions is: This is how things are.'—That is the kind of proposition that one repeats to oneself countless times. One thinks that one is tracing the outline of the thing's nature over and over again, and one is merely tracing round the frame through which we look at it.[6]

This framework of our thought, our definitions of reality and value, the very grammar of our perception, I suggest, is the real problem. Moreover, this framework is by no means as rational as it claims. The myth of progress, for instance, based as it is on neo-Darwinian assumptions, has become the equivalent of fate, with violence, politely called competition, its way of life. Similarly, the myth of happiness, the idea of 'the greatest happiness of the greatest number', is in the long run just that, a myth, since it offers no clear definition of 'happiness'.

We are not as sceptical as we like to think. Even intellectuals live by myths, explaining life in terms of a story they tell themselves to explain why things are as they are, buried though this story may be under rational terminology. Even on their own terms, however, these dominant stories are inefficient, even dangerous, as the current collapse of ethical behaviour in public life and business suggests. Where 'greed is good', might tends to become right, and a few robber barons triumph to the detriment of the well-being, hopes and sometimes even the happiness of the many. Similarly, when 'success' becomes a value, then misfortune, unemployment, poverty, sickness, old age or simply failure to keep up with the Joneses becomes evil, or at least unworthy of sympathy. Faring ill, as Ricoeur remarks, is confused with doing ill.[7] By a merely rational calculus, it is difficult to question these developments. As Max Horkheimer argues:

From the standpoint of positivism, no conclusions can be drawn about morality . . . Scientifically speaking, hatred is no worse than love though its social function may be different. There is no logically conclusive argument to show that I should not hate, as long as I am not thereby placed at a disadvantage in my social life.[8]

To this argument the left seems to have no real answer, apart from the suspicion, inertia and well-meaning muddle that, as Meaghan Morris suggests, characterise the left these days.[9] In this sense, Paul Keating's well-known contempt for the 'basket weavers of Balmain' is perhaps justified. But surrender to the system— Morris's 'mental bureaucratisation' and 'addictive gravy-training'— is not the answer either. That leads to the 'decreased effectiveness and drooping spirit' she observes on the left today.

The real problem is one of belief, of finding the kind of belief that makes for freedom. Patrick White realised this from the beginning when, in his otherwise dreary second novel, *The Living and the Dead*, he made Eden Standish argue for a change that is not merely political, 'the exchange of one party for another, which isn't an exchange at all',[10] but some kind of 'transvaluation of value'. But the question remains, how to discover this alternative set of values? How to escape the limits of historicism, cultural relativity and ideological conditioning?

One way out is the postmodernist one. But that is a way that despairs not only of integration but also of meaning, choosing to play with meaning rather than attempting to discover it. More damaging, it can also be seen as an aspect of consumerism, of a culture based on simulation, on images with no real means of support.[11] Turning away to cultivate one's own postmodernist maze may only confirm a cherished premise of the right, that one of the basic freedoms is freedom from politics. Postmodernism leaves the problem of social freedom unresolved. One does not want to reopen old wounds, but Paul de Man's complicity with Nazism may also point to the possibilities of the *trahison des clercs* implicit in postmodernism's indifference to generality. Solipsism is not the same thing as genuine individualism. It may be a form of social betrayal.

The way I propose is the recovery of some possibility of religious belief, a redirection of thought away from the merely empirical and rational towards the intuitive, to 'realities at present unseen', which are beyond rational comprehension and control but can be argued about rationally. That is not to suggest we should 'get religion' and join the religious fundamentalists or take up with one or other of the various New Age spiritualities on offer. They, too, may be just another consumer product, packaged for comfort and consolation and designed to last for eternity. But it is to suggest that the humanities and social sciences might begin to learn from contemporary mathematics and physics as they move beyond the narrow confines of Enlightenment thought towards a new, more 'poetic' paradigm for thought and exploration. Intellectuals need to rediscover a dialectical sense, to play off the visible against the invisible, the actual against the possible. Otherwise we remain like Archimedes, trying to move the world with the lever of thought but unable to find a place outside it from which to get leverage.

To take an example: the crucial problem facing us in this country may well be our relations with Aboriginal people and their culture, and with the long and brutal history of our invasion and occupation of this country. But this is a problem that appears insoluble in terms of our present culture, Money, as nearly everyone now admits, is not the real answer. Nor is mere legislation. The real problem is ideological. The system of meanings that installs us in imaginary relations to the Aboriginal people and to the land they inhabited for so long sets us apart in mutual misunderstanding, if not hostility. Whether we label it the 'myth of progress', or the 'Manichean allegory' on which colonisation is based, [12] or Orientalism, [13] Western ideology is essentially ethnocentric. We assume that our ways are superior, inevitable and the only ones worthy of decent human beings. Locked within this ideology, most white Australians are unable to grant full humanity to Aborigines or to their culture, much less allow their right to live in their own way. Even more crucially, we are unable to admit that we have committed offences against them. The neo-Darwinist underpinning of 'progress' will not allow that these were offences; as 'primitives', the Aborigines were doomed to die anyway, so their sufferings figure as the result of history at work rather than of human brutality. Similarly, 'progress', defined in terms of economic development, finds no place for a culture for which the land itself and life lived in tune with it are sacred, and money is not. Problems remain even when we do admit some offence and begin to talk of 'reconciliation', since secular culture does not know much about forgiveness and guilt. Reconciliation demands some deeper, transcultural and theological ground.

These examples suggest, then, that the real crisis facing us is one of values, of the basic orientation of our society and culture. As one of Pynchon's Proverbs for Paranoids goes, if 'they' get you asking the wrong questions, they don't have to worry about the answers. But the right questions may have to do with who we are and what we ought to believe and to hope for—questions that, as I have argued, intellectuals these days tend to discount. With these questions, however, the question of 'God', of what White calls a 'grandeur too overwhelming to express', begins to revive.

It is all very well, as Ricoeur says, to take the point of Nietzsche's

The Gay Science that 'God is dead'. But we must also ask 'which god is dead; then, who has killed him (if it is true that this death is a murder); and finally, what sort of authority belongs to the announcement of this death'.[14] Ricoeur has suggested the answer to the first two questions. 'Religious' people themselves killed 'god' by turning him into their own projection. In this sense the ultimate murderer is the cultural process itself and the nothingness at its heart, to which 'religious' people, like the rest of us, have surrendered. That means that the authority that belongs to this announcement is the authority of the will to power that Nietzsche also proclaimed. True, nothing is capable of proving this authority. But it does make possible a new form of life that is its justification and that is also the form of freedom.

The way to this new life, I suggest, begins where we began, with the interrogation of conventional religiosity on the one hand and, on the other, acceptance of the spiritual emptiness in which we find ourselves and the ironic self-awareness that flows from that emptiness. Irony is perhaps the characteristic mark of our intellectual life and of its commitment to secularity. But it is also a mode of interrogation, undermining confidence not only in appearances and conventions but in the long run, as postmodernism suggests, in itself. It has already discredited the god of taboo and refuge who is also the god of accusation and consolation. The next step, I would argue, with Ricoeur, is attentiveness, an acceptance of the emptiness, the situation of non-mastery, in which we find ourselves, an acceptance that is prepared to listen for what might be spoken within it, within the depths of an ironic awareness of self and its situation.

This is the kind of passionately ironic attentiveness evident in the work of many of our best writers, painters and musicians. Unfortunately, it is not characteristic of intellectuals. The reason for this, I would argue, is cultural; it is a matter of language, of the imaginative illiteracy that assumes that if language is not 'descriptive' it has nothing to do with reality. If the limits of our language constitute the limits of our world, a whole range of possibilities for thought and action is excluded by the language of intellectual life. But the arts point a way out, in their concern with ironic possibility, with the duplicities of language and symbols, and thus with the critique of mere 'facts' implicit within this duplicity. This implicitly interrogates a culture and society based upon the merely conditioning power of language and symbol. But it also points to the recovery of a properly religious sense, one that is dialectical, not univocal, since it depends upon the interplay between the seen and unseen, the actual and the possible.

This is bound up with the recovery of the symbol, its liberation from manipulation by advertisers, politicians and the media, its liberation into its fullness of implication. Manipulation tends to devalue symbols, turning them into units in an allegory of power; but if we become aware of the full potency of the symbol, then it points us both to freedom and to belief. Complex, ambiguous and therefore beyond clear definition or control, the focus of a whole range of personal and cultural experiences, memories and association and thus liberating rather than constraining, the symbol properly understood creates new meaning and purpose, challenging the merely literal and upsetting conventional models and modes of apprehension. As something essentially personal and individual that entails the creation of meaning out of experience, it works subversively within a culture that is dependent upon conventional fixities of meaning.

This is a familiar enough argument for those whose profession is 'literature'. How to connect it, however, to the question of intellectual life in general? Once again, Ricoeur is helpful. By definition, he argues, the symbol ' "gives rise to thought" . . . The symbol gives: I do not posit the meaning, the symbol gives it; but what it gives is something for thought, something to think about.'[15] There is a meaning that is already there. But it is one that begins from within language, that has already taken place; so that, as Ricoeur goes on, everything has in a certain sense already been said. The task for thought is to recuperate this meaning and draw out its implications. In this way the symbol restores the possibility of revelation, even of hierophany, opening the way to a restoration of the sacred, of some sense of that-which-is-other, utterly compelling but also utterly active, the giver of meaning and purpose.

This may at first sound a conservative position. But the meaning of the symbol is not tied to the past, to what has already been said historically, but to what lies ahead, to the ways in which readers create meaning, and to what they make of it. As Ricoeur also points out, the symbol is contingent, liable to a 'variety' of interpretations, 'a prisoner of the diversity of language and culture'[16]—just as it is imprisoned in our culture, which uses symbols instrumentally, turning them into mere signs in an allegory of power. The task for thought, then, is to recover the language of symbol, a language that is opaque, not transparent, and whose interpretation is therefore always problematical.

This problematic, I would argue, is crucial, especially since the 'Dawkinisation' of universities, when intellectual life has been driven by a search for certainty and conformity, for operating in the world rather than for interrogating or reflecting upon it. That way tyranny lies. Freedom begins with interrogation, with discovering options, and then making choices between them. But this matter of choice raises the question of belief. The critique of belief that opened our discussion is essentially a critique of its cultural representations, not of belief itself. But the dimension of belief itself—especially of belief in the sacred, what is given to be revered—is important for freedom as well as for thought. Since this dimension has been misrepresented, however, it needs to be approached indirectly, from the bottom up, as it were.

Here, too, the symbol is significant. Since its 'meaning' lies ahead of it, constituting a task to be achieved, it emerges that consciousness and the self also constitute a task rather than a given; existence is thus open rather than closed to possibility. Moreover, to the extent that this task is achieved dialectically, in a debate between one's physical and social circumstances and ideological conditioning and the further possibilities revealed in the symbol, it points to the need to be informed and empowered from beyond the self, by what is 'given' in the symbol. Read in this way, therefore, the symbol belongs within the myth of freedom that presupposes a 'call to go further'. Personally, I would also want to argue that this is the essential Judaeo–Christian myth, however much it may have been occluded and distorted by the ideological overdeterminations of Western culture.

This is not the place to try and justify this proposition, but only to point to the way in which an understanding that reopens the possibility of belief as interruption overturns the notion of religion as a mere projection. Instead of being part of a general theory of culture, as it was for Marx, Nietzsche and Freud, religion understood in this way becomes instead a part of the critique of culture, challenging the god of refuge and taboo in the name of freedom. That puts it generally, but I want to look more specifically at the social consequences of this move.

The simplest way is to draw on another continental philosopher and theologian, Max Horkheimer, who takes as his starting point the 'longing for justice' that he sees as characteristically human. This longing, Horkheimer argues, is not and cannot be fully satisfied within secular history—a fact that recent history underlines, to the consternation and demoralisation of many on the left. But it therefore implies a belief in, or at least a hope for, some reality different from the one we know at present. This reality, he says, is bound up with the notion of 'god', of an other for which we long, an intuition that 'over and above suffering and death there is the longing that this earthly existence may not be absolute, not the ultimate reality'.[17]

Admittedly, this argument is dangerous to the extent that it echoes Marx's idea of religion as the 'sign of the oppressed creature' and 'the protest against real distress'. But it goes beyond Marx by posing the existence of this other, a contra-factual dimension, as the other side of the dialectic of freedom. Nor is this other simply a refuge, a mere projection of need, since it demands action; the longing for justice implies that the present order is not the final order, and unites and empowers all those who will not and cannot come to terms with its injustice. In this way 'theology' involves a social critique. At the same time, it points to an alternative that may rescue the left from its demoralisation. Where positivism is unable to find any final authority and the liberalism that has been the ultimate basis of many on the left is similarly helpless, religious belief of this kind, based as it is on a myth of freedom that it reads out of Scripture, grounds the longing for justice in a narrative that guarantees such notions as freedom, justice, community and so on. As Horkheimer remarks, a 'politics that does not contain theology [as defined] within itself may often be shrewd but remains in the end no more than a business'.[18]

That is a good point at which to conclude, commenting as it does on the proliferation of Royal Commissions and the exposure of the politics of mere shrewdness. The task for intellectuals concerned for freedom is therefore, in my view, the recovery of a belief of this kind. True, this recovery may seem an un-Australian activity. But if intellectuals have locked themselves in a narrow and parochial confine, there is no reason why they should stay there permanently, much less snarl at those who come to the door, even if they come from elsewhere and with different ideas. The newcomers may be offering a key to open out new possibilities of thought, and exploring those possibilities may also bring us in from the margins of society, where we have been condemned to a merely aesthetic existence, without influence or consequence. As for those intellectuals who have become willing servants of the economy, this kind of thinking may at least give them pause.

NOTES

1. Patrick White, *The Vivisector* (Cape, London, 1970), p. 612.
2. Ian Turner (ed.), *The Australian Dream* (Sun, Melbourne, 1968), p. x.
3. David Martin, *A General Theory of Secularisation* (Harper Colophon Books, New York, 1978), p. 12.
4. Clifford Geertz, *The Interpretation of Cultures* (Basic, New York, 1973), p. 89.
5. Hannah Arendt, *On Revolution* (Penguin, Harmondsworth, 1973), p. 139.
6. Ludwig Wittgenstein, *Philosophical Investigations*, trans. G.E.M. Anscombe (Blackwell, Oxford, 1974), pp. 114, 115, 48e.
7. Paul Ricoeur, *The Symbolism of Evil* (Beacon Press, Boston, 1969), p. 27.
8. Hans Kung, *Does God Exist?* (Collins, London, 1989), p. 490.
9. Meaghan Morris, 'Politics Now: Anxieties of a Petty Bourgeois Intellectual', in *The Pirate's Fiancée: Feminism, Reading, Postmodernism*

(Verso, London, 1988), p. 176.
10. Patrick White, *The Living and The Dead* (Penguin, Melbourne, 1967), p. 253.
11. Jean Baudrillard, *Simulation* (Semiotexte, New York, 1983).
12. Abdul JanMohamed, 'The Economy of Manichean Allegory: The Function of Racial Difference in Colonialist Literature', in H.L. Gates (ed.), *'Race', Writing and Difference* (Chicago University Press, London, 1986), pp. 78–106.
13. Edward Said, *Orientalism* (Penguin, Harmondsworth, 1985).
14. Paul Ricoeur, 'The Conflict of Interpretations', in Don Idhe (ed.), *Paul Ricoeur: Essays in Hermeneutics* (North Western University Press, Evanston, 1974), pp. 445–6.
15. Ibid., p. 288.
16. Ibid., p. 317.
17. Kung, p. 491.
18. Ibid.

THE ARTICULATION OF SILENCE
FINDING WHAT HAS BEEN BURIED ALIVE

for Dorothy Green

I hope that this title does not sound too lurid—we play it cool in these postmodern days. But Dorothy Green was not afraid of passion. To the end of her life she retained the sense of urgency which was perhaps the gift as well as the burden of her generation, fortunately unfortunate enough to be caught up in World War II. To the end of her life she contested what she saw as the technological and ecological madness of our Western culture, its murderous propensity to war, and in Australia, 'the rot in high places', the 'scrupulous unscrupulousness' which has replaced the notion of public service and a media dedicated to 'infotainment' which enables political and social lies to flourish on an unprecedented scale today. To the end of her life she continued to believe in what has been largely silenced, the connection between writing, reading and 'humanity' and in the need, as she put it, 'to think the vital thoughts of life all over again'. She wrote:

The question, has literature a place in society, is a non-question. Society in any significant sense of the word is simply not possible without literature in some form . . . Literature is the memory of a society which provides it with its continuity and its enduring personality. To deprive children of a knowledge of it . . . is to deprive them of most of their humaneness and to return them back towards the status of solitary animals.[1]

Again:

Literature in the end is a great corporate effort in every way . . . on the part of writers and readers, or speakers and hearers . . . Either spoken or written, [it] is humanity thinking aloud—communicating its experience of all that is, holding a great continuous discussion throughout the ages and across the world.[2]

In these self-conscious days, however, it is difficult to say that kind of thing, however much one may believe it—and I suspect that most of us do. Today we don't have such a robust sense of community and what she calls 'humanity'; humaneness is a suspect term. So, too, is the word 'literature'. In the light of high theory it sounds rather precious, class-conscious, even—heaven forbid!—elitist and/or old hat. We prefer words like 'writing' and 'communications'. But that is our loss, since it represents a loss of what Hannah Arendt calls 'the specific and usually irreplaceable in between which should form between [the] individual and [her] fellows'[3] and which constitutes civil society—Habermas calls it 'communicative action'.

This is why Dorothy Green matters. She believed in literature. But she was no simple idealist and denounced what she called 'windy reformist rhetoric'.[4] Having read Adorno and Althusser, she knew that no writing or reading is innocent and was aware of the ways in which we are all affected by ideological bias. 'Most of us [she wrote] . . . are as much unconsciously at home with the elements of production-consumption for profit as a mole is at home underground, unable to conceive that any other kind of world could exist'.[5] But she had no patience either with those who despaired of change, the 'so-called realists chanting you cannot change human nature'. All the evidence, she said, was to the contrary, from the industrial revolution to the present. Literature, she believed, could be an agent for change. But only under certain conditions—conditions of reception:

One of the saddest things to have to admit is that the accumulated wisdom of the ages, repeated in different ways in every generation, sits on my study shelves, yet none of the powerful people who control our lives take the faintest notice of it.[6]

The answer is not to give up reading and writing, it is to make it transformative. Nor should we give up the notion of 'humanity'— if we define it, as John Passmore has, as a moral attitude which is 'universalistic' rather than 'particularist' and assume that 'we have moral responsibilities towards other human beings simply as such, whatever their sex, race, age, national group, position in society'.[7] This is an attitude which many of us like to associate with 'the' Australian tradition. But it is beginning to look rather forlorn in a society in which the media rules us with its 'indifferential' inert passions. Jack Davis, who as an Aboriginal writer might be expected to be more optimistic, puts it this way:

THE WRITERS

They say
we are the makers of history
we inspire others
to laugh and to cry and to kill
They say
we are the sages
we write the pages
and out of the figment
Of what they imagine
men come steel clad
over the brow of the hill.[8]

At the other end of the scale, with its disdain for representation, its games with the very notions of 'reality', purpose and value, postmodernism undercuts political concerns—indeed, freedom from politics is often seen as one of the basic freedoms.[9] Criticism is not allowed to be 'interpretation' any more, and theory often becomes an aspect of the larger exaltation of signs based on denying the reality of things. In contemporary universities, too, preoccupied with serving the economy, literature increasingly becomes an optional extra which we are unable to afford in our slide to—or is it on?—a banana republic.

Dorothy Green would not have agreed. Nor should we. But we cannot merely repeat her ideas, fine as they are. Nor would she want us to do so, aware as she was of the ways in which thought is constantly threatened by inertia. Let us begin, then, where she left off and see where that leads us.

In the first place she believed that it is the writer's and reader's task, to be adversarial—'let no one represent you' was her motto. That is one reason, she argued, why we no longer have a democracy in Australia today but a 'Kakistocracy', rule by the worst—a word which needs to be reinstated.[10] She criticised, therefore, what she saw as the contemporary *trahison des clercs*, the 'blandness, the willingness not to rock the boat, the shifty silence' she saw in intellectuals as well as politicians drawn into what Gail Jones calls the 'fluid and non-participatory, effortless and ineluctable dream' of consumer society.[11] It is not criticism which undermines society, Green declared, but lack of it.[12] If, as she argued, we live in 'the Age of the Institutionalised Lie', it is the 'duty of writers to call things by their true names and to distinguish myth from reality'.[13] If Australian writers can be said to have created a tradition she argued, 'it is one marked by a strong social conscience'.[14] In this respect—mistakenly, I think—she saw a decline, finding 'little or nothing [in contemporary writing] which *threatens* those who make the real decisions behind the smoke screen of the franchise'.[15]

We must, then, be 'on the side of life rather than of death'. Fine words. But what does this mean? It is not as empty of content as it sounds. First of all it assumes that the disasters of our time which she attacked so eloquently, the wars and threats of war, the waste of billions on armaments while millions starve, the destruction of the environment, the cult of endless and useless consumption and so on, are essentially the result of imaginative failure. There is plenty of support for this view in the work of the Frankfurt School she admired as well as more recent thinkers like Foucault, Barthes and Baudrillard.

For Green, language was the key and 'literature' for her represented language working at its most intense. It constitutes what Barthes called 'a liberating theory of the signifier' because it makes a writer of a reader, opens out beyond the merely utilitarian to the bodily and the physical, the domain of pleasure. If the answer to the crisis facing us today is, as she asserted, 'to fall in love with this planet', then literature as pleasure, the word made flesh, may lead us to this love. The change that is required is one of perception.

Literature can be the occasion of the change, putting us in touch with the past on the one hand and with an imagined future on the other. Obviously, Green would not put it this way, the fact that she does not perhaps is a point in her favour but this corresponds to Barthes's proposition: 'the writer can only be maintained in present society as a sort of pervert who lives his [her] work as a utopia and tends to project his [her] perversion, his [her] "for nothing" into a social utopia'.[16] But this Utopia comes out of the past. As Green reminds us, none of us create out of nothing what we have or what we are. What we do is discover, imitate, rearrange—or destroy—what is already there.[17] That is why she insisted on hope; 'to deprive a child of a sense of the future is [she declared] a cardinal crime, a sin against the Holy Ghost'.[18] This duty to hope rests on the fact that 'we are human subjects not things'.

This is a crucial point in contemporary thought, explored also by thinkers like Habermas and Althusser at one end of the scale and Derrida at the other. The question of subjectivity is bound up with the question of language, especially today when we are ruled from within by the means of the language of the media which plays upon our desires—obsession replaces fate—and by language which delimits the possibilities of thinking and feeling: computer language, for instance, is merely instrumental language. Believing we are tracing the nature of a thing, as Wittgenstein noted, actually we are only tracing around the frame through which we look at it. A picture holds us captive. As Green knew, this is a peculiar kind of captivity and peculiarly absurd:

Why does a species which has become dominant through its intelligence, use its intelligence to destroy what it knows nothing about [the complex mysteries of our plant life], information on which its own existence depends? Whom the gods wish to destroy they first make mad.[19]

This picture tends to preclude poetry, the language of symbol, which bespeaks a reality beyond language which is not complete, however, until it is spoken in language, thus reminding us that 'no reality belongs to me (to us), we all live somewhere else, beyond where we are, we are all a reality different from the word I or the word we'.[20]

It is this language, which, by and large, has fallen silent and been buried. Yet it may be necessary for our survival as human beings and for the survival of the planet. It is still alive, however, and its recovery and reinstatement may be the most important thing we can do, to the extent that it may lead to the recovery of what is crucial, a sense of community and of bodiliness, what Habermas calls the 'language of communicative action', seeing it as the way to rescue what is human, liberating the 'life world' from the rule of the 'system' of productivity, efficiency and technological appropriateness to stipulated economic ends.[21] In Green's words:

[The answer to] the difficulties that modern society has created for itself in the nuclear age [is] the extension of consciousness, the growth of awareness that the challenge . . . now comes mainly from [our] spiritual environment, the impoverishment of which is rapidly impoverishing our material environment.[22]

This sounds theological—a forbidden category—and indeed it is. But what if the 'theological' dimension were what we most need today. The word, as Kevin Hart points out, need not imply religious connotations nor is it necessarily the enemy of thought. It 'pertains . . . to the use of any vocabulary in which meaning or being is said to be wholly resolved by a reference to an origin, end, centre or ground'.[23] Nor does talk of 'centres' or 'grounds' offend against the insights of contemporary theory, much less return us to the fanaticism of fundamentalities. The ground at issue here is that of language itself.

Green was not a theoretician. But she thus points us to a theory of reading, asking us to interrogate the idea of 'reality' and language's relationship to it, like Derrida at one end of the scale and Althusser at the other. For her the proper end of writing was not mere representation and of writing mere description, more of the same, but 'the enlargement of the intellect'.[24] She calls this enlargement 'wisdom', not, of course, a word which contemporary theoreticians would use, though it is worth reflecting that in its root meaning it has to do with dwelling within the shape of things—'wis' is the old Saxon equivalent of *arete*, an idea not unlike Derrida's notion of 'grammar'.

Like Althusser and Derrida, Green questions current notions of reality and thus the idea of representation. Implicitly, though not explicitly, she problematises the assumption that texts are transparent like windows, and that 'reality' is a matter of resemblance. This is perhaps the reason for her interest in Grant Watson who also, as she says, in his day moved 'against the prevalent . . . desire . . . to account for all [we] experience in a rationalistic way, to argue for imaginative and intuitive interpretation'.[25] This interpretation might be called 'theological' in the sense we have defined, as a point from which we may begin to break out of the circle imposed upon us by current forms of representation and ideas of reality. But it is also a radical one.

As Green keeps reminding us, the problem with single-minded materialism is not just with what it does not see but also with what it does see. The more it establishes the criterion of visibility, the more it establishes knowledge as presence, as fixity, and so guarantees itself and the present order of things,[26] persuading us that we live in the best of all possible worlds with the supermarket just around the corner, automatic banking at our fingertips and a Coke at hand. As she insisted, however, echoing Baudrillard this time, these complacencies hide from us not only the increasing poverty, racial hatred and environmental disasters which confront us but also the compassion, dissent and creativity which may rescue us and return us to a richer, more joyous and more powerful existence. Representation as resemblance locks us in a circle of abstraction growing increasingly vicious.

Significantly, therefore, Green's first love was poetry; equally significantly, her first book was entitled *The Dolphin*. As its epigraph reminds us, in legend the dolphin ferries the souls of the dead to new life:

Poeta agit de inferno isto, in quo

*perigrinando ut viatores, mereri et
dememeri possumus.*

So, too, the writer's task is transformative. She 'lives to serve a god/whose absence is the night' but whose presence she is to seek:

*Stay your hand before you cloud
The dolphin's candid eyes:
When swiftness, diligence and love
Are gone, the whole world dies.*[27]

Agreeing with Marx that it matters not just to interpret the world but to change it, Green saw her task as reader as well as writer in these terms. In this sense her practice interrogated the fixity of logocentrism, of the notion of the world as one great book to be pored over and mastered. Like Derrida, she was seized with the importance of language as metaphor, that things are not so much things but words, metaphors, words for other things, so that we are not so much readers as read. What we ought to be seeking, therefore, is not some unity between words and things but what Kristeva calls 'heteronymy', the 'power of an open infinity' in which 'meaning' becomes a matter of possibility and representation dissolves into intuition and desire.[28] This kind of language and the reading which goes with it abolishes what is given, transforming it by putting the emphasis not on the power which controls it but on what exceeds this control.

Women writers have been pushing us in this direction for some time, of course, as have our poets and poetic novelists; they keep reminding us of the textuality of texts and of the fact that what we call 'the world' is itself a text. Just as importantly, the more we come to know of Aboriginal culture, especially as Aboriginal artists mediate it for us, the more we also realise that it represents this other which we have repressed, a polyphonic and reverential rather than a unitary and dominative sense of reality. Our problems are not just economic and political but ideological. We are not reading the world properly. We need to read symptomatically, with an eye for the gaps and absences, in which can be heard hitherto silent voices of suffering and desire, and of creation as something living, not a mere machine. These are the voices which speak in Aboriginal poetry, in Mudrooroo's '*Song Circle of Jacky*', for instance:

Underground—don't try to find us;
Underground—how we hurt, aching
For the last of all of us.
Dried up tears in cheap hotel rooms,[29]

and in voices of forgotten women writers like Lesbia Harford and Louisa Lawson, reminding us of a different kind of history, that of the losers, not the winners. We can only break out of the closed circle of our present society by inhabiting it in a different way, producing meanings differently, expressively, so that reading a text is not a matter of interpretation but of negotiating with it in a way in which it deconstructs itself and our certainties, enabling new concepts, new ways of thinking and feeling and thus of acting.

The meaning which matters is thus not what is obvious but 'what words emit, what is beyond them, what escapes' the silence within them which it is our business as critics to articulate.[30] True, this may spell the end of the humanism which implies a coherent, continuous and rational subject. But it replaces it with a new openness and adventurousness which make possible once more the qualities of awe, wonder and worship which have been crucial to human beings throughout the ages. Articulating this silence thus brings us in touch with who and where we are. As Octavio Paz put it:

Poetry . . . is the necessary momentary perception (which is all that we can bear) of the incommensurable world which we one day abandon and to which we return when we die . . . Language is the consequence (or the cause) of our exile from the universe, signifying the distance between things and ourselves. At the same time it is our recourse against this distance.[31]

Non-Aboriginal Australians know about this sense of exile. But

Aboriginal Australians remind us of the resource hidden within the space we inhabit, apparently empty yet magnetised over thousands of years by their beliefs and practices. There is no time to explore this point, however, except to point out that Dorothy Green knew about this distance, this exile, which we ignore at our peril and that of the world we hold in trust for future generations.

Dorothy Green was someone who thought carefully about her ultimate convictions and expected others to do the same, to 'think the vital thoughts of life all over again'. This business of literature is not something marginal, then, but central. These lines, not by Dorothy Green this time but Gwen Harwood, tell us why:

I hold
in my unhoused continuing self
the memory that is wisdom's price
for what survives and grows beneath
old skies, old stone.
            Fresh mornings rise
the carapace of night with gold.
The sand grains shine, the rock pools brim
with tides that bring and bear away
new healing images of day. [32]

NOTES

1. Dorothy Green, *Writer, Reader, Critic* (Primavera Press, Sydney, 1991), p. 14.
2. Ibid., p. 16.
3. Hannah Arendt, *Men In Dark Times* (Cape, London, 1970), p. 4.
4. Ibid., p. 8.
5. Ibid., p. 7.
6. Ibid., p. 87.
7. John Passmore, 'For Us, European Need Not Be a Dirty Word', in *The Australian Higher Education Supplement*, 17 June 1992, p. 19.
8. Jack Davis, *Black Life: Poems* (University of Queensland Press, Brisbane, 1992), p. 32.
9. Hannah Arendt, *Men in Dark Times* (Cape, London, 1970), p. 4.
10. Dorothy Green & David Headon, *Imagining the Real: Australian Writing*

in the Nuclear Age (Penguin/ABC, 1987) p. 104.
11. Dorothy Green, The Music of Love: Critical Essays (Penguin, 1984), p. 15.
12. Ibid., p. 17.
13. Green, Imagining the Real, p. 105.
14. Green, Writer, p. 19.
15. Ibid., p. 23.
16. Roland Barthes, 'Literature/Teaching', in Peter Botsman (ed.), Theoretical Strategies (Local Consumption Publications, Sydney, 1982), p. 70.
17. Ibid., p. 109.
18. Ibid., p. 104.
19. Green, Music of Love, p. 36.
20. Octavio Paz, The Monkey Grammarian (Peter Owen, London, 1989), p. 55.
21. Jürgen Habermas, The Philosophical Discourse of Modernity (Polity Press, Cambridge, 1990), chapter XI.
22. Dorothy Green (ed.) Descent of the Spirit: Writings of E.L. Grant Watson (Primavera Press, Sydney, 1990), p. 35.
23. Kevin Hart, The Trespass of the Sign (Cambridge University Press, Cambridge, 1989), p. 32.
24. Green, Writer, p. 41.
25. Green, Descent of the Spirit, p. 35.
26. Here I am relying heavily on David Holmes, 'The Politics of Negative Theology' in Melbourne Journal of Politics, 20, 1991, pp. 95–121.
27. Dorothy Auchterlonie, The Dolphin (Australian National University Press, Canberra, 1967), p. 1.
28. Julia Kristeva, 'The Novel as Polylogue', in Desire in Language (Colombia University Press, New York, 1980), pp. 159–209.
29. Colin Johnson (Mudrooroo Narogin), Song Nineteen: The Song Circle of Jacky (Hyland House, Melbourne, 1986), p. 30.
30. Holmes, pp. 106–7.
31. Paz, pp. 129–30.
32. Gwen Harwood, 'Carapace', in Bone Scan (Angus & Robertson, Sydney, 1988), p. 56.

THE SHAPE OF STILLNESS

There is a sense, I think, in which many women in the Church today feel themselves to be on the frontier, on some kind of boundary between the known and the unknown; between order, custom, and the grace and ease of habit and a feeling of darkness, confusion, doubt and anxiety. This is the feeling generated by moving out into strange new country, moving out into territory as yet unmapped. Yet in another sense, this feeling or at least this situation is the proper, even the normal, one for Christians. We are by definition a pilgrim people, called always beyond our certainties to explore ever more fully the mystery of the 'realities at present unseen' which are for us the crucial realities. But it is also perhaps a situation characteristically Australian, whether we be non-Aboriginal people come into a strange, new country, 'wanderer(s) on the way to the self' or Aboriginal people whose lives centre on the mysterious but potent presence in their midst which they call the 'Dreaming'.

What I would like to do first of all, therefore, is to spend some time on this notion of the journey, of moving across the frontier, because this is the notion that will enable us to make sense of our lives in general and of our present situation in particular. Let us take as our text a passage from one of Kafka's parables. 'Where are you going to, master?' the passage begins, to which the reply is, 'Away from here, anywhere, but away from here'.

'So,' he said, 'so you know your destination?'

'Yes, didn't you hear me? It's away from here. My destination is away from here.' [1]

'Anywhere, but away from here', that seems to me to be an important element in any story of change, but especially in the story of women in the Church, a story which has to do on the one hand with a great dissatisfaction with our present definitions of value and purpose, as well as with the present order of the Church; and on the other with a great longing for something more, for some place or way of being in which facts and values are not at odds but in harmony with one another, where the human and the spiritual are not the opposite of the real or the practical.

I think we can see something of this exemplified in the story of Ruth. After the death of her husband, first of all, and then of her sons, Ruth's mother-in-law Naomi, you will remember, decided to return home to her own country. Her two daughters-in-law, Ruth and Orpah, went with her. But when they reached the frontier, Naomi said goodbye, bidding them return to their own mothers. Naomi turned to go, but Ruth refused to move.

Do not press me to leave you and to stop going with you, for wherever you go, I shall go, wherever you live, I shall live. Your people will be my people and your God will be my God. Where you die, I shall die and there I shall be buried. Let Yahweh bring unnameable ills on me and worse ills, too, if anything but death should part me from you![2]

At the moment, there may be a particular appositeness in the story for those of us who are Roman Catholics as we watch Anglicans move closer to the frontier, preparing for the crossing involved in being admitted to the ordained priesthood. Many of us are saying, if not 'Let us go with you', at least, 'we shall be with you'.

But it applies more generally, to the fact that what impels us to the frontier and to the crossing is not ambition, not hunger for power, but the logic of love, the desire to move even more deeply into the mystery of love and service which is the mystery of the Christian God. It is also a mystery of diminishment: 'If you would go to the All, you must go by a way in which you have nothing' (St John of the Cross). For the fact is that there is no external road to this goal, which lies at the heart of who and what we are and long to be. There are no maps, because the goal is what Is, the mysterious one whose name is the unnameable and the unspeakable one who is love.

That brings us, then, to our title, 'The Shape of Stillness'. Our best guide to the unseen and unknown is listening, listening to what is being spoken to us here and now, on the frontier in the time before the crossing, in the kind of no-woman's land in which we find ourselves. What do we have to listen to? It is, I suggest, what we have: our apprehension and our anxiety.

If it is true that, as Schillebeeckx puts it, 'the hermeneutical principle for the disclosure of reality is the scandal, the stumbling block',[3] then our problems can also be the occasions of grace. Truth for the Christian is marked by the sign of the cross and, in a sense, is the cross. The desert, literally or metaphorically, may therefore be the special place of God's speaking and coming towards us.

The story of Ruth is part, therefore, of that larger story, central to the Judaeo-Christian tradition, the Exodus, and therefore also the story of all who see themselves as people on the way.

This story, of course, begins with affliction, with the oppression of God's people by the Egyptians. It was important if they were to move forward, into the destiny God placed before them to make their own, for them to realise, first of all, that they were oppressed; and then that Pharaoh, the authority, was the source of their oppression, realising, therefore, that power and goodness are not necessarily to be identified with authority—even, we might suggest, in the Church. What is provided here and now, the 'onions and leeks of Egypt', is not, it seems, what matters most. Certainly here, it is in the sense of being oppressed, of feeling powerless, which provides the occasion for God's call. In the present instance, as far as women in the Church today are concerned, this feeling may well be the occasion not only to be aware of God but to broaden our compassion, to be aware, beyond our own relatively privileged plight, of all the others throughout the world who are subject to oppression of far worse kinds, of all the others who are grieving, often for much more terrible losses, and join, with them, in discovering the God whose special predilection is for 'the little ones'.

But—to continue the story—in the midst of that oppression, a child, Moses, a sign of new hope, is born, and lives because of the courage and solidarity of women. Egyptian law had it that every male child born to the people of Israel had to be put to death. But a group of women, including even a daughter of Pharaoh, one of the privileged, disobey that law, separating obedience to the law of Pharaoh from obedience to the law of God. Catching a glimpse of a different future and believing in it, they made a gesture of love and compassion, and it was this gesture, saving the life of Moses, God's person, the liberator, which made possible the liberation of the whole people. They were not prepared to accept that Pharaoh's rule would prevail forever and were prepared to challenge it, if not openly, at least effectively, risking themselves in the process.

The next stage is the positive 'call'. We have a good deal to learn, I think, from Moses. He did not take the call upon himself; his decision was not in a sense his own choice. He was the one who was chosen to bring about change, to liberate his people—men as well as women. It was because he was called—gifted by God—that he had not only the vision but the courage to fulfil it.

Nothing really effective for God takes place without this touch of God, without the glimpse of another kind of logic and power; Moses learned this in his vision of the burning bush, which was burning but never consumed—something which is not merely beyond our understanding but challenges it.

Here, then, was the first frontier he had to cross, a frontier of understanding and thus of control. Moses had to let go, let God's logic prevail, and trust in God's love for his people, which seemed to be asking him to do the impossible. The Judaeo-Christian God is the one who is always intent on leading us into new country. He will not let us stay still, being a God who is life and movement and promise, the source of our energy as well as of our hope.

In the present context, in which our need is for conciliation, not contestation, it may be well to pass over the next stage of the struggles to make the break from Egypt: the battles with Pharaoh, his opposition, his bullying, his changes of mind and the various plagues that were sent to punish him.

Let us move instead to the stage of the desert. When they passed over the frontier, when they left Egypt, the people of Israel did not go out into easy or fertile country. They found themselves in the desert, in what seemed a place of desolation, without most of the things they regarded not only as pleasant but also necessary. Above all, they felt very much alone, suspended between what had been and what was not yet—as many women in the Church feel themselves today. But their confidence, and ours, was surely that the place in which they found themselves was not in the first instance the result of their own choice, was not a response to merely social factors, but a response to God's call. It was God who called them—and us—out, away from their previous certainties, to be here. We are going where God bids us go, doing what God bids us do—at least we hope so.

What one needs most of all in the desert, however, is trust, the readiness and ability to wait, trusting that we shall find manna, just enough for each day, and water even from a rock. But for us, as for the Israelites, the temptation is to look backwards, to mourn lost comforts and certainties, as the Israelites mourned the 'onions and leeks' of Egypt. But the God who calls us is often not comfortable; what he offers instead is himself. On the way, though, we need to cherish one another, share what we have and live simply, day to day, trusting that what we need will be provided as it was for the people of old. Then, finally, in the midst of the desert, there will be the Sinai experience, the thunder and lightning.

This encounter with the awesomeness of God is perhaps the most important stage of all. I suspect that what we women in the Church need most at the moment is to think a great deal more about 'spirituality', about prayer. With all that we have had to do and say, we have perhaps sometimes lost sight of this encounter, this central experience of our faith and hope and love, the meeting with the God who is Other—not just a mirror reflection of ourselves but the Other who is the ultimate partner, the goal of all our loves. This God is love—of course—but also, as the Sinai experience shows, terror, the kind of experience expressed, for instance, in Blake's 'The Tyger', especially in the wonderful opening lines:

Tyger, tyger, burning bright
In the forests of the night

It seems to me that women's experience is often of this kind, anyway. In birth especially, but also in the insistent and intimate relationship women have with their bodies, power and sexuality and energy are caught up and fused, hammered out, if you like, in the furnace of creation. And that is also where God is, in this terrible, sometimes terrifying, even drunken, energy, just as much as in gentleness and serenity. The biblical God is not the God of the philosophers, a reasonable God who fits the calculations of the human mind. This God is or can be violent, urgent, transforming. Gwen Harwood understands something of this in her poem, 'I am the Captain of my Soul':

But the Captain is drunk, and the crew
hauling hard on his windlass of fury are whipped
by his know-nothing rage. Their terror
troubles the sunlight. 'Now tell me,'
the Captain says, as his drunkenness
drifts into tears, 'what's to keep me
at ease in this harbour?'
               'We'll tell you,'
say Hands, 'in our headlong chase through a fugue

for three voices, you heard a fourth voice naming
divisions of silence. We'll summon
that voice once again, it may tell you
of marvels wrung from sorrows endured.'
'We have seen,' say Eyes, 'how in Venice
the steps of churches open and close
like marble fans under water.'

'You can rot in your sockets,' the Captain cries.

'I have children,' says Body, haloed
in tenderness, firm in rightness still.
'I grew gross with their stress, I went spinning
in a vortex of pain. I gave my breast
and its beauty to nourish their heedless growth.

They jump on my shoulder in mischievous joy.
On their lives your astonishing sorrows
flow easy as water on marble steps.'

'Lass sie betteln gehn,' roars the Captain
as his old wounds burn, and he gulps
from his flagon of grief. 'You servants, you things,
stand up there! You *with the ageing choir-boy face,*
and you *with your facile dexterity,* you
with your marble hallucinations, COME!'

Hands, eyes, body keel to the void as the drunken
Captain sings in his wilderness of water.[4]

Over the frontier, in the wilderness, it can seem as if the world is falling to pieces in this way, and yet the call keeps coming, a call, I think, which is not so much to power as to community with all those others who are wounded, whose worlds or lives also seem to be falling apart, yet who are actually—we must believe—giving birth to something new. In this country, this is truest perhaps of our Aboriginal sisters and brothers, but it is the case also with many others—young people, immigrants, old people—as well as women.

The desert, then, is a dangerous place. But it can also be exhilarating. We church people in particular have been clinging to the fringes of self and of experience for too long. But now we begin to realise that we are out—to use another metaphor—'forty thousand fathoms deep', on the great ocean of being, open to 'the heart pain and profoundly vulnerable to the world pain' (Conrad), as we were not before perhaps.

We need all of our strength in this situation, but that is, I believe, the strength which comes from powerlessness. In the past our great gift as women, painful as it may have been, has perhaps been this powerlessness. Power, as we know, corrupts very easily, can kill off certain sympathies and initiatives. But women mostly have been able to sit more easily by the wells of life, to know what it is to be solitary, less pressured to conform because less powerful socially, economically and politically. It is important not to move too far away from this solitude, from this inwardness which is the place of the living God and of prayer, to listen to the muse Anne Elder invokes in her poem, 'Crazy Woman', sitting

. . . musing under the lyric tree
plucking and plaiting the thoughtful branches
deep in the heart of the public gardens . . .[5]

What one learns is that there is a secret wisdom, something not much acknowledged in larger society, in the world of affairs or even, I am afraid, by the institutional Church. Indeed, this wisdom will sometimes seem crazy and must be expressed diffidently. Elder's poem knows this:

I debated how to say it aloud,
to their alarm. Before our death
there is much to communicate that goes by the board
because it is thought unusual indeed crazy
to gather the fallen leaf and the daisy,
the magpie lark and the private lark
in the public park,
the eternal cherubic spout, the nakedness
and lovingness of loneliness
into the right word
to bless our other selves in the name of the Lord.[6]

But this is our task: to be prayerful, to be strong, to be prophetic and to dance that prophecy, as it were, to shout for joy at what we have heard and seen; the promise of the Lord that we shall enter into even richer possibilities of love, worship and service—like Miriam shouting for joy after the passage through the Red Sea, and like so many of the other great women of the Judaeo-Christian tradition.

The source of this joy, however, is the notion of God, the 'One who is Mighty' who has done such great things for, in and through us, who perhaps asks us to bring alive once more the true meaning of a word which has been obscured by so much misunderstanding, self-interest and cant, obscured sometimes by the Church which exists to proclaim it. It is for us to witness to the fact of this, the essential Word without which nothing else has meaning, and that is what our journey is about, the journey to the God who calls and who Is, the love which draws us, *'amor meus, pondus mea'* (St Augustine). The weight that draws me, the dynamic that empowers me, is the God who is the love through whom and in whom we are able to love ourselves in the first place and then others.

That is what we may call the ecstatic side of the equation. There is another side, however, and it is summed up in the image of the Crucified God. To love is to be vulnerable. But it is also to know oneself personally, not just the other, as vulnerable, because God's love goes out particularly to those who are wounded—that is the point of Matthew's parable of judgment,[7] the culmination of his series of parables of the Kingdom.

In this way, it becomes possible to see God in the wounds inflicted upon us, often in the name of God, as we attempt to remain true to the liberator God we believe in. Some, perhaps many, of us have difficulty with the notion of Church at the moment. But if we think of it as the group of those called (*ecclesia*) out into the desert to live, in all our woundedness, we may be recovering a truer sense of Church than if we were to concentrate on institutional matters.

This community is called out to search for God, not to own God, but to have God as the one who goes before, at once guiding us and our goal. But, and this is our last point, this is a community not of the powerful or the important, not the winners but the little ones, people who often seem to ourselves and others to be foolish and to be failures. In our journey, as we look forward to the community of love, freedom and justice we believe in and hope for, it is important also to recover the great memory, enshrined not only in the story of the Exodus but also of the God who became the Poor Man of Nazareth. This, of course, is a memory of suffering, dangerous because counterfactual, a challenge to the false values of the world which crucified and goes on crucifying God.

At present I would argue that Australian society by and large worships false gods, an unholy trinity of Mammon (God of wealth and possessions), Moloch (God of struggle and ruthless competition) and Marilyn Monroe (emblem of the murderous power of the mindless search for pleasure and sensation). But this great memory contests their power and constitutes the revolution we are looking for, a revolution of values, which works on the one hand to change the world for future generations and on the other unites us in the present with the whole suffering and wounded, joyous and loving community of God's people. In this view, the value of history is not to be found only or even especially in the successful, the conquerors. Its most important centre lies with those who might otherwise be called the losers, those who have managed to survive, who go on through the desert, hoping against hope.

What we really want and need, then, is to believe in God's call and to remain faithful to it. It is, of course, a long process—one of the significant elements of the Exodus story is that, in a sense, when God's people thought they had arrived in the promised land, they had not. You never really arrive there in this world, although in another sense you are always in it—so long as you are listening to God and thus learn that you must continue to move on because God is movement.

In the long run, therefore, it is a matter of perspective. The great English woman mystic of the fourteenth century, Julian of Norwich, had a glimpse of the perspective we need, I think, when she saw 'all thing that are . . . as it were a little hazelnut in the Divine Hand'. It was this vision which gave her the deep confidence that 'all shall be well, and all manner of things shall be well'. But she also had a glimpse of God as Mother, a vision to balance the fierce God of the desert. Let us end, then, with this vision since the desert in which we find ourselves may thus be said to be an aspect of her kindness:

Thus, Jesus Christ, that Doeth good against evil, is our very Mother. We have our being with him, for there the ground of Motherhood begineth, with also the sweet keeping of love that endlessly followeth. As truly as

God is our Father, so truly is God our Mother. That showeth He in all. And especially in those sweet words where he sayeth 'I It Am'. That is to say, I am the might and the goodness of Father God. I It Am, the wisdom and the kindliness of Mother God. I It Am, the light and the face that is all blessed love. I It Am, the Trinity. I It Am, the unity. I It Am, the high sovereign goodness of all manner of things. I It Am, that maketh thee to long. I It Am, the endless fulfilling of all true desires.[8]

NOTES

1. Quoted in Robert W. Funk, *Parables and Presence* (Fortress Press, Philadelphia, 1982), p. 130.
2. Ruth 1:16–17.
3. Edward Schillebeeckx, *Christ: The Christian Experience in the Modern World* (SCM, London, 1980), p. 35.
4. Gwen Harwood, 'I am the Captain of my Soul' from *Selected Poems* (Angus & Robertson, Sydney, 1990), p. 21.
5. Anne Elder, 'Crazy Woman' from *Crazy Woman and Other Poems* (Angus & Robertson, Sydney, 1976), p. 5.
6. Ibid., p. 6.
7. Matthew, 25:31–46.
8. Julian of Norwich, *A Showing of God's Love*, (ed.) Anne Maria Reynolds (Sheed and Ward, London, 1974), p. 38.

REFERENCES

The publisher wishes to acknowledge the sources of those essays in this book which have been previously published:

'A Properly Appointed Humanism: Australian Culture and the Aborigines in Patrick White's A Fringe of Leaves', *Westerly*, 28, 2, June 1983.

'Caught in the Draught: Burning Bush and Blowing Wind', *Freemantle Arts Review*, 6, 5, May 1991.

'Emerging from the Shadow', *The Way*, 31, 1, January 1991, pp. 38–47.

'Intellectual Belief and Freedom', *Meanjin*, 50, 4, Summer 1991, pp. 533–542.

'Over the Frontier: The Poetry of Rosemary Dobson', in David Brookes and Brenda Walker (eds), *Poetry and Gender*, University of Queensland Press, Brisbane, 1989, pp. 105–127.

'Patrick White: A Tribute' in Clayton Joyce (ed.) *Patrick White: A Tribute*, Collins/Angus & Robertson, Sydney, 1991, pp. 141–146.

'Polyphonies of the Self: The Challenge of Aboriginal Australia', *Proceedings of the Inaugural Conference of the European Association for the Study of Australian Literature*, Berne, 1991.

'Racism', *Indian Ocean Review*, 3, 3, September 1991, pp. 1–4.

'The Articulation of Silence: Finding What Has Been Buried Alive', the Inaugural Dorothy Green Lecture, Conference of the Association for the Study of Australian Literature, delivered at Ballarat, 1992.

'The Men Who Loved Children' in Penelope Hetherington (ed.), *Incest and the Community: Australian Perspectives*, University of Western Australia Press, Perth, 1991, pp. 79–95.

'The Shape of Stillness', in Marie Louise Uhr (ed.), *Changing Women: Changing Church*, Millenium Press, Sydney, 1992, pp. 24–33.

'Thinking as Feeling: Bill Neidjie's Story about Feeling', *Westerly*, 35, 1, 1990, pp. 87–92.

'To Be or Not to Be: The Verbal History of Patrick White', *Westerly*, 37, 2, 1992, pp. 61–68.

'Towards Reconciliation?' in *Briefing Paper No 3*, Indian Ocean Centre for Peace Studies, Perth, 1992.

'What Will Suffice: Les A. Murray's The People's Otherworld', *Helix*, 21 & 22, 1985, pp. 112–119.